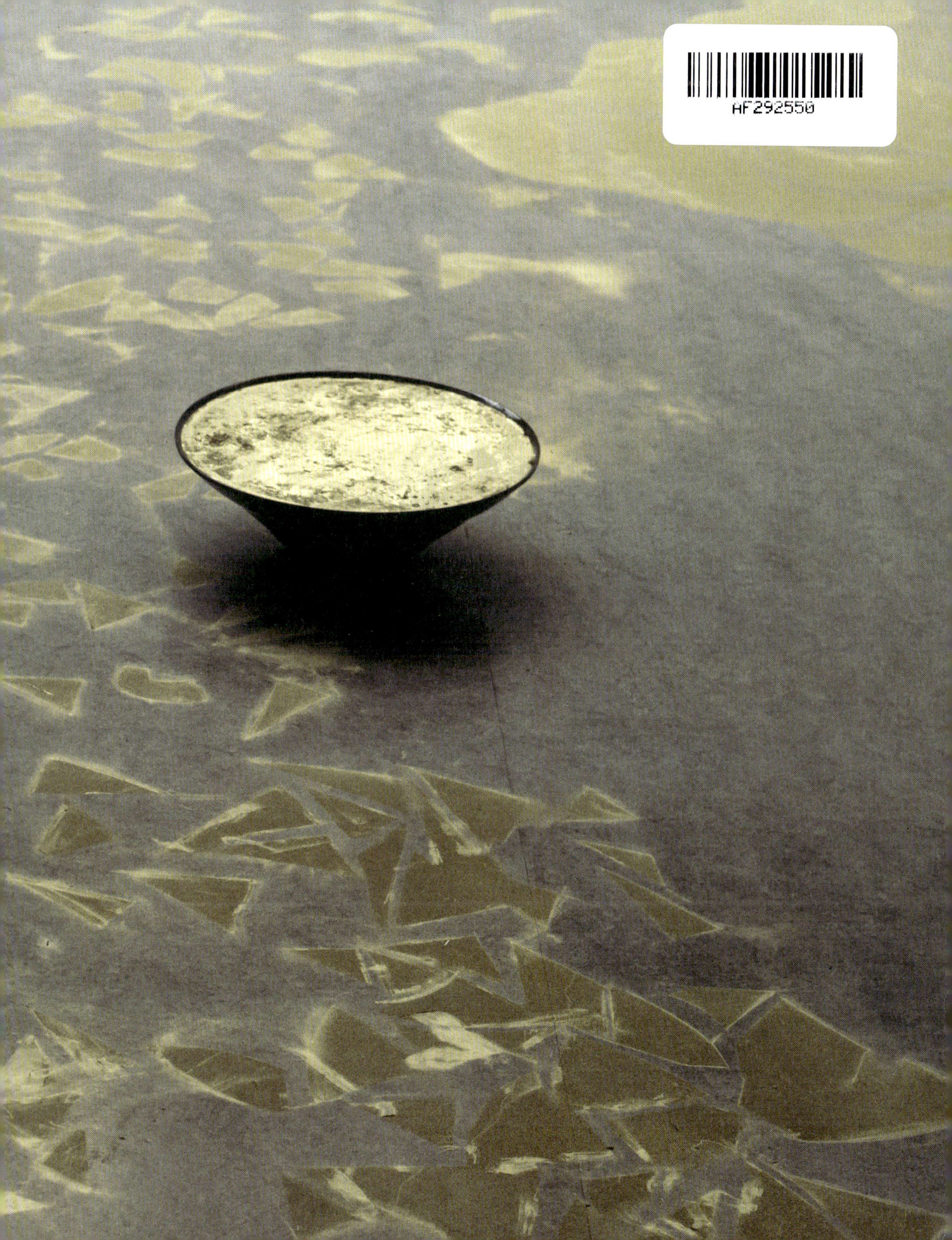
HF292550

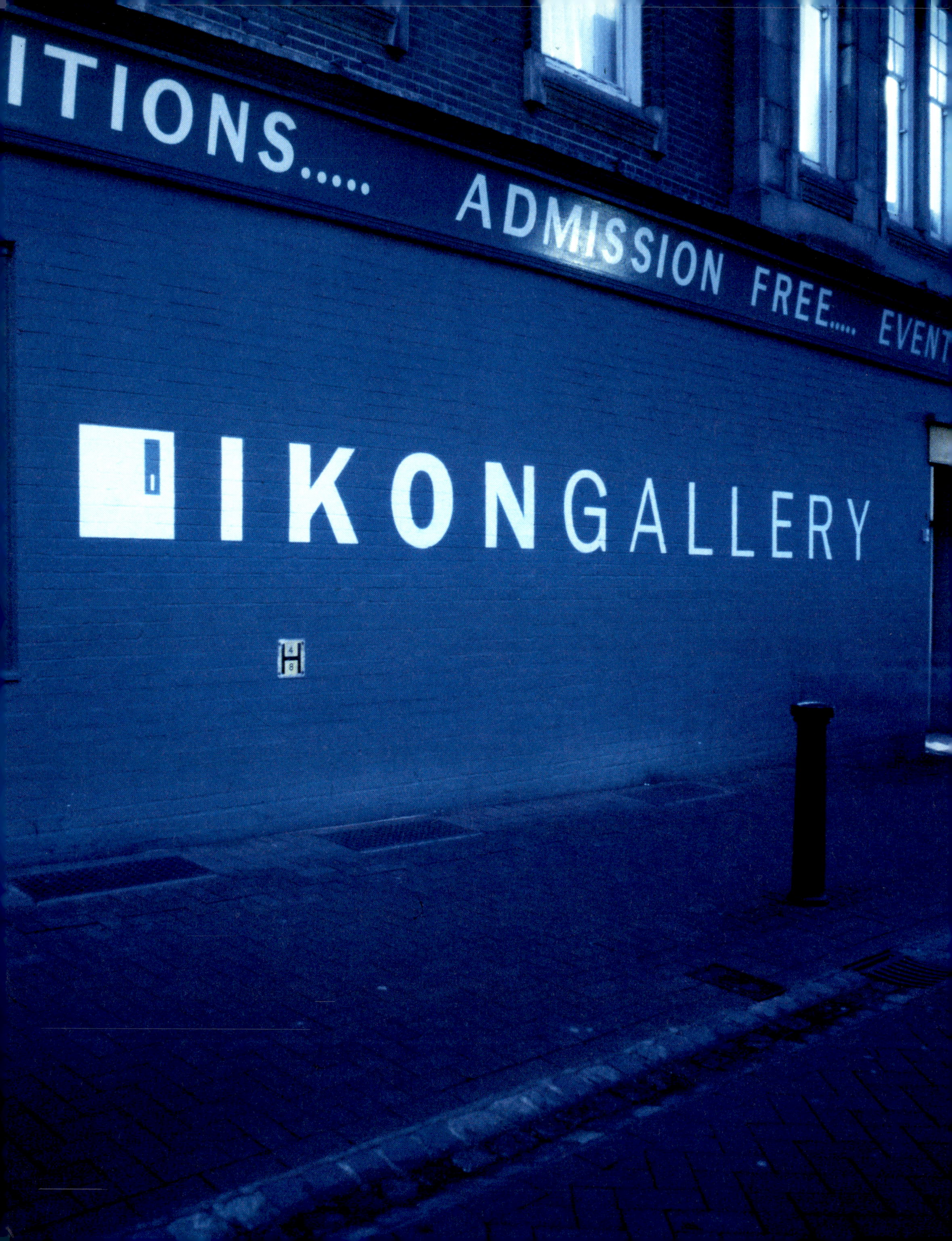

ITIONS.....
ADMISSION FREE.... EVENT
IKONGALLERY

A Very Special Place

IKON IN THE 1990s

IKON

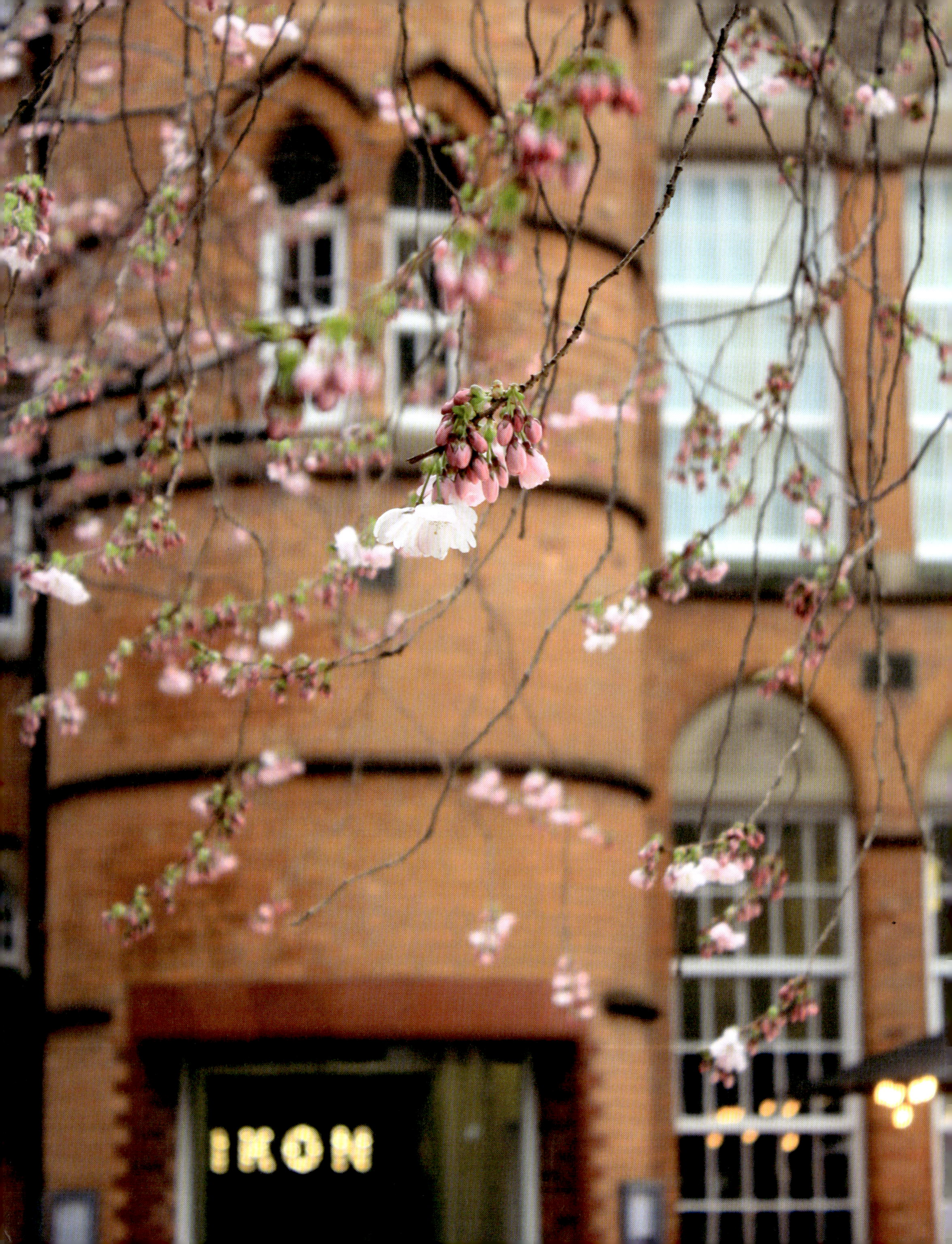
IKON

Contents

Introduction

The fourth in a series of surveys of Ikon's artistic programme, this exhibition is a review of the 1990s. It comprises work by artists who featured in exhibitions and other projects that happened at the gallery in John Bright Street during 1990–1997 and then at Ikon's current premises in Brindleyplace until 1999. These were the years during which Elizabeth Ann Macgregor was Director, prior to her departure for the Museum of Contemporary Art, Sydney.

In keeping with the ethos espoused by its founder artists, Macgregor summarised a vision for Ikon in a policy statement that still holds true, more than twenty-five years later: "The ambition is to break down all the boundaries which act as a deterrent to greater understanding of the role of the contemporary artist today. Ikon can provide a new model where the gallery is at the hub of a wide range of art practice and audience engagement." The John Bright Street building, with its leaking roof, insufficient heating, toilets running with damp and lack of disabled access, might have had bohemian charm but it was holding back the audience development that Macgregor wanted, and so the hunt for another, more suitable, address was on. Finally, it stopped at the door of the dilapidated neo-gothic shell of the old Oozells Street School, Brindleyplace. Through a concerted fundraising campaign, drawing in a game-changing grant from the new National Lottery, an award-winning refurbishment was undertaken and so Ikon reopened in March 1998.

Certainly Ikon was no stranger to moving, having taken up residence in four venues since its inception in 1965, but this latest relocation was completely transformative, providing artists and audiences alike with an attractive building that was user-friendly whilst meeting the stringent environmental conditions required for museum loans. Brindleyplace is a corporate precinct, off the Broad Street leisure strip, and its neighbourhood of Ladywood is one of the most characterful and culturally diverse in the country. Ikon is also within walking distance of Symphony Hall, the Birmingham Repertory Theatre and the new Library of Birmingham, and at the heart of the city's extensive canal system. Macgregor put the gallery in a good place, geographically and strategically, and much of what has happened since at Ikon, both in terms of artistic programme and audience development, would not have been possible without her achievements.

Ikon rode high in the 1990s. It received an incentive funding award from the Arts Council of Great Britain in recognition of a sound business plan setting out the gallery's proposals to expand its income generation within the terms of its artistic policy. This was followed by a new deal with Birmingham City Council increasing its funding almost to the desired 1:2 ratio with that provided by the Arts Council. In 1997, Macgregor delivered an extremely good progress report to her Board, concluding that the gallery "has consolidated its reputation as one of Britain's leading contemporary art galleries and has developed a significant international reputation. Ikon's work has featured at a number of important conferences in Britain and abroad. Ikon was shortlisted three years running for the Prudential Awards for the Arts, as well as for the Sainsbury Art Education Awards in 1993, and a Gulbenkian education award and a National Art Collections Fund award in 1994."

When Macgregor arrived at Ikon, the artistic programme was in the process of becoming more international, and she continued in that vein, placing particular emphasis on the Americas and, towards the end of the 90s, Australia. Concerning the representation of British artists, she resisted the fashion for "Young British Artists" in favour of an eclecticism ranging from painters such as Basil Beattie and Lisa Milroy to the more overtly experimental practices of artists such as Georgina Starr and Mark Wallinger. As during the 1980s at Ikon, there was a distinct openness to black and minority ethnic artists, often raised locally, such as Keith Piper, Donald Rodney and Zarina Bhimji.

Transcontinental, organised by Ikon in collaboration with Cornerhouse Manchester and curated by Guy Brett, was a seminal exhibition for Ikon. Taking place in 1990, it featured nine artists from Latin America, including Juan Davila, Eugenio Dittborn, Victor Grippo, Cildo Meireles and Tunga, whose work was very varied in terms of style and media – often as installation – and smartly political. Group exhibitions – such as *Mothers*, about motherhood (1990), *With This Ring ...*, an exhibition about the union of individuals in marriage and through sex (1991) and *Clean* and *Dirty*, offering multiple perspectives on society's preoccupation with purity (1994) – occurred often at Ikon, with themes derived from current affairs or topical issues. These informed the 1990s programme overall, with racial and sexual politics to the fore. Concerning the latter, Martha Rosler and Nancy Spero were the most renowned, both having solo exhibitions at Brindleyplace. Also from the US Adrian Piper used photography and text to explore the nature of otherness and ostracism; Ellen Gallagher, on the other hand, was making minimalist work with narratives derived from race-related themes.

Australian artist Gordon Bennett exhibited paintings with a cut-and-paste postmodernism that conveyed the predicament of his Aboriginal identity; likewise, Juan Davila appropriated art historical imagery in a searing critique of colonialism. Yinka Shonibare combined "exotic" fabric design and Victorian imagery with a smart sense of humour to articulate a proposition that has since led to world-wide acclaim, and Edward Allington was similarly knowing in his conflations of popular culture and art history. With different but equally postmodern propositions, Amikam Toren took aesthetic analysis to exciting extremes while Avis Newman followed a more poetic, contemplative path.

This rich artistic mix provided a foil for the process-based abstraction of Callum Innes' paintings, shown towards the end of Macgregor's time at Ikon. In many ways it anticipated the kind of non-referential work that was to feature more prominently during the

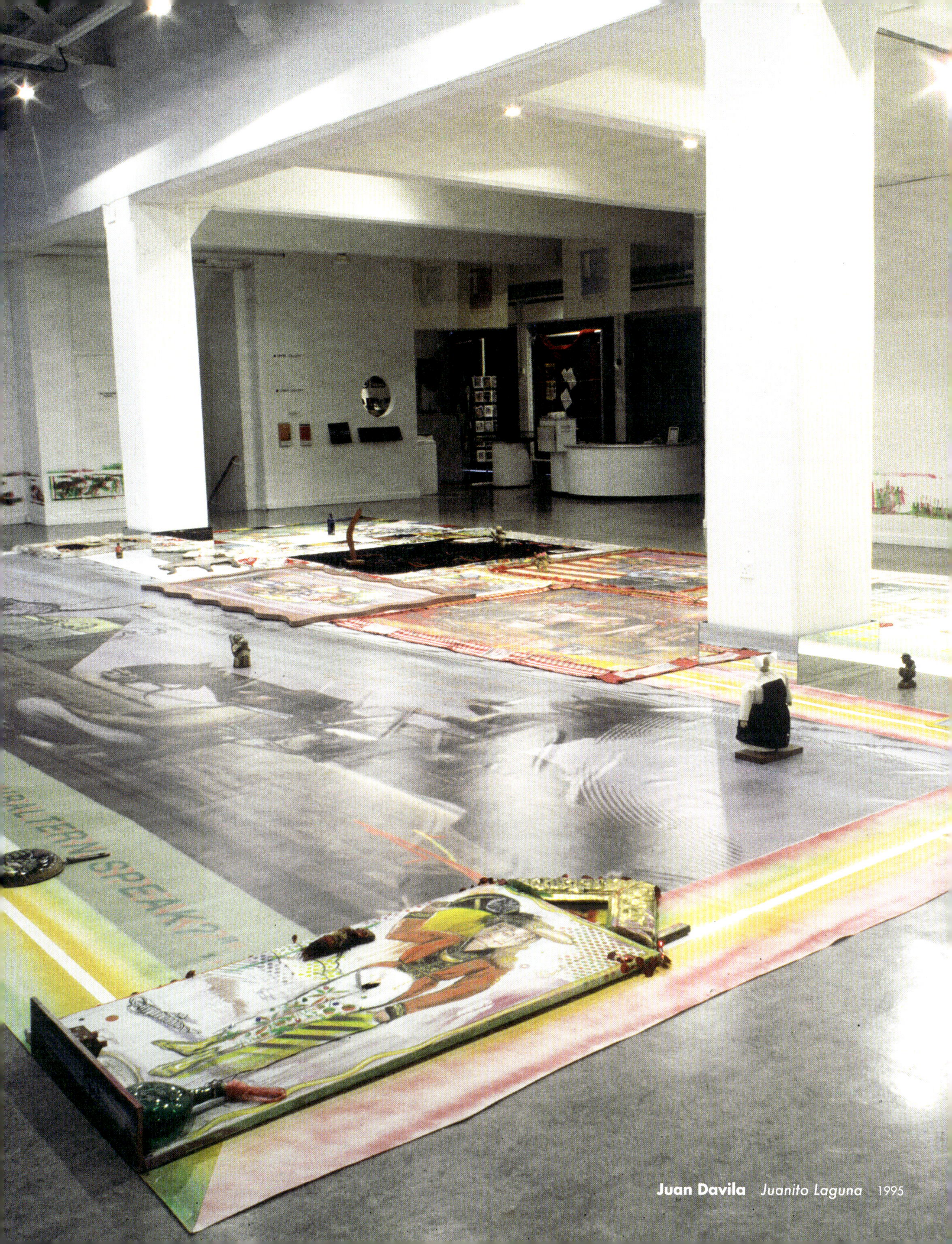

Juan Davila *Juanito Laguna* 1995

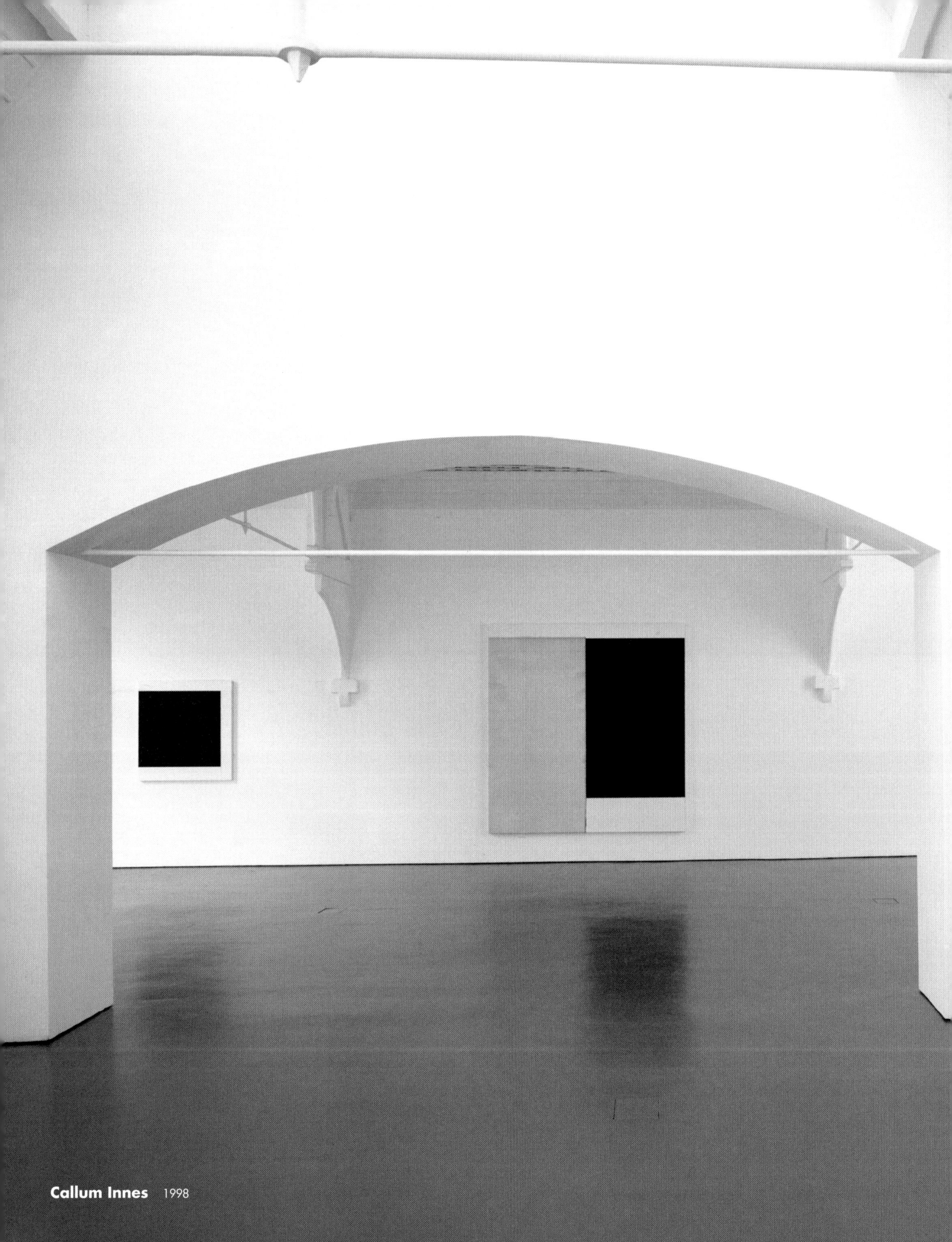

Callum Innes 1998

2000s by artists such as Ding Yi, Olafur Eliasson, Bernard Frize, Katharina Grosse, Ann Veronica Janssens and Francois Morellet. This was part of the next chapter in Ikon's story, post-millennial, coinciding with a zeitgeist shift, mainly due to the geopolitical fallout from 9/11 and a heightened awareness of climate change. As Ikon was settling into its new location in Brindleyplace, the world around it started to move faster and more erratically.

Most recently, the ongoing c-19 pandemic has constituted a major challenge but, despite it, many of our supporters have remained true, in fact redoubling their helpfulness in the face of adversity. A thousand thanks first and foremost to my predecessor, Liz Ann – as she is affectionately known – and Adrian Bland, Chair of Ikon's Board for much of this pivotal decade, and we gratefully acknowledge their continuing goodwill. How much too we appreciate the contributions of members of various boards and advisory committees since and staff, past and present. The advice and practical support received from colleagues in museums and other institutions – Arts Council Collection, Tate, Birmingham Museums Trust, British Council Collection, The Museum of Contemporary Art Australia, New Art Gallery Walsall, the National Galleries of Scotland, Collection Adrian Piper Research Archive Foundation and the Estates of Edward Allington, Rose Finn-Kelcey and Donald Rodney – have been invaluable. Furthermore, many private collectors and galleries, as indicated by the catalogue list, were unstinting in response to our loan requests. And the contributions of Elonex, The Grimmitt Trust, Paul Mellon Centre and The Owen Family Trust have provided a vital supplement to the core funding we receive from Arts Council England and Birmingham City Council.

Finally, to the artists, not only those exhibiting on this occasion, but to all who have joined in with us since the beginning, we extend our heartfelt thanks. They, above all, have made Ikon a very special place.

Jonathan Watkins
Director

A Very Special Place

Jonathan Watkins

In 1987 the Arts Council of Great Britain undertook an organisational appraisal of Ikon. In her annual report to her Council of Management Ikon's Director Antonia Payne described it as being "in general […] extremely supportive of the gallery's work", reflecting "a shared sense of purpose". It strongly recommended "that the Director should spend a greater proportion of [her] time travelling and working on research for the exhibitions programme, and that Ikon should continue to develop the international components in its programme."[1] Plans for 1988–1991 were then drawn up towards Ikon increasing its international programming, but by the time they were being realised Payne had left Ikon.

Elizabeth Macgregor, Payne's successor, was appointed in early 1989 and proceeded to develop a programme that significantly extended beyond Europe and the US, beyond the subcontinent to South East Asia, Australia and especially to Latin America. Macgregor and Payne also shared an enthusiasm for audience development that was very much in keeping with the original vision for Ikon. The founding artists opened a gallery in Birmingham's Bull Ring in 1965 to make innovative contemporary art more accessible, and every subsequent Ikon venue was landed on with the same spirit. Swallow Street (1968–72) was bigger, more accommodating, the Birmingham Shopping Centre (1972–78), above New Street Station couldn't have been more central and John Bright Street (1978–97), nearby, was bigger still. The latter, the ground floor and basement of a four-storey commercial building, was inherited by Payne and by 1988 she had raised the funding necessary for a renovation that included repairs to the roof, walls and floors. At the same time she was envisaging that Ikon would take the first floor of John Bright Street for more office space and storage.

Similarly, shortly after she arrived, it dawned on Macgregor that something would have to be done about Ikon's premises. In a Strategic Plan presented to the Council of Management in July 1989 she proposed a refurbishment of the entrance and shop. The offices were cramped and so she was open to an idea that the City Council would acquire the building for Ikon to share with other arts organisations. The area was run down, with a concentration of disreputable night clubs, but, she explained, "remaining in its current site offers Ikon the advantages of a city centre location close to the station and excellent exhibition spaces … recent pedestrianisation [of John Bright Street might] improve the ambience and encourage more day-time activities …"[2] Shortly afterwards the Council of Management formed a Building Committee.

Macgregor, whose first job involved driving an arts bus which took exhibitions throughout Scotland, had recently been working in London for the Arts Council and Ikon was her first gallery job. She was keen to get cracking and, besides building issues, she immediately prioritised the artistic programme and marketing. Concerning the latter she commissioned

Arts Council of Great Britain, Ikon Gallery Birmingham: July 1987. Appraisal Report, p.19

Strategic Plan July 1989, p.18

Tony Arefin, the graphic designer of choice for progressive arts organisations in the early 90s, to revamp Ikon's publicity material and develop a new corporate image. His brief was to convey an identity that was "non-elitist, prestigious, friendly, young, not intimidating, stylish", and the result was a distinctive logo, based on an upper-case "I", a fresh san-serif brand font and a fashionable range of colours to be used for signage as well as print.

Concerning the artistic programme, in the 1989 Strategic Plan she observed, "One of the problems in attracting new visitors lies in the programme's emphasis on presenting new work by unknown artists. While this commitment must be maintained as the core of the programme, it is possible to provide variation by occasionally presenting touring exhibitions by major twentieth century artists, thematic exhibitions and exhibitions which contribute to debates around the boundaries between fine art, craft and design".[3] Already Ikon had been occasionally touring in exhibitions of work by major twentieth century figures – often courtesy of the Arts Council – and "thematic" group shows were a feature of Payne's programme, but the idea of including craft and design was new. As it turned out, craft did not really come through, whereas, pertinently, by the mid-90s there were exhibitions of work by architects.

Macgregor's vision for Ikon became more clearly articulated by the time she wrote her 1991 Business Plan, with a policy statement, as follows:

> To encourage great public understanding and enjoyment
> of the contemporary visual arts
>
> To promote and support the work of living artists
>
> To forge a role within a regional and national matrix
>
> To promote increased fair and equitable access to
> visual arts provision

Under the heading of "Key Issues" was an acknowledgement of a national economic recession that was having profoundly negative effects – exacerbated by Thatcherite initiatives – but despite this, Birmingham City Council increased ikon's revenue grant to £80,000 per annum, within conceivable reach of the 1:2 ratio match funding preferred by the Arts Council. This encouraged Ikon to look into the possibility of gaining access to the top three floors of John Bright Street as the lease there was coming up for renewal in the following year. By expanding within current premises Ikon would have "the opportunity to develop its full potential as a dynamic cultural centre of national significance, providing people with the opportunity to engage with British art in an international context and challenging the dominance of London based provision".[4]

3
Ibid. p.10

4
Ikon Gallery. Business Plan 1991

Within months however Macgregor was starting to change her mind about Ikon staying in John Bright Street, enumerating in a report serious problems with the premises. Besides the shortage of office space, there were leaks again in the roof, cracks in the basement ceiling, insufficient heating, toilets running with damp and no disabled access to the lower ground floor. At the same time her attention had been drawn to a dilapidated school building on Oozells Street, still standing in an inner city wasteland that was to become Brindleyplace. As she explained to the Council of Management: "[It is] on a site due to be developed by Rosehaugh behind the [International Convention Centre] … Rosehaugh has indicated that it is willing to grant Ikon a 99 year lease at a peppercorn rent if Ikon undertakes the refurbishment of the building."[5]

Architect Axel Burrough of Levitt Bernstein was quickly commissioned to undertake a feasibility study. He came to the conclusion that a conversion was possible although there would be less floorspace than at John Bright Street. "A sealed building will be most appropriate, both for security and to control the environmental conditions by air-conditioning and pollution control [as required for museum loans] … The school will provide good spacious galleries without any really large spaces".[6] As the lease for John Bright Street was due to expire in February 1993, the idea of moving into the school soon afterwards was seriously entertained – "The option of moving into Oozells Street [School] requires immediate action" – but actual events unfolded differently.

●

Meanwhile there was the business of developing a continuous programme of exhibitions, both at the gallery and for regional touring – the latter, since 1980, being smaller, more portable shows devised for community centres, schools, hospitals, libraries and smaller galleries and museums throughout the West Midlands. As well there was Ikon Education, a learning programme also with a regional remit, including artists' residences for schools, and events and activities related to exhibitions.

In June, Macgregor presented a report to the Council of Management on developments at Ikon since 1986, and in light of her experience at the Arts Council she was forthright: "The context for all arts organisations has changed dramatically in the past five years. A more business-like approach is expected at all levels …"[7] and, evidencing Ikon, she circulating publicity material and catalogues designed by Arefin. Recently returned from research trips to the US, Russia and Estonia, and having realised *Transcontinental*, a seminal exhibition of contemporary Latin American art initiated by Antonia Payne, the year before, she was clearly keen to preside over a more geographically expansive programme: "Five years ago, international exhibitions were beyond the gallery's means. Presenting exhibitions from abroad widens horizons and places British artists firmly in

5
Director's Report, April 1991–
March 1992

6
Axel Burrough, 'Oozells Street
School, Brindleyplace', December
1991

7
Elizabeth Macgregor, 'Report
on Developments since 1986/87'

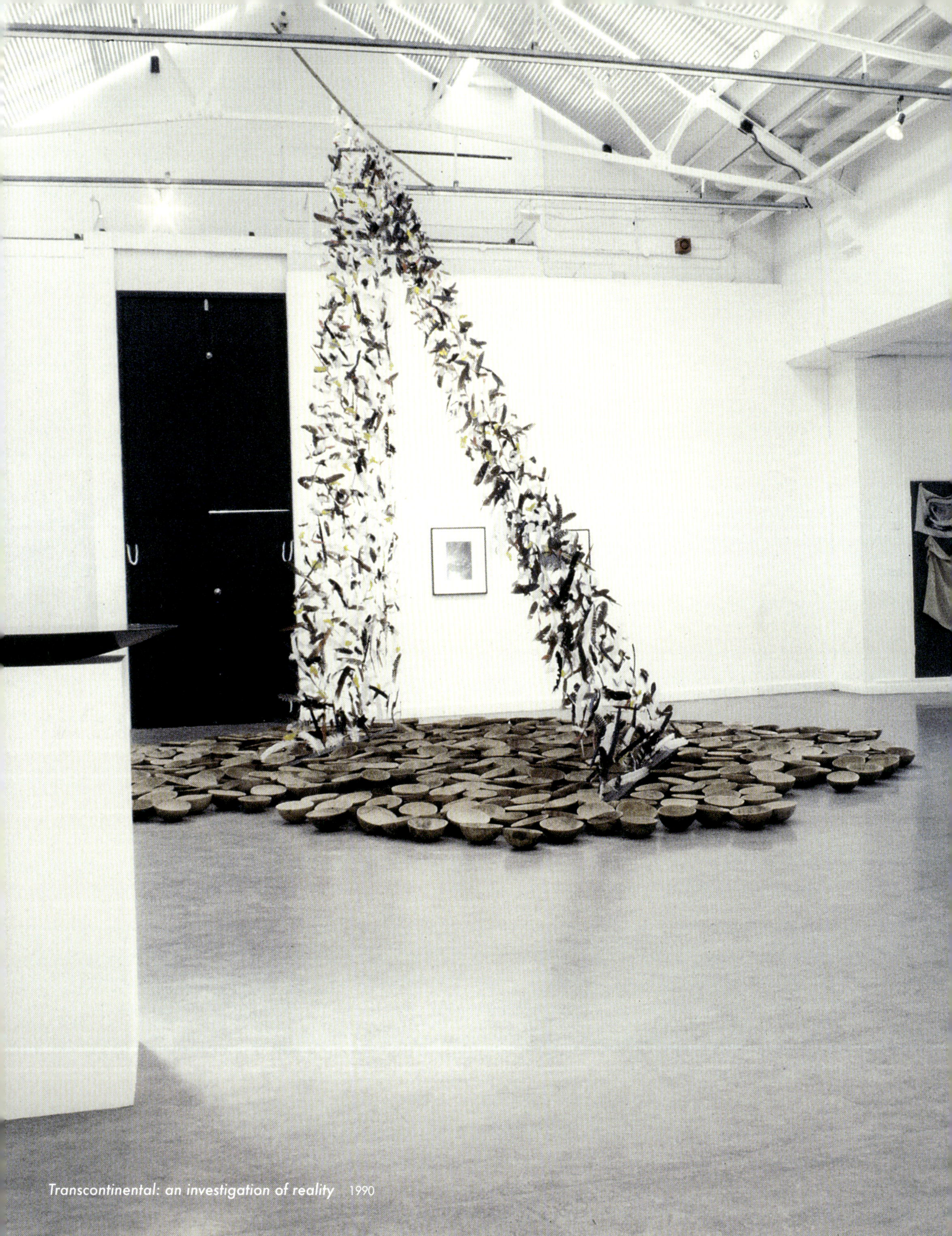

Transcontinental: an investigation of reality   1990

an international context".[8] The Council accepted this idea without demur and, more generally was supportive of Macgregor's plans for the programme overall: "It was agreed that Council should not be involved in artistic decision making, but members found it useful to have the opportunity to talk about exhibitions and activities."[9]

Transcontinental: an investigation of reality, organised by Ikon in collaboration with Corner-house Manchester and curated by Guy Brett, was an extraordinary achievement. Featuring nine artists from Argentina, Brazil and Chile – Waltercio Caldas, Juan Davila, Roberto Evangelista, Eugenio Dittborn, Victor Grippo, Jac Leirner, Cildo Meireles, Tunga and Regina Vater – it challenged familiar misconceptions of art work from Latin America as being either traditional and folkloric, or a poor imitation of modernism. Exemplifying a strong experimental tendency, smartly responsive to geopolitics, *Transcontinental* was a postmodern critique of an art historical model that pitched peripheral cultures against those in the "First World" centres of Europe and the US. In an insightful and lucid catalogue essay, Brett posed a series of rhetorical questions around the possibility of a "'third way' which goes beyond these alternatives of homogenisation and polarisation and all that they entail":

> Is there a more sophisticated model that takes into account the movements and journeys of artists themselves, or the common patterns that arise in attitudes towards experimental art? Is it possible to speak of the meeting and clashing of cultures both in terms of profound differences – and therefore of inevitable misunderstandings – and also in terms of the creation of non-essentialist, multiple identities?[10]

Through a wide variety of styles and media – often manifested as installation – *Transcontinental* had a strong positive impact in terms of critical reception and subsequently resonated through Ikon's programme. Arguably, Birmingham's regional status only served to make those arguments against the insidious dichotomy of periphery and centre more pertinent, and informed Macgregor's tenure as a whole, from shortly before *Transcontinental* through to a major survey of work by Australian Aboriginal artist Gordon Bennett, realised after she left Ikon in 1999.

Two artists from *Transcontinental*, Victor Grippo and Juan Davila, went on to have solo exhibitions at Ikon in 1995, and prior to that were two group shows that included Latin American artists. *In Fusion*, curated by Macgregor, Gavin Jantjes and Roger Malbert, was an Art Council touring exhibition – at Ikon during early 1993 – that brought together eleven artists living and working in Europe, "but whose cultural roots [were] elsewhere in the world"[11] – as if to reiterate Brett's point about the "movements and journeys of artists themselves". Four of them were from Latin America, others from Algeria, Armenia,

8
Ibid.

9
Minutes of Council of Management of Ikon Gallery, 11 June 1991. Certainly this had not always been the case. Twelve years earlier the Council had felt that "[Ikon is] no longer in a position to afford [the Director] the opportunity for the unrestrained exercise of a personal view … [and that] an undue percentage of resources being used for foreign shows would be wrong." (Council of Management Policy Discussion, Director's summary of meeting on 13 June 1978).

10
Guy Brett, 'Border Crossings', *Transcontinental*, exhibition catalogue, Verso, in association with Ikon Gallery, Birmingham & Corner-house, Manchester, 1990, pp. 11–12

11
Foreword, *In Fusion: New European Art*, exhibition catalogue, Arts Council and South Bank Centre, 1993, p. 5

the Caribbean, China, Iran, Senegal and Turkey, making work that was, by and large, pre-occupied with issues arising from colonisation, displacement, alienation and appropriation. A year earlier there had been *Turning the Map: Photography from Latin America*, a show originated by Camerawork, London. Including Dittborn and Brazilian artist Rosângela Rennó, it marked the 500th anniversary of Columbus' 'discovery' of the Americas:

> America of course was not discovered, but colonised, its indigenous
> nations suffering genocide on a mass scale. *Turning the Map* [provided] an
> antidote to Europe and white America's Quincentenary fever by showing
> the contemporary work of Latin America, Chicano and Native American
> photographers from both North and South. For America today, contrary
> to popular belief, is not a country, but a continent: not one place but many.[12]

Ikon's programme at the time made a number of references to the anniversary of Columbus' voyage, but none so much as Antoni Miralda's *Honeymoon* project (1986–92, at Ikon spring 1991). Smart and Spanish, Miralda had the idea of "marrying" the Christopher Columbus Monument in Barcelona to the Statue of Liberty in New York, culminating in a 1992 wedding ceremony in Las Vegas. Along the way other cities would contribute: New York a 110 foot high engagement dress, Columbus' suit designed by Tamami Nakano from Tokyo, a 300 foot long veil from Barcelona, a wedding cape and necklace from Philadelphia and Sète respectively, and a gondola shoe from Venice. Birmingham, thanks to Ikon, provided an eternity ring for Miss Liberty, produced in the Jewellery Quarter in conjunction with Miralda's team in Barcelona and filled with hundreds and thousands of rings donated by people from all over the UK. There was a procession, camp in the extreme, by canal boat and on foot, as part of the official programme to celebrate the opening of the city's International Convention Centre and an exhibition at Ikon, including the ring and shoes, associated correspondence, planning and press materials, "on the theme of ritual and ceremony".

Despite the inclusive nature of the project, bringing together community groups, artists living locally and other arts organisations, there was a harsh backlash from the press and more generally, as Macgregor explained to her Council of Management: "It became a political issue, being used by the Conservatives to attack the local Labour group's spending on the arts in national broadcasts before the local elections. It was perhaps unusual in being criticised by both the right and the left, the latter because of its association with the upcoming Columbus 'celebrations' … [the project was ironic, but] this was difficult to put across in the context of a pageant event."[13]

Preceding Miralda's *Honeymoon* in 1991 was *A Ship Called Jesus*, an exhibition by Keith Piper. This artist, Birmingham-raised, London-based, wrote extensively within the pages

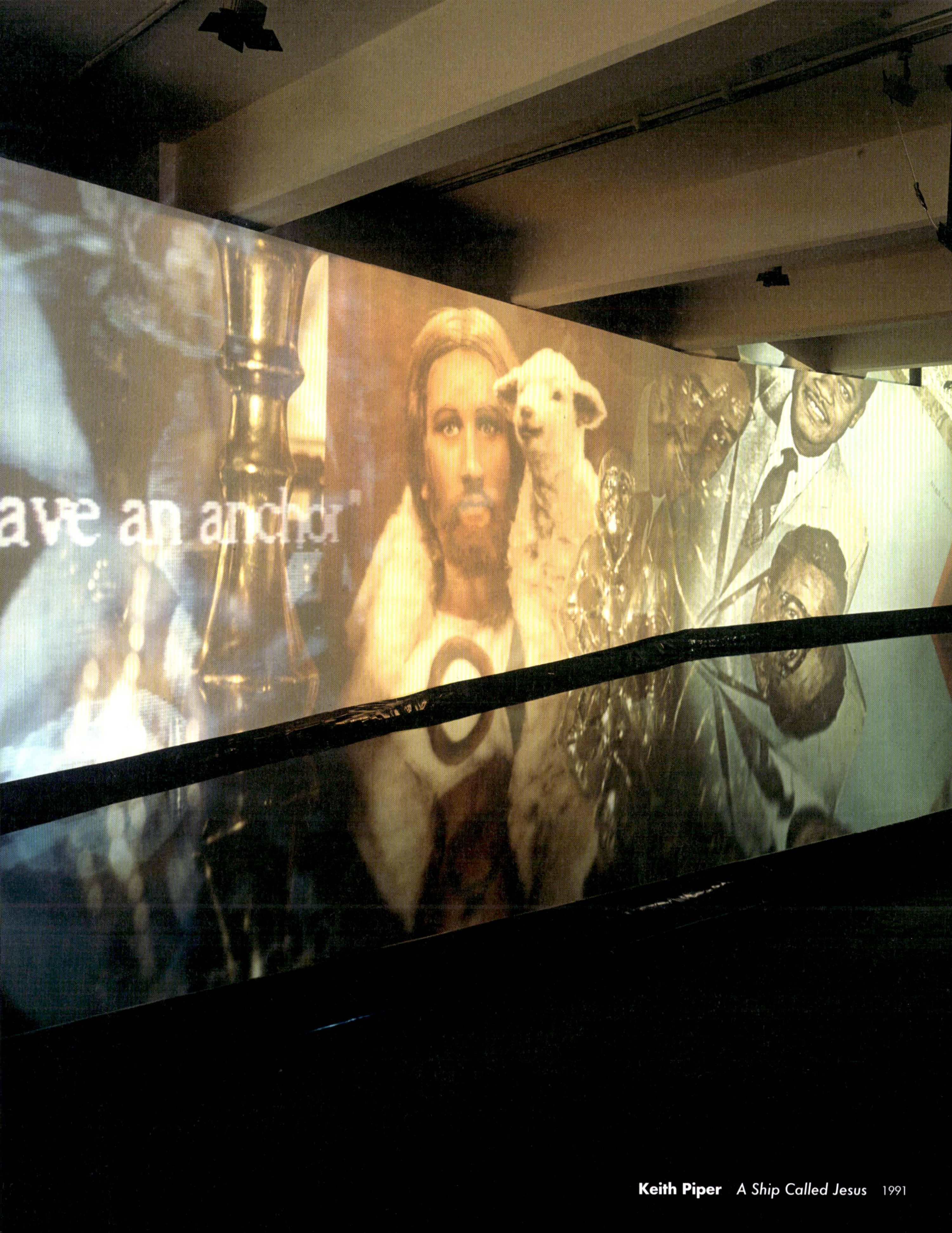

Keith Piper *A Ship Called Jesus* 1991

of the catalogue, beginning at the beginning: "From the point at which Columbus claimed the 'New World' for the Catholic Spanish monarchy in 1492, Colonialism and Christendom became firmly locked in an unholy alliance of mutual self-interest. When a Papal Bull of 1455 authorised the 'reduction to servitude of all infidel peoples', it gave initially the Portuguese, and then also the Spanish an effective monopoly on Colonial expansion."[14] The slave trade evolved out of this assumed superiority and the English became competitively involved, in the 1560s, when Queen Elizabeth I chartered for a ship for four voyages to West Africa and the West Indies under the command of Sir John Hawkins. The ship was *Jesus of Lübeck*.

Piper proceeded, both in his writing and art work for this exhibition, commissioned by Ikon, to make observations on Black British experience and the phenomenon of Black Christianity – paradoxically, "the Christian church [being] a centre and focus from which many of our parents derived their strength". An installation in three parts, the exhibition combined sculptural pieces with segmented framed photographs, projected images and reflecting pools of water. At the heart of the show was a tombstone inscribed with the words "the name of the ship was JESUS OF LUBECK. We've been sailing in her ever since". The catalogue was designed (by Arefin) "to exist not solely as a record of the exhibition, but also as a study and a piece of work in its own right".[15] In his introduction, Piper makes the observation that he and fellows members of the Blk Art Group, a "loose grouping of young Black artists, based initially in the West Midlands … [including] Eddie Chambers, Donald Rodney and myself, [who] were all the products of Fundamentalist Christian backgrounds engaged in that (largely unspoken) process of extreme rebellion against that background." Clearly *A Ship Called Jesus* was as personal and heartfelt as it was research based, and this came across to visitors so that Macgregor could report to her Council of Management that it had "received a good response".[16]

At the same Council meeting Macgregor announced that Ikon had recently appointed a new "Exhibition Trainee", supported by an 18 month Arts Council bursary. He was Donald Rodney. Born in Birmingham in 1961, Rodney studied Fine Art at Trent Polytechnic in Nottingham and there he met Keith Piper, subsequently claiming that it was Piper who then inspired him to make work with a political edge. A close friendship quickly formed, to be terminated by Rodney's tragic early death in 1998 from complications arising from sickle cell anaemia. Despite the condition, punctuating his traineeship with periods of hospitalisation – to the extent that the traineeship could not be completed – he organised *White Noise*, an exhibition at Ikon during the summer of 1992 comprising five sound installations by artists from marginalised cultural backgrounds. Also he helped Macgregor organise a major exhibition of work by American artist Adrian Piper in partnership with Cornerhouse, Manchester. Macgregor explained in her introduction to the catalogue, "Piper raises the spectre of miscegenation and seeks to tackle racism right

14
Keith Piper, 'A Ship Called Jesus',
A Ship Called Jesus, exhibition
catalogue, Ikon Gallery,
Birmingham 1991

15
Ibid.

16
Minutes of Council of Management
of Ikon Gallery, 12 March 1991

in the bastion of white liberal activity, the art gallery. Piper's target is specific: those who don't think they have a problem. This, says Piper, is the problem".

Working with photography, performance, installation, video and text, Adrian Piper was exploring the nature of otherness and ostracism in ways that chimed in with Rodney's and Keith Piper's art practices. In this vein, the catalogue introduction is one of Macgregor's best pieces of writing for Ikon. She argues forcefully for "subversive and politically orientated work" and within a British context makes a case for regional venues such as Ikon and Cornerhouse: "most of the important initiatives have come from outside London and as a result can still be regarded as marginal from the metropolitan perspective that predominates." Post-Brexit, her closing paragraph with its observations on the prospect of a unified Europe, is especially poignant:

> Debates about national identity take little account of the diversities of populations which exist in every country and the increase in racism in the form of physical attacks and strident calls for stringent immigration policies. The implications of the economic relationship of a strengthened Europe to the so-called Third World has yet to be addressed. The function of Piper's work is to force us to confront our attitudes and ultimately take action to change ourselves and the systems under which we operate. After all, the personal is still political.[17]

Rodney returned to Ikon in 1994, exhibiting with London-based artist Rose Finn-Kelcey. A work by him, *Visceral Canker*, combined plastic tubing filled with his own blood and the coat of arms of Sir John Hawkins to suggest an entanglement of heredity and slavery. Another, *Truth, Dare, Double-Dare …*, was a sound installation he made in collaboration with Finn-Kelcey, inspired by the children's game of Truth or Dare, where participants challenge one another to say what they really think about each other. The voices of the artists were assumed by actors and heard through different loudspeakers.

The honesty of *Truth, Dare, Double-Dare …* is as searing as it is compelling with much of the dialogue dwelling on Rodney's illness. It is made more poignant in light of Finn-Kelcey's having had polio as a child and her own death in 2014 from motor neurone disease. Rodney explains succinctly that he and Rose are "mis-matched": "At times in the past I really wanted to work with other artists / Rose won't work with other artists again / Rose won't work collaboratively again." Other excerpts are equally candid, as follows:

> Rose relishes the opportunity to say what she feels about me.
> Rose is angry at me and feels I've let her down.

17
Elizabeth Macgregor, Introduction, *Adrian Piper*, exhibition catalogue, Ikon Gallery, Birmingham and Cornerhouse, Manchester 1991, pp. 7-9

> Rose didn't think about the practicalities
> I didn't think about the realities.
>
> I needed pain killers to keep our meetings going.
>
> I don't get to sleep till late at night.
> I take "amitriptyline" tablets to sleep
> I take "co-proximal" to get out of bed
> I inject "Desferal" to keep my heart and liver working
> My images will now be bleaker and old
>
> At times Rose is like an Inferno Hellion.
> We have survived and pioneered
> This has been a thorn in my side for some time

Finn-Kelcey similarly played the game in earnest:

> Donald's illness is his site of manipulation
> Fear of betrayal is my site of manipulation
> Manipulation is a fact of life
>
> I hated Donald for a while
> Once I had decided to pull out of the show I loved him
> But when Donald decided he didn't want to pull out, I hated him again
>
> I criticised Donald in my notebook but tore it out just in case I left the
> book at his house
> One entry read 'Fat black baby'
>
> Am I a monster
> Does Donald think I am a slave driver
> Is this art
> Is this therapy
>
> Donald told me that black artists can't afford to play. They have to be out
> there exhibiting otherwise they lose the ground they have gained.
>
> Women artists of my generation had the same anxieties.

In his obituary, Guy Brett observed that Finn-Kelcey's art practice was empowered by the feminism she grew up with during the 1960s and 70s, paradoxically to the extent that she could express feelings of vulnerability and a lack of confidence.[18]

18
Guy Brett, 'Rose Finn-Kelcey obituary', *The Guardian*, 24 Feb 2014

Brett also wrote the catalogue essay for Finn-Kelcey's Ikon exhibition and later was the author of a substantial monograph on her work (2013). A very influential London-based writer and curator, he has been a champion of many important artists, from all over the world who, if not from the periphery, were often out of the mainstream. After *Transcontinental*, during the 1990s, he was very involved with Ikon. He was close to many exhibiting artists, including Lucia Nogueira, Shelagh Wakely, Juan Davila and Victor Grippo – also writing catalogue essays on Davila and Grippo – in tune with the gallery's emphasis on marginalised communities and cultures.[19]

Wakely, who grew up between the UK and Kenya, at the end of 1991 made an expansive installation directly onto Ikon's ground floor of stencilled baroque swirls made from powdered turmeric. The pattern and assertive materiality of the work betrayed both her experience as a fabric designer and her keen interest in Brazil where she had many artist friends such as Tunga, to some extent thanks to Brett. Nogueira, arrived in London from Brazil in 1973, was drawn to such kindred spirits – also including art critic Adrian Searle and gallerist Mario Flecha – and her exhibition of new sculptures, assemblages from found objects, took place in 1993.

With a wealth of experience derived from lives lived elsewhere, neither Wakely nor Nogueira were explicitly autobiographical. Likewise Permindar Kaur, whose exhibition *Cold Comfort* (1996) was clearly derived from personal experience, as she explained, "[drawing] influence from my Indian and British background" but conveyed more general observations on "the complications and contradictions that arise from cultural fragmentation"[20]; and Vong Phaophanit, an artist from Laos, who spent formative years in France before settling in the UK, making an installation of bamboo and lead at Ikon with similar intent, deliberately avoiding "biographism".[21] Its title could not have been more gently poetic: "tok tem dean kep kin bo dai. what falls to the ground but can't be eaten".

By contrast, Zarina Bhimji, arriving in the UK from Uganda at the age of eleven, explained how she needed to negotiate aspects of everyday life usually taken for granted: "[I am] … trying to make sense of my history. To do this I need to project back into the feelings I had as a child … the clothes I wore, the food I ate with my parents. These things are so relevant to what I do now." Bhimji's exhibition, at Ikon in 1992, was highly charged with symbolic significance. Photographic subjects could not have been more meaningful and likewise found objects – for one work encased in 85 glass shoebox-like vitrines inspired by her residency at the Victoria & Albert Museum. Three years later, in an article for The Sunday Times, Macgregor recalled Bhimji's show as evidence in her case for the defence of contemporary art: "In the Ikon, we had a very moving piece by Zarina Bhimji. She filled the gallery with tiny children's shirts she had burned holes in. People cried."[22]

19
Besides Brett, Cathy de Zegher, then Director of the Kanaal Art Foundation (Kortrijk, Belgium), was very involved with Ikon's artistic programme during Macgregor's directorship. She made contributions to the catalogue of *Transcontinental*, and shortly afterwards organised exhibitions of work by Antoni Muntades and Ilya Kabakov & Ulo Sooster that took place at Ikon. Ikon's Victor Grippo exhibition was a collaboration with the Kanaal Art Foundation. After the reopening of Ikon at Oozells Street School de Zegher wrote an essay for the Nancy Spero exhibition catalogue, and edited *Martha Rosler, Positions in the Life World*, co-published by Ikon, the Generali Foundation and The MIT Press.

20
Permindar Kaur, Proposal for *Cold Comfort*, unpublished 1995

21
Claire Oboussier, 'tok tem dean kep kin bo dai. what falls to the ground but can't be eaten', *tok tem dean kep kin bo dai. what falls to the ground but can't be eaten*, exhibition catalogue, Chisenhale Gallery, London 1992

22
Elizabeth A Macgregor, This is art we should all understand', *The Sunday Times*, 13 August 1995

The article, 'This is art we should all understand', was upbeat in its overview: "In the end, perhaps, the ultimate question for all art is one of quality: what is going to last? It is history that will decide, but the popularity of galleries gives us some indication of whether we are getting things right. The signs are encouraging: there were 110m visits to museums and art galleries last year, 25m to football matches. We are the only art form that can claim rising audiences. Contemporary art is a great British success." But, essentially, the motivation for Macgregor's putting pen to paper was to counteract ongoing tabloid newspaper attacks on Ikon's programme. It would be wrong to assume that these were provincial – or "peripheral" – as all London galleries and museum were similarly targets during these years of muscular "red top" journalism, but what made this press antagonism particularly galling was that it played on the fact that Ikon had just been awarded £3.67m of national lottery funding for the renovation of the Oozells Street School building. Four years since Axel Burrough's optimistic plan for Ikon moving in 1993, there was still a long way to go before confirmation, and while negotiations were going on with stake-holders – especially Birmingham City Council – negative publicity was the last thing Macgregor needed.

She referred to artists Damien Hirst and Hamad Butt, to Duchamp, in order to make the point, simply, that art wasn't what it used to be, no longer oils on canvas and cast bronze: "At the Ikon Gallery in Birmingham, we have had our fair share of ridicule. When the gallery won [...] lottery funding, some newspapers picked up on an exhibition from earlier in the year. Under such headlines as 'Spuddy Stupid', scorn was poured on an installation by the important Latin American artist Victor Grippo which happened to be made of potatoes …"

Ikon's Victor Grippo exhibition in 1995 is legendary – Birmingham's equivalent to Carl Andre's "Tate bricks". It was a retrospective for an important Argentinian artist who survived formative years under political dictatorships to positively assert relationships between art, science and everyday life: "The materials he uses, and their associations with the daily lives of people in his homeland … give his work a powerful symbolic and political significance."[23] His installation, *Analogia I* (1970–77), a work which involved the generation of electricity from trestle-table tops laden with potatoes – as an analogy of human consciousness despite oppression – provided the trigger for an avalanche of philistinism from both press and politicians. An editorial in *The Sun* asked for a "Lottery Shake-up": "How can anyone give close on £4million to a gallery which thinks a hundred-weight of potatoes wired for electricity is art?"[24] But it wasn't just the tabloids. Robert Clark writing for *The Guardian* was condemnatory – "In Britain's tired cultural climate we'd need a massive dose of irony for rotting potatoes to become anything other than rotting potatoes."[25] – while Peter Aspden from the *Financial Times* circumspectively observed that "Sadly no one seems to think that artists with exotic designs on vegetables

23
Foreword, *Victor Grippo*, exhibition catalogue, Ikon Gallery and Société des Expositons du Palais des Beaux-Arts Bruxelles in collaboration with Kanaal-Art Foundation, Kortrijk 1995, p. 4

24
'Time for Lottery Shake-up', *The Sun*, 28 April 1995

25
Robert Clark, 'Spuds U don't like offer little spark', *The Guardian*, 3 May 1995

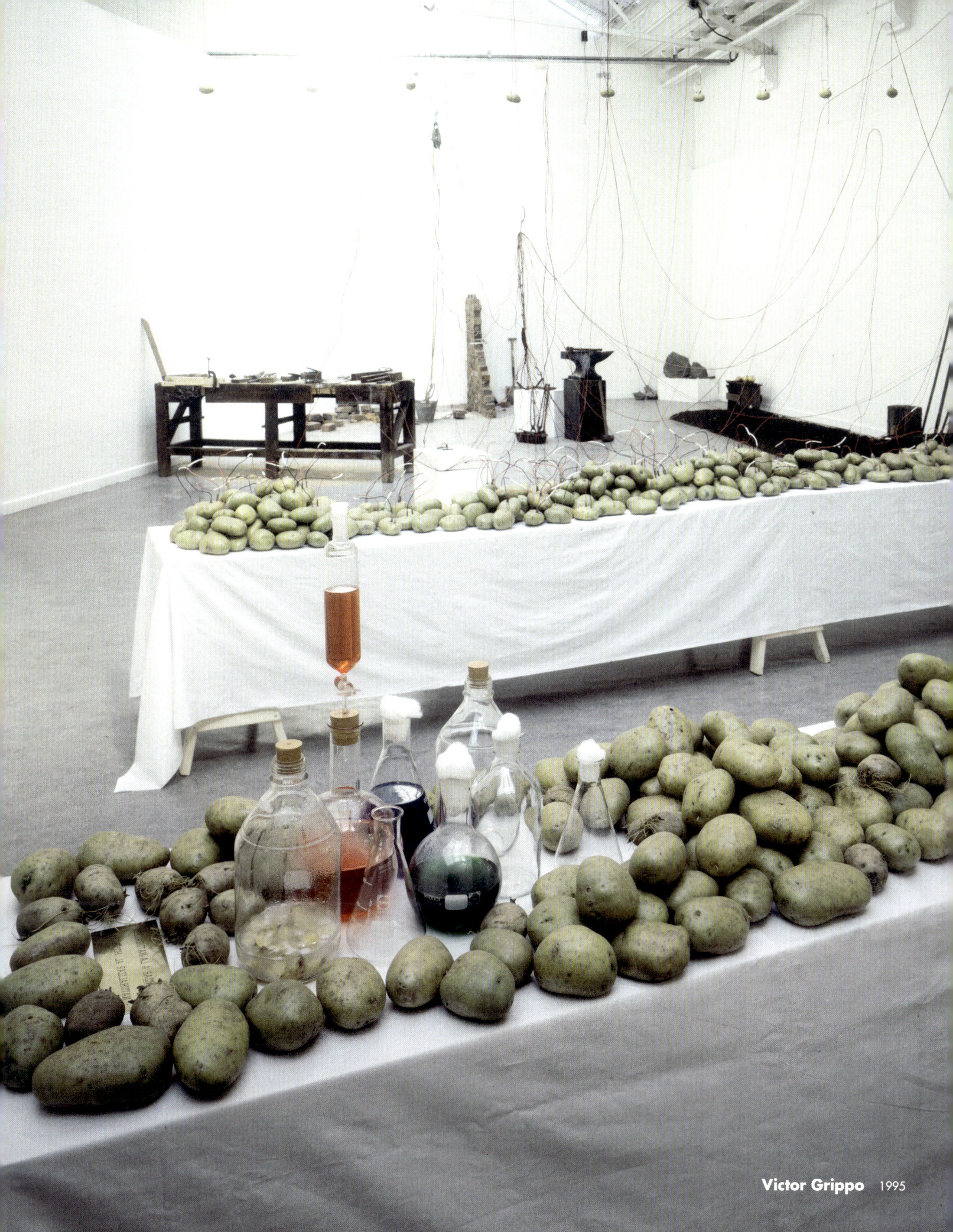

Victor Grippo 1995

are terribly important at all; but then, whoever said that life in the *avant garde* would be easy?"[26] Closer to home, *The Shropshire Star* couldn't resist the temptation of word play: "A King Edwards-sized row has erupted over plans to fork out £100,000 of National Lottery cash to a gallery where the star exhibit is … potatoes on a table. Tory councillors in Birmingham are outraged by the handover of the grant to the local Ikon Gallery … Councillor Alan Blumenthal demanded, 'How can the public be supporting ideas like this when we are constantly hearing of spending cuts?'"[27]

The Daily Mail assumed a familiar moral high ground with its suggestion that the money spent on Grippo's exhibition "could have been used to alleviate any number of social problems … Medical experts said it would have bought an X-ray machine with £20,000 to spare or paid the annual salary of eight junior nurses or seven junior doctors … 'What a waste', said Councillor Ken Hardeman. 'How can anyone see this as art? These potatoes should be handed over to homeless organisations and put to some practical use.'"[28] This position couldn't have been more beside the point, given that cost of the exhibition – £50,775 – had been more or less covered by grants from Argentina and subsidiaries of the Arts Council. The local hostility was unfortunate, especially for a city keen to prove its internationalist credentials, as according to Macgregor's Director's Report March – June 1995, "The Beunos Aires local council faxed through a list of motions put down in their council questioning the behaviour of Birmingham councillors in criticising a leading Argentinian artist."[29]

The political opportunism in Birmingham carried on with momentum. The next victim was Avis Newman, a British artist exhibiting shortly after Grippo, whose work could not be more poetically subtle. "Councillor says Ikon Gallery displays are 'tripe'", was the headline in the *Birmingham Post*: "… Coun Graham Green said he was angered after being sent an invitation to the exhibition at the Ikon Gallery which featured *Webs*, one of four minimalist paintings being exhibited." … Coun Green said: 'To think that we are spending £100,000 a year keeping this art gallery going, whilst at the same time we are closing down elderly people's homes and reducing services across the city, is nothing but a disgrace, especially when they turn out what is in my opinion nothing but a lot of tripe … The £100,000 spent on nursery education could have produced better pictures than this."[30]

It turned out, predictably, that Coun Green had not seen Newman's exhibition before condemning it. In response, Macgregor accused him of trying to score cheap political points: "… It's getting boring. The critics never come and see the paintings and no-one can possibly tell what they are like without seeing them".[31] She was right; it was boring, tedious and all-too-familiar as a ruse of the press, with local politicians happy to be complicit with "outrage", more or less up until the time, around 2005, when tabloid newspapers,

26
Peter Aspden, 'Telling your money where it should go', *Financial Times*, 15/16 July 1995

27
'Gallery roasted over spuds they don't like', *The Shropshire Star*, 24 April 95.

28
Stephen Wright, 'This week's lottery good cause, 500lb of artistic potatoes', Daily Mail, 24 April 1995

29
Elizabeth Macgregor, Director's Report, March – June 1995

30
'Councillor says Ikon Gallery displays are "tripe"', *Birmingham Post*, 5 October 1995

31
Ibid.

especially those in the regions, were becoming superseded by social media a decade later – when the people themselves became, for better or worse, "the voice of the people".

Antony Gormley's exhibition at Ikon in 1995, including *Field for the British Isles* – a floor-based installation of forty thousand small clay figures – was the highest weekly attended exhibition of the year, "very popular with a variety of visitors".[32] And it was timely, given the recent installation of the *Iron Man*, the artist's large public sculpture in nearby Victoria Square in 1993. In an interview with Terry Grimley, art critic for the *Birmingham Post*, he spelt out the connection: "The *Iron Man* wouldn't have been possible without the *Fields* and they have a lot in common. Although the *Iron Man* carries the baggage of the body case, that fact that it's patently buried in the earth means that it contains the same questions – to what extent human beings are different from mineral beings or vegetable beings".[33] A year later, in a "comment" for the *Post*, Grimley declared that "… the *Iron Man* is a major piece of late 20th century British sculpture and a significant asset to the city".[34] He had been moved to defend the sculpture in light of a backlash campaign started by the *Post*'s tabloid sister, *The Evening Mail*, protesting against TSB, the bank that commissioned *Iron Man*, moving its headquarters from Birmingham to Bristol: 'Now YOU say *Iron Man* must go!' … "seventy-four per cent of those who voted in our special poll said the bank's £120,000 gift to Birmingham should be shifted from Victoria Square when the TSB moves its headquarters".[35] Another *Mail* headline was in typical British tabloid style: 'Stick it in Bristol with your new HQ'.[36]

Juan Davila's exhibition, one of the most promiscuous – aesthetically and in terms of subject matter – staged at Ikon during the 1990s, was strangely passed over by the local press, with the exception of a letter to the editor of *Metronews* from a Mr Walter Block: "As a mere father I do my level best to monitor filth, as I see it as a moral duty. So after an hour of inspecting this trash, I left … it seems to me that the poor benighted ratepayer is unwittingly subsidising yet another nail in the coffin of the British way of life".[37] Davila, born in Chile, living and working in Australia, personified "peripheral" culture being catapulted back into the centre with a muscular postmodernist eclecticism. He apprehended what was considered violent, pornographic and insulting in polite society and meted it out in concentrated doses as works of art. Pictorially he was revelling in the "inauthentic", as Brett explained: "… in his ability to mimic a whole host of other people's styles, including styles themselves based on the mimicry of other styles […] also in his appropriation of resources which mock that very skill, from computer-guided auto-mated painting at one extreme to debased handicrafts at another."[38]

Like Wakely, Davila spread his work over the ground floor of Ikon, but not with an idea of beauty; rather as "a hybrid format drawn from the displays of AIDS quilts and pavement sellers".[39] The protagonists in this multi-layered installation were, on one hand, Juanito

32
Minutes of Board Meeting of Ikon Gallery Limited, 18 June 1996

33
Terry Grimley, 'Gormley's field of 40,000 figures', *Birmingham Post*, 25 May 1995

34
Terry Grimley, 'Iron Man is a true symbol of our city', *Birmingham Post*, 7 June 1996

35
'Now YOU say *Iron Man* must go!', *Evening Mail*, 22 May 1996

36
'Stick it in Bristol with your new HQ', *Evening Mail*, 21 May 1996

37
Letter to the Editor, *Metronews*, 16 February 1995

38
Guy Brett, 'Montage as Mestizaje', *Juan Davila. Juanito Laguna*, exhibition catalogue, Chisenhale Gallery, London 1995

39
Ibid.

Laguna – sweetly standing in for Davila – an imaginary boy from the slums of Buenos Aires and Simon Bolivar, a saint-like figure from Latin American history re-imagined as a transvestite prostitute. Davila could not have arrived from a place further from Birmingham but interestingly, in the early 1990s, another radically gay artist, John Yeadon, closer to home from Coventry (but equally "peripheral"), had resorted to a similar strategy in his storytelling. His alter-ego was Blind Bifford (Biff) Jelly, a kind of theatrical wise-fool, whose travels through the "British Isles" were analogous to a journey through life, a là Candide. Interestingly, in an essay for his Ikon catalogue, he made reference to carnival in Latin America and its subversion of a colonialist dynamic: "In Brazil [carnival] is an explosion of popular culture. In European Carnival style, the poor of Brazil become Kings and Queens for a few days, celebrating African goddesses. Carnival in Latin America has its roots both in Europe and West Africa, an historical pageant remembered through slavery."[40] He and Davila (and Guy Brett) were very much on the same wavelength.

The appropriation of motifs and themes from popular culture was pervasive in contemporary art during the 1990s and this was clearly reflected in Ikon's programme. For Mark Wallinger, sport, and the ways in which it shed light on the class structure of British society, was a major preoccupation. He showed *Royal Ascot* (1994), a video installation in which we see the Queen and Prince Philip in a horse drawn carriage, on four different occasions, regally waving to other racegoers. Nearby was a photographic portrait of himself as Emily Davison, the suffragette who threw herself under King George V's horse at Epsom in 1913, dressed up as a jockey. He/she is wearing the colours of the suffragette flag.

With a syndicate the year before, Wallinger had bought a racehorse and called it *A Real Work of Art*, thereby drawing comparisons between the speculative worlds of racing and the art market, with all the class complexity involved. The horse ran its first race (in suffragette colours) at the EBF Mornarton Maiden Stakes, Bath in September 1994, broke a leg bone and was then sold to a German collector.

Israeli born, London-based artist Amikam Toren, similarly problematising the values that underpin the art market, had his first major exhibition at Ikon in 1990. The proposition of his work is neat, confusing subject and object to the extent that, in his *Armchair Paintings*, works of art are made from works of art. This ongoing series involves paintings, oils on canvas bought cheaply from second-hand stores and junk shops, from which he cuts out stencilled letters revealing the wall behind. These are short sentences or phrases taken from songs, graffiti, signs and such like, and so we read found words inscribed into found (art) objects. And what might once have been looked down upon as old fashioned kitsch, epitomised by paintings for sale at the Bayswater Road Sunday Art Exhibition, is transformed into real works of art, as endorsed by a gallery like Ikon.

40
John Yeadon, 'Laughter, a Peoples' Culture', *John Yeadon. The Travails of Blind Bifford Jelly*, exhibition catalogue, Ikon Gallery and Third Eye Centre, Birmingham and Glasgow 1991, pp. 34-35

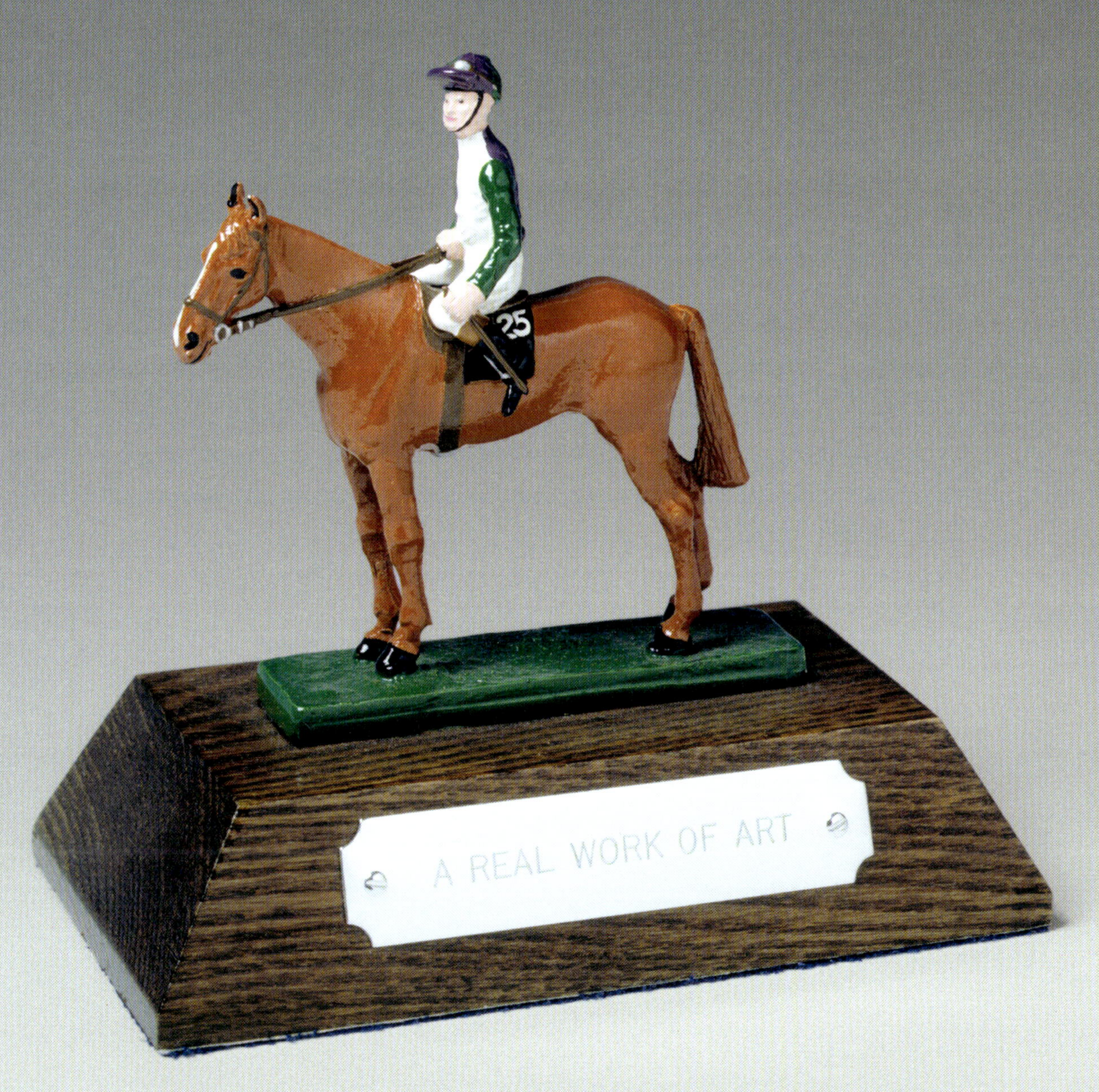

Mark Wallinger *A Real Work of Art* 1993

Edward Allington's art practice was very postmodernist, despite curators protesting too much in the foreword of the catalogue that accompanied the exhibition touring to Ikon in 1993, and accordingly he embraced kitsch. Work from the 1980s, with which he first attracted international attention, involved plastic fruit and souvenir-like miniatures of classical sculpture, mixing things up to the extent that Annelie Pohlen, Director of the Bonner Kunstverein, referred to the "loss of center [sic]" in her catalogue essay: "That center freed of mindless honored or consumed fetish fills itself up with the wealth of the many energy carriers in diversified dialogue over the nature of form or the form of the spirit that strives for beauty". In other words, "Today culture stands no longer against the department store"[41] and, aesthetically, anything might go. In much of his work Allington played on classical architectural forms, and the ideas of eternal beauty and truth that they signified, effectively to convey at once his admiration and scepticism, with the same kind of knowing humour that permeates Mark Wallinger's work.

The architectural dimension in Allington's work fitted in well with Macgregor's idea of an emphasis on the built environment, to the extent that she was proposing an "architecture season" in 1995. This was when Diller and Scofidio presented their *Slow House* installation at Ikon, very early on in what has since become a brilliant career, a year after Siah Armajani's exhibition of *Sculpture and Public Art Projects*, featuring models that emphasised "disorder"

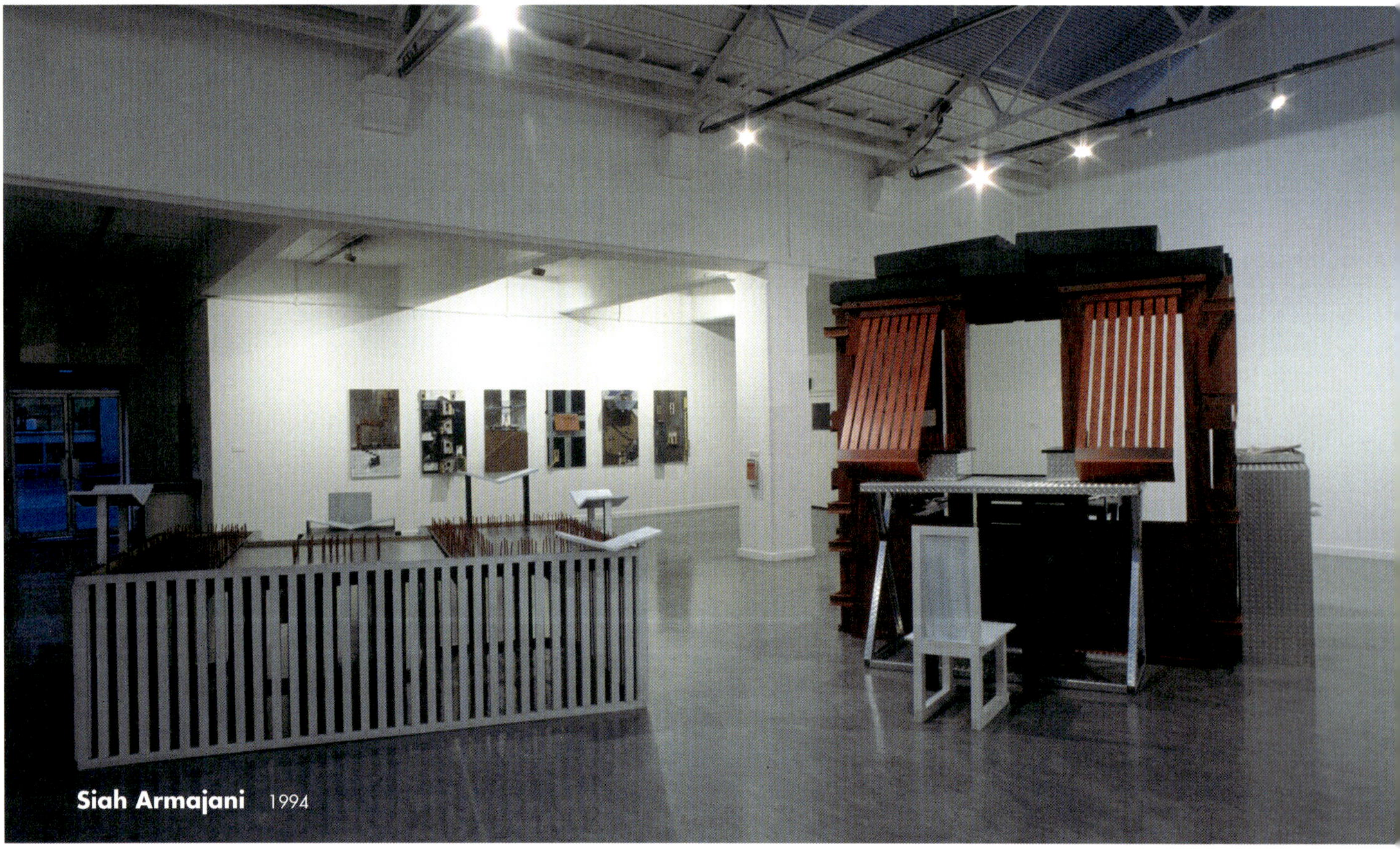

41
Annelie Pohlen, 'The Ideal Form of the Loss of Center', *Edward Allington*, exhibition catalogue, Bonner Kunstverein, Stadtische Galerie Göppingen, Cornerhouse, Manchester 1993, p. 49

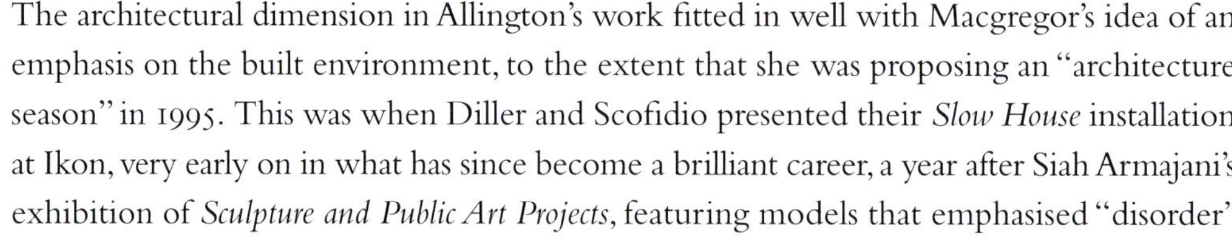

through his dedication of edifices (*Gazebos*) to anarchists rather than establishment figures. Again audiences found themselves in a cultural periphery – also, indirectly at least due to Armajani's Iranian heritage – that was as politically loaded as it was essentially postmodern.

Lisa Milroy's paintings at this time often depicted architecture. Already renowned for her ordered repetition of types of motif – shoes, fans, plates, vinyl records – wittily referencing the modernist grid, she was seeking out a corresponding inherent abstraction in Kyoto houses, Renaissance buildings in Rome and twentieth century modern edifices in central London. This was the predominant subject matter of Milroy's *Travel Paintings* exhibition, toured from Chisenhale, that reached Ikon at the beginning of 1996. Painting towards the more overtly abstract end of the aesthetic spectrum, Basil Beattie had a solo exhibition at Ikon in 1994, whereas Suzanne Treister, invited to show very early on by Macgregor (1990), made work that was figurative in a semiotic kind of way. The surrealism of her earlier pictures, heavy with symbolism, was then giving way to imagery that was distinctly "readable", if elliptical, about the ways we navigate the visual world and how visual experience is mediated. She was drawn to kitsch, like Allington – thereby signifying a similar "anything goes" pictorial democracy – and, increasingly, to the virtual worlds of video games.

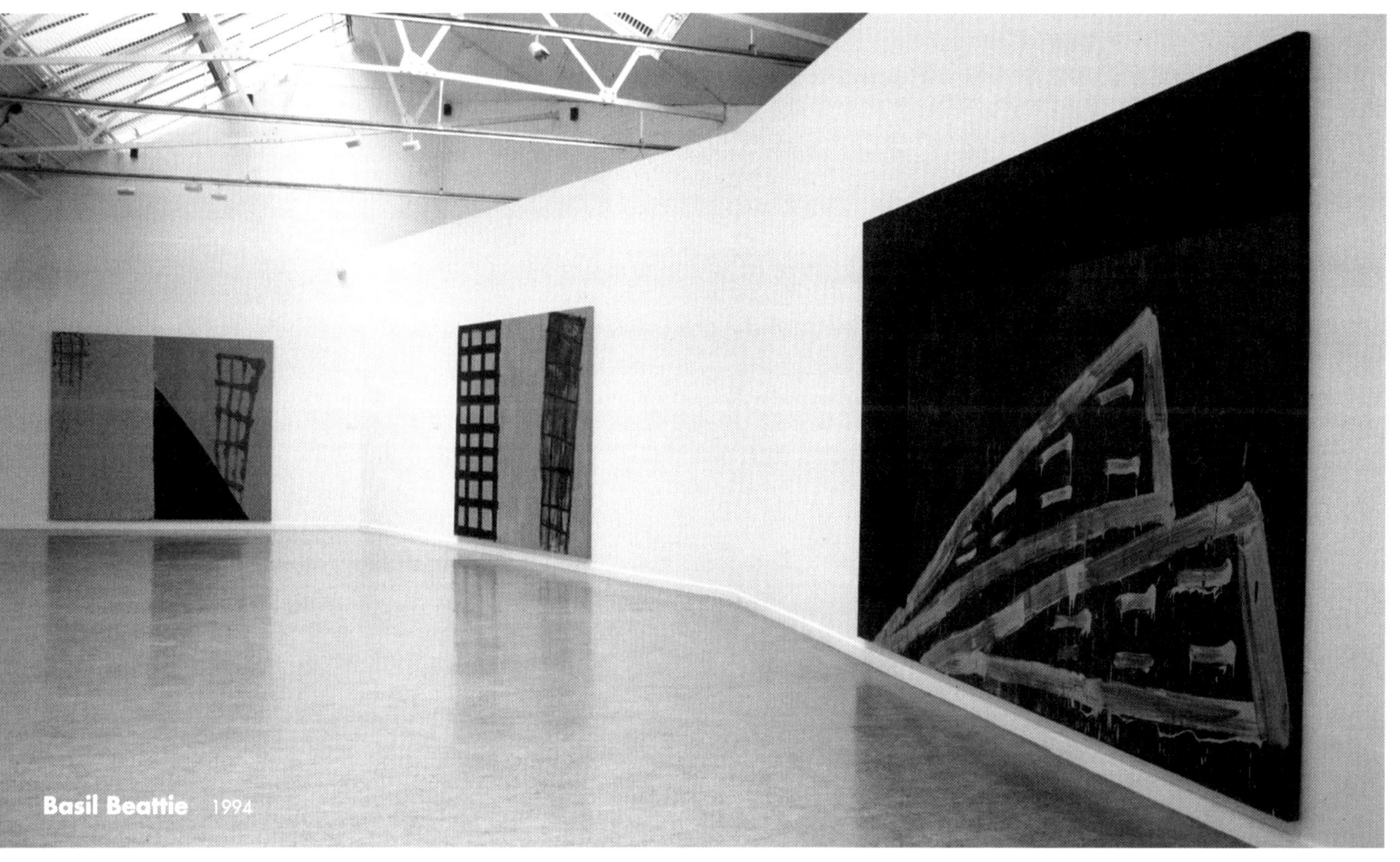

Basil Beattie 1994

There was a remarkable openness to painting at Ikon during Macgregor's years in John Bright Street – from Beattie to Davila, from Milroy to Newman, from Toren to Treister – as had previously been the case, under Antonia Payne's directorship. But now it was the decade following the declaration of a "new spirit in painting" which had been translated stylistically into a "neo-expressionism", painterly and figurative. In 1983 Adrian Searle and Tim Allen were guest curators of *paint, presence, other stories*, an exhibition or work by British artists painting with the new spirit, and *Bruise, Painting for the Nineties* was a rejoinder. Curated by Ikon's Exhibitions Officer, Angela Kingston, it was "a highlight of the exhibition programme", according to the 1992 Director's Report, picking up on a preoccupation with a kind of unwholesome beauty shared by the six participating artists – Mikey Cuddihy, Roger Kite, Nicholas May, Estelle Thompson, Alison Turnbull and Joseph Mark Wright – to suggest a sea change across the country. Writing for *The Independent on Sunday*, Tom Lubbock concurred: "… the proposal is that if the Eighties saw a revival of figurative painting, what we are seeing now is a revival of abstraction. It may sound like an answer that anyone could have devised on a wet afternoon, but it is not a complete fiction. There is a faint quickening of this particular pulse, and IKON [sic.] has put a finger on it."[42]

Four years later there was another painting show, curated by Terry Shave, including his own work and that by a number of other British artists – Mark Hammond, Alexis Harding, Louise Hopkins, David Martin, Victoria Morton, Cathy Wilkes and Richard Wright – who were, likewise "intrigued and stimulated by the process and materials of painting itself and the way painting is negotiated as a credible practice at the end of the 20th century".[43]

For some reason, painting has been and continues to be interrogated unlike any other art form. Painting exhibitions came around every five years or so at Ikon during the 1980s and 1990s. Otherwise group shows, deemed to be more popular than solo shows, tended to be "thematic" focused on current affairs and issues that were threaded through the fabric of the gallery's artistic programme as a whole, with racial and sexual politics to the fore. *With This Ring …,* an exhibition about "the union of individuals in marriage and through sex … [cutting] right into the gloss of weddings and romance",[44] was actually organised to coincide with Miralda's *Honeymoon* project. It was preceded a few months earlier by *Mothers*, a "very personal" curatorial exercise for Angela Kingston – touching "upon differing aspects of a notion of 'mother' that matter very much to me"[45] – and involved a number of important feminist artists such as Felicity Allen, Bobby Baker, Marysia Lewandowska and Jo Spence. In her erudite catalogue essay, art theorist Hilary Robinson puts the exhibition into wider cultural and political contexts, accounting for the taboo of the body of the mother.

42
Tom Lubbock, 'Cruisin' for a bruisin' in Brum', *The Independent on Sunday*, 19 July 1992.

43
What's On, Birmingham, 2 – 15 November 1996

44
Angela Kingston, *With This Ring …*, exhibition catalogue, Ikon Gallery, Birmingham 1991

45
Angela Kingston, Introduction, *Mothers*, exhibition catalogue, Ikon Gallery, Birmingham 1990, p. 5

Robinson also referred to the phenomenon of "the so-called 'new man'" and the sexual abuse of children, very much in the news at that time due to the Cleveland scandal and the growing AIDS crisis: "[The exhibition] also coincides with increasing heterosexual concern about AIDS, rising homophobia and the valorising of heterosexual fidelity".[46] *Mothers* had immediately followed *Ecstatic Antibodies*, a touring group exhibition curated by artist and writer Sunil Gupta to disrupt the politically laden mythology of HIV and AIDS. This also was an aspect of Juan Davila's exhibition at Ikon five years later. Between the two exhibitions, in early 1994, was a pair of shows curated by Kingston, *Clean* and *Dirty* occurring simultaneously – one on each floor of Ikon – to offer "multiple perspectives on society's preoccupation with purity".[47] In *Dirty*, two artists were making reference to AIDS: Locky Morris and Alistair Raphael. The latter's work, according to Kingston, "is centrally concerned with notions of illness. His use of the gallery building itself becomes a metaphor for the ways in which we have been 'infected' by current images of AIDS in the media … the work is extraordinarily calm, counteracting the furious moralising often associated with this issue. Raphael quietly addresses the hysteria of the so-called 'Gay Plague', creating a space in which we can contemplate the presence of this virus."[48]

Clean and *Dirty* were curated by Kingston as a visiting curator, as she had left Ikon at the end of 1993 to pursue a freelance career, to be replaced by John Leslie the following spring. He is remembered at the gallery mostly for his exhibitions of Mark Wallinger and Mark Dion, both characterised by sharp wit and humour to foil the serious political points that they were making. For Dion, fascinated by the systems of natural history, the ideas he conveyed of homo sapiens as an endangered species due to environmental neglect were ahead of their time in the art world. When it came to group shows, Leslie was not so concerned, as Kingston had been, with social problems close to home, but rather was more inclined to be philosophical – with an epistemological twist. He curated *Close Encounters* in 1994, an exhibition of work by seven artists, including Gregory Crewdson, Graham Gussin and Marcus Hansen, that blurred the line between reality and fiction with sci-fi overtones. *into the void*, two years later, was an exploration of nothingness.

●

In 1994, in a discussion paper, 'Ikon Gallery: a new way forward'[49], Macgregor explained that, in light of a preoccupation with the possibility of new premises – also the unlikelihood of a move happening within the next three years – with other staff members, she was interested to "redefine what it is the gallery is trying to achieve." This is an important document, not only because it reflects Ikon's curatorial strategy at the time, but also the extent to which it anticipated the artistic programme for years to come, well after Macgregor's departure:

46
'The Body of the Mother: Paradoxes and Absences', *Mothers*, exhibition catalogue, Ikon Gallery, Birmingham 1990, p.7

47
Clean and *Dirty*, exhibition brochures, Ikon Gallery, Birmingham 1994

48
Dirty, exhibition brochure, Ikon Gallery, Birmingham 1994

49
Elizabeth Macgregor, 'A discussion document. Ikon Gallery: a new way forward', as part of Ikon Gallery's Appraisal Submission to the Arts Council of Great Britain, July 1994

[Ikon] has developed a way of working which puts the artist at the centre while experimenting with different ways to engage a wider audience and in doing so has attracted attention on a range of levels … The intention is to create new ways of exploring the relationship between the art as presented in the 'institution', the artist and the audience.

In essence, the gallery would seek to work with different groups on a more intensive level, to involve them with contemporary art practice outside the gallery but without giving up the notion of the gallery as a very special place in which all kinds of ideas can be presented and discussed in ways that do not happen anywhere else. Producing quality exhibitions must be the core of the activities but there is room for a redefinition of the ways in which education and outreach programmes operate and the way in which the gallery works with artists.

A programme of artists working on specific projects with particular interest groups, over a period of three months to a year … The gallery would also like to offer more short-term possibilities for artists to visit and work in the city whether in a studio or on a project which has a public manifestation. In some cases, the artists may be involved in an exhibition

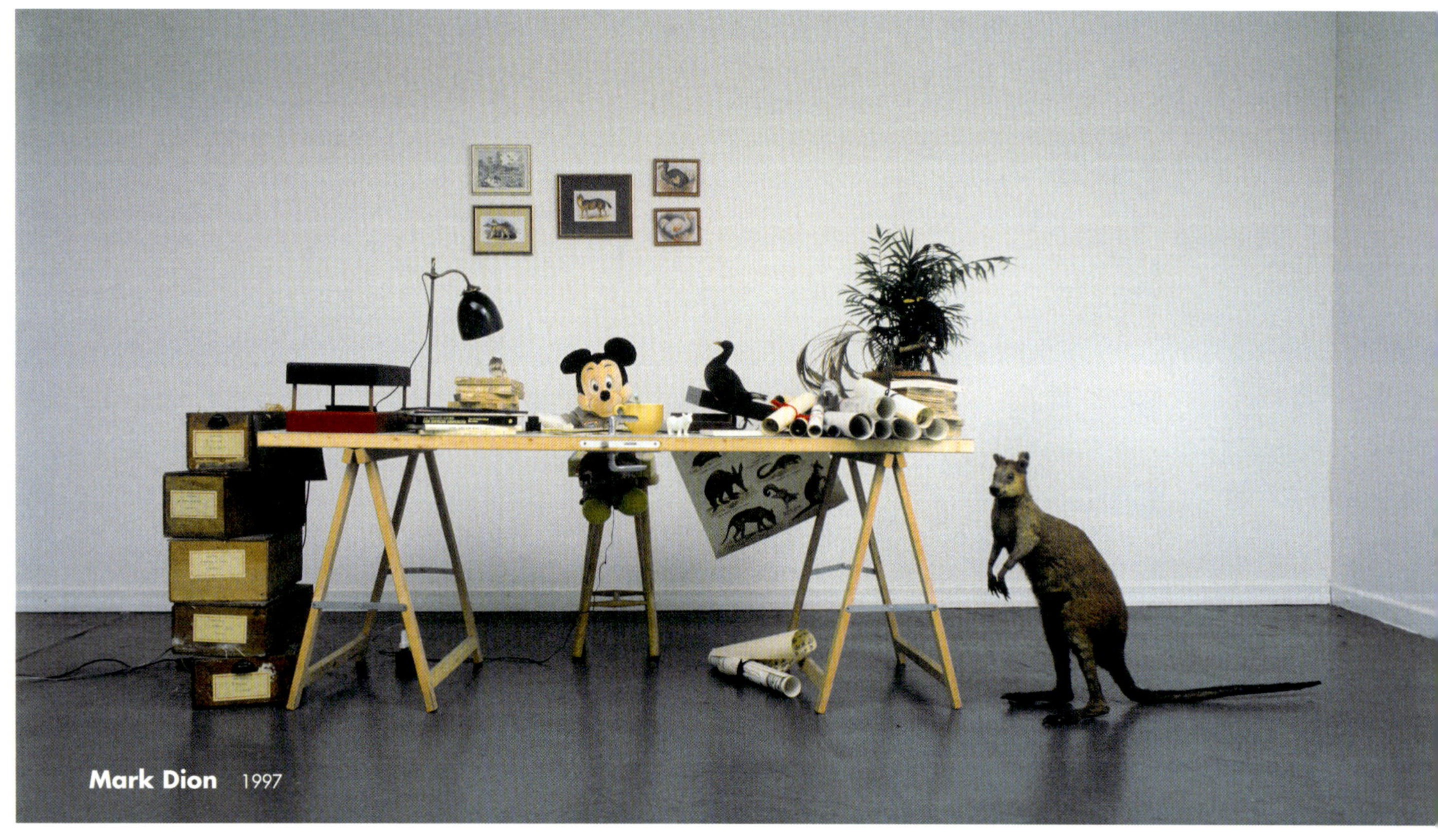

Mark Dion 1997

at Ikon, or in presenting a new piece of work elsewhere, supported by Ikon. (Birmingham has a plethora of new public monuments. Ikon would like to be able to present occasional site-specific work as an antidote!) On occasion it may be that a completely different form of exhibition may be more appropriate, such as a newspaper. Above all it is essential that the artists involved are of the highest calibre and continue to reflect the culturally diverse nature of the city.

The ambition is to break down all the boundaries which act as a deterrent to greater understanding of the role of the contemporary artist today. Ikon can provide a new model where the gallery is at the hub of a wide range of art practice and audience engagement.

This paper was submitted to Ikon's board in July 1994. Much discussion ensued about "what kind of image we wish to project in the new building (although this can also affect what we do now)". Again the question was raised about widening the range of exhibitions in the programme "to include craft, design and historical work or whether we should continue to forge a strong identity by concentrating on new work by living artists." The latter was clearly Macgregor's preference by this time, and, as outlined in the discussion paper, this would involve an unusually dynamic integration of off-site and learning activity with exhibition programming. The gallery would continue to be acknowledged as a "very special place" – a place for the freedom of expression as well as artistic excellence – but not an ivory tower as so often was assumed to be the case. Certainly this shift in actual practice started to happen, but then Macgregor would often refer to the distraction of the impending move. At the same board meeting she explained that Ikon would not be producing exhibitions as much as normal: "Due to the Director's time being diverted to securing a new building for the gallery, more exhibitions will be toured in. e.g. Gormley, Boyd Webb, Ron Haselden, Juan Davila, Lisa Milroy."[50]

Macgregor was consistently wanting to support living artists, aiming "to extend public engagement with significant new art and contemporary issues". When listing "specific objectives" she was anticipating her article in *The Sunday Times* a year later:

The gallery is committed to providing opportunities for artists to present new work which inevitably means taking risks and presenting difficult, challenging and even uncomfortable work. But this has been done within a context of trying to encourage greater public involvement. It is not so much the content of contemporary art that alienates a wider audience but the context in which it is presented. Hence rather than trying to devise a more "popular" programme, (and it is debatable what would succeed

50
'Projections of Income and Expenditures to 31.3.1996', Minutes of Council of Management of Ikon Gallery, 14 July 1994

without departing from the gallery's aims) effort has gone into making the experience of visiting Ikon more enjoyable.

In what would be later referred to as a "SWOT" analysis Macgregor painted a bigger picture. The threats included poor visual arts infrastructure within the city, tabloid attacks and a lack of leisure tourism. The weaknesses: cramped working conditions, degeneration of John Bright Street and, compared to London venues, a lack of national press coverage. The opportunities included Birmingham's ambition to change the image of the city and its European aspirations, and the business profile of the city transforming itself from an industrial to a financial and service sector.

At the same meeting Macgregor reported that Brindleyplace was extending Ikon's option on the Oozells Street School building to the end of March 1995 when presumably Ikon would know the result of its application to the National Lottery. She summarised: "having looked at various options, including the Custard Factory, Oozells Street was undoubtedly the best option." A local authority depot on Holiday Street had been considered; also Digbeth – although intended as Birmingham's media zone, was deemed "not central enough" – and properties in the Jewellery Quarter were both too small and too expensive.[51]

The feasibility study for Oozells Street, drawn up by Axel Burrough in 1991, coincided with a board meeting at which Macgregor was asked how Ikon's programme might change as a result of a move to this site. She replied "that the new location would permit a greater variety of shows and would accommodate more intimate work. The drawback of the new and more high profile location is the possibility of its being open to more intervention in the event of controversial shows."[52] The following year it was becoming clear that John Bright Street itself was becoming controversial. The pedestrianisation of the street, rather than having a gentrifying effect, made it "seedier" with a proliferation of night clubs. This was reported by *The Birmingham Voice* newspaper in October, that it was influencing Ikon's interest in moving, and Brindleyplace made sense as a new address for the gallery given that the city's focus was now shifting to Broad Street.[53]

Due to the recession, wheels were turning more slowly – or falling off, as in the case of Rosehaugh, and they were replaced as developers of Brindleyplace by Argent. The end of 1993, rather than being the time of Ikon's (optimistically projected) relocation, saw the negotiation of a new five-year lease for the gallery at John Bright Street and the completion of another, more thorough, feasibility study by Burrough. According to Macgregor, this document helped to convince the Arts Council and the Chief Executive of Birmingham City Council that "the move to the school was very important"[54] – and timely, as an exhibition of Roger Hilton's paintings, toured by the Arts Council to Ikon, had to be closed in November because of flooding in the basement space. At a Council of Management meeting a few weeks later, Macgregor was clearly exasperated: "Given the events of the past three weeks and the damage it has done to us physically and in terms of our reputation, we are now convinced that if we stay here, it is only a matter of time before something really disastrous happens. The extent to which the building is inhibiting our ability to operate, never mind develop, cannot be underestimated [sic]."[55] In the same meeting she presented a 'Resumé of current position as regards premises', more or less a list of arguments for Ikon's taking up residence in the old Oozells Street School building. They included a 150 year lease and "peppercorn rent", better visitor and income generating facilities – with a view to attracting more private sector support – museum standard security and environmental control and, finally, the support of the local authority. Arguments against included no room for expansion but, as Macgregor pointed out with some prescience, "this could be a benefit!"

At the same time, questions about the nature of Ikon's programme in the new premises were occurring to Terry Grimley in his end-of-year round up of local cultural activity for the *Birmingham Post*. He thought the former Oozells Street School building would make a superb gallery, "but would Ikon's line in austere, politically correct installation art win it any more friends there than it has in John Bright Street".[56] Having anticipated the idea of the exhibition programme being less experimental to suit a more "high profile" venue, Macgregor by this time was asserting a determination that this wouldn't happen, that there would not be a popularising of content, but rather Ikon would be more attractive in its new home, made a more enjoyable place to visit.

This was the stance that eventually released funding necessary to refurbish Oozells Street School: grants from the National Lottery amounting to £4.5 million and almost £1 million each from The Foundation for Sport and the Arts and the European Regional Development Fund. The latter was announced in January 1996 and two months later Ikon's Board (ex-Council of Management) announced that the gallery would close at John Bright Street in March 1997, confident that the lease on Oozells Street would be signed as indeed it was by the time building work commenced there on 13 May 1996.

Ikon stepped up its activity beyond the gallery to coincide with its fundraising campaign. Most notably, and promoted within the context of Ikon Touring, was *England's Glory*, an off-site exhibition at Witley Court, a derelict stately home in Worcestershire, during August – September 1995. Part of a wider initiative, encouraging artists to respond to this asset of English Heritage by West Midlands Arts, it included new site-specific art work by Helen Chadwick, David Fryer, Brighid Lowe and Nicola Petrie ostensibly to "encourage greater public understanding and enjoyment of the contemporary visual arts".[57] At the same time, it provided an elegant setting for a summer party devised as a development opportunity, targeting the great and the good of the West Midlands. It was

55
Council of Management Meeting of Ikon Gallery Ltd, 14 December 1993

56
Terry Grimley, 'The year Christ went missing', *Birmingham Post*, 28 December 93

57
England's Glory, exhibition brochure, Ikon Gallery, Birmingham 1995

a brave attempt, but lost money (predictably) in a regional economy that still was lagging provincially – peripherally – behind the metropolis.

There were a number of off-site commissions that happened in Birmingham between the closure of Ikon at John Bright Street and the opening on Oozells Street. Perhaps most visible was a mural 22 metres long spelling out the word "Ocean" by the Portuguese-American artist Rigo. Located on a wall of a multi-storey car park in Brindleyplace, it was a constant reminder for residents and visitors that the city could not be more landlocked until it was obscured by the construction of an adjacent building. Other projects were "undertaken within the community"[58], engaging people from all walks of life in the process. These included the production of a comic book out of a collaboration between artists Simon Grennan and Christopher Sperandio and a group of local teenagers, and Yinka Shonibare's *Portable Personal Histories Museum* involving eight residents from inner-city Aston. Each was allocated a display case and encouraged to question the conventions within museums for displaying other people's culture, and the results were exhibited in Aston Hall, a Jacobean mansion open to the public. Built in the heyday of the slave trade, it could not have been a more suitable venue for such reflections on cultural heritage and diversity.

Shonibare went on to have a solo exhibition at Ikon in Oozells Street School that included *Portable Personal Histories Museum*, thus exemplifying the strategy that Macgregor had outlined in her 1994 discussion paper, later described as the "[fusion] of outreach and gallery work … breaking down the distinction between artists who show in the gallery and artists who undertake outreach projects, working with targeted groups … [taking] advantage of the relocation to focus on audience development".[59] This applied also to Adam Chodzko and Clement Cooper, two other artists who showed at Ikon, post-reopening.

The developments in programming at Ikon, whereby exhibitions, learning and outreach activity were becoming more integrated gave rise to a staff restructure, so that curators would become more involved in each area. Claire Doherty, appointed as Exhibitions Co-ordinator in 1995, to work alongside John Leslie, became a curator in a team with Deborah Kermode and Alessandro Vincentelli as the reopening drew near. Leslie left shortly after the closure of the gallery at John Bright Street, where he had curated the last exhibition, Mark Dion's *Natural history and other fictions*. Fittingly, amongst other things, it touched on themes of extinction and evolution.

Ikon's new premises on Oozell Street opened to the public on 20 March 1998. The reincarnation of the old school building – now with galleries on the two upper floors, spaces dedicated to learning activities, well-appointed toilets, and a shop and café downstairs – was very well received by the press. The elegant unpretentiousness of the refurbishment

58
Ikon Gallery Limited, Annual Report and Accounts, 31 March 1998

59
'Insight Ikon', Ikon's application for funding from Arts 4 Everyone, 1997

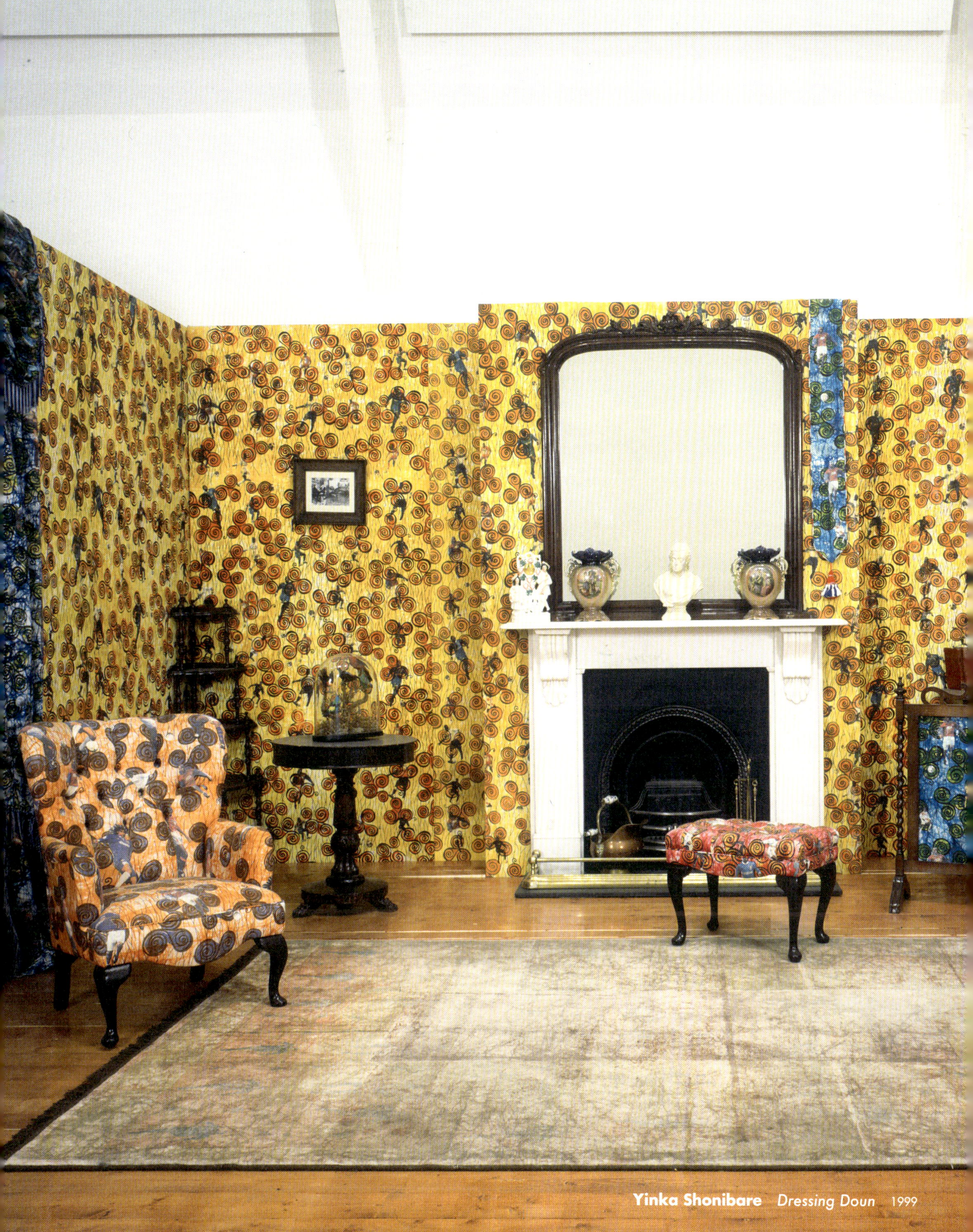

Yinka Shonibare *Dressing Doun* 1999

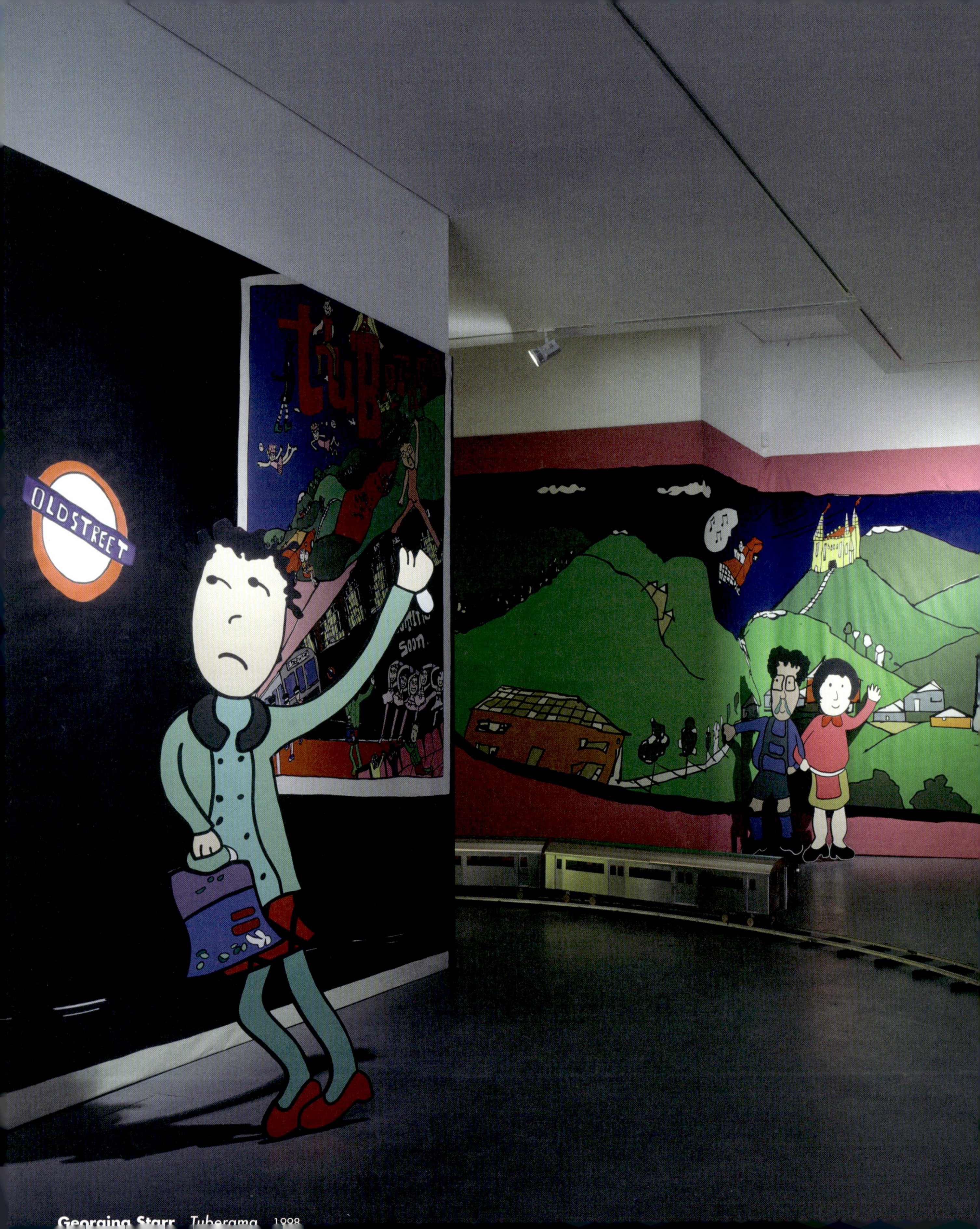

Georgina Starr *Tuberama* 1998

was often remarked upon, reflecting a good relationship between architect and client. Macgregor explained, "I wanted a gallery that artists could muck about with … So they can drill holes and paint the floors and move partitions about. Our defining test was for an artist to be able to fill a room with water. And they can."[60] The involvement of artist Tania Kovats in the architectural design team had been very beneficial. Not only did she offer practical advice that maximised the versatility and resilience of the galleries, she also proposed a "plinth" for the entire building, so that it "becomes a kind of sculpture".[61] In black slate, "in order to highlight and differentiate the building from its surroundings"[62], it is a foil for the red brick and terracotta finish that characterised the work of the original architects, Chamberlain and Martin, responsible for many of the distinctive neo-gothic schools and libraries throughout Birmingham towards the end of the nineteenth century.

Macgregor later reported to her board that the whole business of moving Ikon to Oozells Street had been stressful, but that the launch "was a great success with the building being praised in every national newspaper". On the other hand, "The opening exhibitions did not fare so well in the hands of the aging white male critics!"[63] She was referring, specifically to Adrian Searle's damning *Guardian* review of Georgina Starr's installation on the first floor, *Tuberama,* and this touched a nerve especially because he referred to it as typifying the whole access and education philosophy of the gallery: "The story is stupid, the animated drawing dismal … the installation sadly uninvolving. And Starr can't sing. Is *Tuberama* meant to be this bad? … Starr's earlier installations and little films had a perverse edge, a strangeness that I often enjoyed. *Tuberama* hasn't."[64] Other (middle-aged) white male critics, including Tim Hilton and William Feaver were actually more generous, and Richard Cork and Terry Grimley, writing for *The Times* and *Birmingham Post* respectively, quite positive.

The inaugural exhibition on the second floor comprised new work by the acclaimed American artist Nancy Spero. In her foreword for the exhibition catalogue Macgregor explained why the choice of Spero was appropriate on this occasion, given the ethos of Ikon:

> Making decisions about which artists to exhibit is an exacting, but exhilarating, task in the normal course of putting together an exhibition programme. When the exhibitions mark the opening of a major new building, the decisions take on an additional significance.
>
> For the first time, Ikon has a building which befits its national and international reputation. Moving from a back-street converted warehouse with good galleries but limited visitor facilities into a specially converted, magnificent Grade II listed building in the heart of Birmingham inevitably raises questions about the effect on the programme. The inaugural exhibitions

60
Joanna Pitman, 'Modern Ikon',
The Times Metro, 14–20 March 1998

61
Minutes of Board Meeting of Ikon Gallery Limited, 2 April 1996

62
Minutes of Board Meeting of Ikon Gallery Limited, 17 September 1996

63
Minutes of Board Meeting of Ikon Gallery Limited, 10 September 1998

64
Adrian Searle, 'And now for something totally mindless …',
The Guardian, 31 March 1998, p. 10

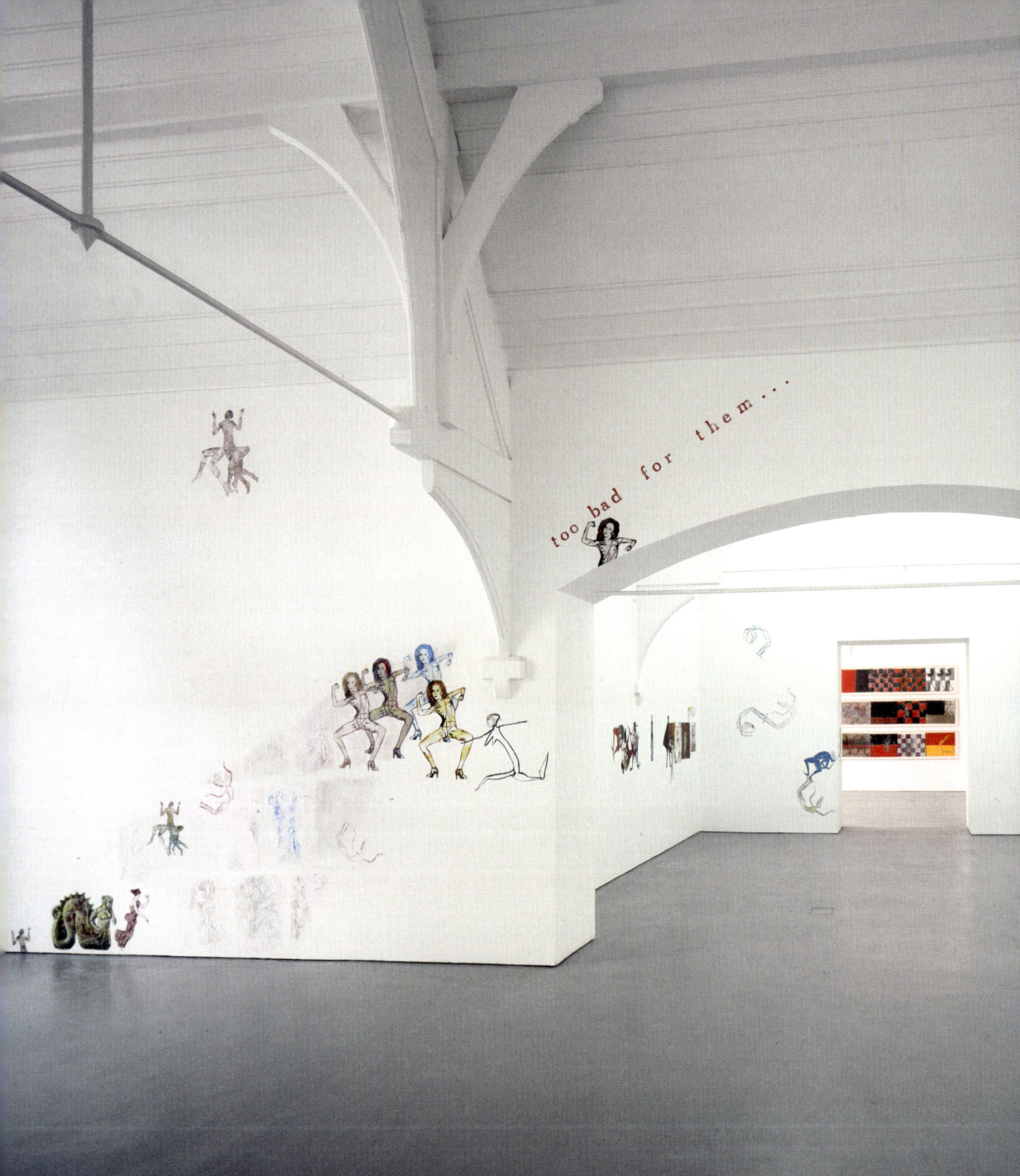

Nancy Spero 1998

therefore signal Ikon Gallery's intent at one of the key moments in its history.

Ikon Gallery is committed to supporting and promoting living artists and to encouraging new audiences to engage with their work. In its programming the gallery has always given a platform to work which addresses social and political as well as aesthetic issues.

It is highly appropriate that Nancy Spero should undertake one of the first major commissions in the new gallery. The celebratory nature of Spero's recent work is ideal for the opening of a new building. Spero takes great pleasure in her very particular portrayal of images of women from across the ages. Her installation is a paean to the possibility of the empowerment of women.[65]

Spero's figures were drawn from ancient Greek, Egyptian and Mesopotamian sources as well as contemporary pornography and photographs of bodybuilders in order to assert a lively feminism. Some were scantily clad, others unashamedly naked, none more so than what she referred to as "the chorus-line", a row of sheela na gigs printed directly onto the walls of the small central space. These grotesques, displaying their exaggerated vulva, are Celtic goddesses of fertility – incidentally warding off evil spirits – and probably the reason for the cancellation of a dinner at Ikon booked for the wives of world leaders at the G8 Summit held in Birmingham during May 1998. The idea that the dinner would take place in Spero's exhibition was a stroke of genius – and, we imagine, something that Hillary Clinton would have appreciated – but it didn't sit well with the British Home Office. In an interview with *The Observer* newspaper, Spero sounded more amused than upset: "When it comes to religion and sexuality, that's when everyone goes bonkers. Maybe [the wives] might have enjoyed my work if they had had the chance to see it."[66]

Spero was one of three women artists from the US shown at Ikon within the first year at Oozells Street. The others were Ellen Gallagher and Martha Rosler. For the latter, her exhibition was a long-awaited retrospective, combining video, performance, installation, photography and text works. Its counter-cultural slant – highlighting sexism, the stupidity of war, racial discrimination, homelessness and other iniquities inherent in capitalism – epitomised the kind of political and social relevance that Ikon's programme aspired to under Macgregor's directorship. Ellen Gallagher's work was less explicit, although often derived from race-related themes. Of West African and Irish heritage, New York based, she had recently arrived as an artist, having starred at the 1995 Whitney Biennial, with paintings that combined a subtle abstraction with a repetition of blackface details including "Sambo lips" and "bug eyes". In an interview for the Ikon exhibition catalogue, Gallagher cited other women artists, such as Agnes Martin and Gertrude Stein, as formative influences and also made reference – significantly for Ikon – to Adrian Piper.[67]

65
Elizabeth Macgregor, Foreword, *Nancy Spero*, exhibition catalogue, Ikon Gallery, Birmingham 1998, p.2

66
Roger Tredre, 'Wives spared the thrust of Nancy's image', *The Observer*, 29 March 1998

67
'This Theatre Where You Are Not There. A Conversation with Ellen Gallagher by Thyrza Nichols Goodeve', *Ellen Gallagher*, exhibition catalogue, Ikon Gallery, Birmingham 1998

Besides the Americans, the artists who featured in Ikon's opening programme were an interesting British mix. Callum Innes' solo show of paintings, made from the broad application and erasure of colour, was paired with Gallagher's exhibition – his abstraction derived from process, rather than subject matter. Previously there had been *Relocating the Remains*, a survey of Keith Piper's work toured by InIVA comprising three interactive installations, and then, following Rosler, Shonibare's exhibition. Alongside display cases from *Portable Personal Histories Museum* and installations characteristically involving pseudo-African fabric, he showed two panels from his *Diary of a Victorian Dandy*, a photographic series that depicted the artist as a young nineteenth century gentleman of independent means. Sending up a popular taste for costume drama and nostalgia for the past, and anticipating the artist's postmodern acceptance of establishment honours – in 2019 he was appointed a CBE, a Commander of the Most Excellent Order of the British Empire – it is a masterstroke of insinuation.

Shonibare's exhibition was very well received by local audiences and press. In his review for the *Birmingham Post*, Terry Grimley observed that "Shonibare's work is colourful, witty and rich in its cultural allusions", and then asked "Couldn't Birmingham adopt him in some way?"[68] He didn't ask the same question about Adam Chodzko who was next up in Ikon's gallery programme. This artist, also then based in London, was one of the earliest British practitioners of "relational aesthetics", a movement involving (non-artist) others in the production of artwork, reaching its peak in the late-1990s. His seminal *God Look-Alike Contest* was included, neatly complemented by *Nightvision* (1998). This new work, exhibited as a two-screen projection, was produced by a group of technicians, specialising in lighting for clubs, raves and concerts, put together by Chodzko with the simple instruction that they "light a wood at night as though it was heaven".[69]

There were more exhibitions that Macgregor had planned for Ikon, three of which were solo shows for Australian artists – Gordon Bennett, Simryn Gill and Lyndall Jones – but by this time she had resigned, having accepted the position of Director of the Museum of Contemporary Art in Sydney. Despite a strong desire to stay with the gallery in its new premises – "I've been living, eating and sleeping this building project. Now I want to run it"[70] – she was in her prime professionally and ready for a new adventure, as she explained to Terry Grimley: "It was a close decision, but I sat down and asked myself where I would really like to go. I'm a huge fan of Australia. I've been there a number of times. It's just a fabulous lifestyle and Sydney is a beautiful city."[71] On the same day that Grimley's article was published in the *Birmingham Post* Ikon's Finance and General Purposes Committee met and "on behalf of the Board [thanked Macgregor] for her contribution to the organisation over the last ten years and added that she would be a very hard act to follow."

68
Terry Grimley, 'Yinka's strangely familiar world', *Birmingham Post*, 23 February 1999

69
Adam Chodzko, 'Seeing the light', *Tate Magazine*, Summer 1999

70
Giles Worsley, 'A building you want to stroke', The Daily Telegraph, 19 March 1998

71
Terry Grimley, 'Head-hunted for top job down under', *Birmingham Post*, 25 May 1999

Macgregor's departure for Australia was in keeping with the curatorial position that she had articulated on her arrival at Ikon. She was then clearly championing cultural practices that had been conventionally regarded as peripheral, and Australia was a postmodern exemplar, with a strong track record of theoretically inverting the relationship between centre and periphery. Meanwhile, about Ikon, Birmingham-born art critic Tim Hilton declared in an article for *The Independent on Sunday* that it was now "[really] post-modernist":

> … we all know in our hearts that dignified regional museums are a thing of the past. Their day is done, if only because they have been so neglected that they can never catch up. The future belongs to galleries like the Ikon. They will be successful and fashionable places close to commercial and entertainment centres. They will have a fast turnover of shows, energetic publicity departments and high-profile directors. No such gallery would ever dream of forming a permanent collection. They will be competitive and international rather than local in their outlook and, at least for the moment, they will exhibit neo-conceptual art.[72]

Applied to the art world as a whole, Hilton's predictions were not far off the mark. Communications and development have since become much more prominent in the management of galleries and museums, feeling the impact of an exponentially increased globalisation and hyperactivity in international art markets. Artistic experience for many on the outside certainly has come to resemble a kind of fashion world, a place where people with too much money have an obscure, refined kind of fun. But this does not mean that independent, publicly funded "galleries like the Ikon" were to be inevitably seduced. Macgregor was forthright in her political convictions and social commitment, as were her predecessors, and so Ikon entered the new millennium on a trajectory that tended to go against the flow of a neoliberal mainstream. And so? Exactly what happened next was directed by me, as Macgregor's successor, undertaking new initiatives for this extraordinary institution whilst being very appreciative of what had gone before.

72
Tim Hilton, 'It's a real post-modernist Ikon', *The Independent on Sunday*, 29 March 1998

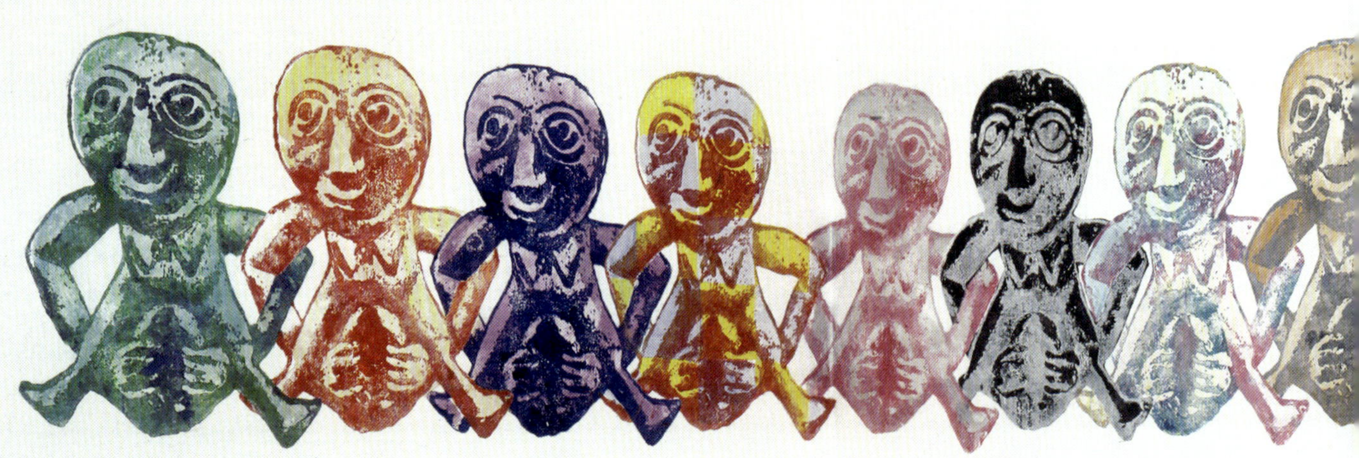

Nancy Spero 1998

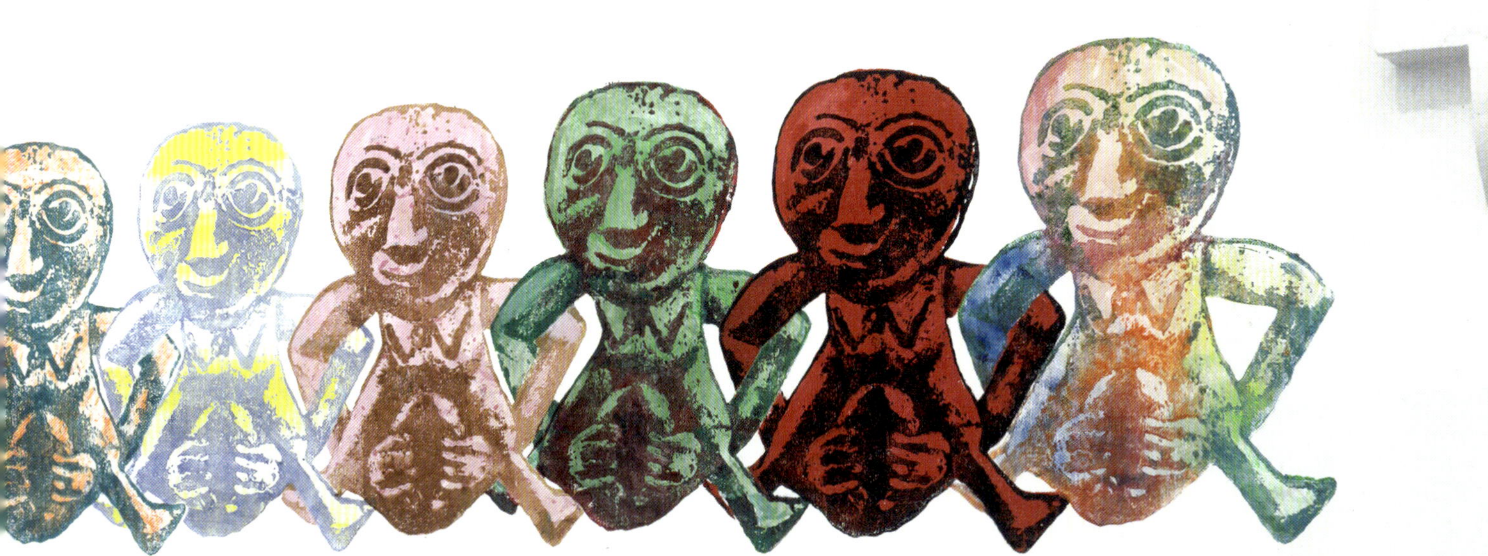

Felicity Allen

Edward Allington

Siah Armajani

Basil Beattie

Gordon Bennett

Zarina Bhimji

Ansuya Blom

Adam Chodzko

Juan Davila

Mark Dion and Jason Simon

Eugenio Dittborn

Rose Finn-Kelcey

Ellen Gallagher

Antony Gormley

Víctor Grippo

Graham Gussin

Callum Innes

Permindar Kaur

Tania Kovats

Cildo Meireles

Lisa Milroy

Antoni Miralda

Avis Newman

Lucia Nogueira

Vong Phaophanit

Adrian Piper

Keith Piper

Donald Rodney

Martha Rosler

Yinka Shonibare

Nancy Spero

Georgina Starr

Amikam Toren

Suzanne Treister

Alison Turnbull

Shelagh Wakely

Maxine Walker

Mark Wallinger

John Yeadon

Felicity Allen
Baby II   1989

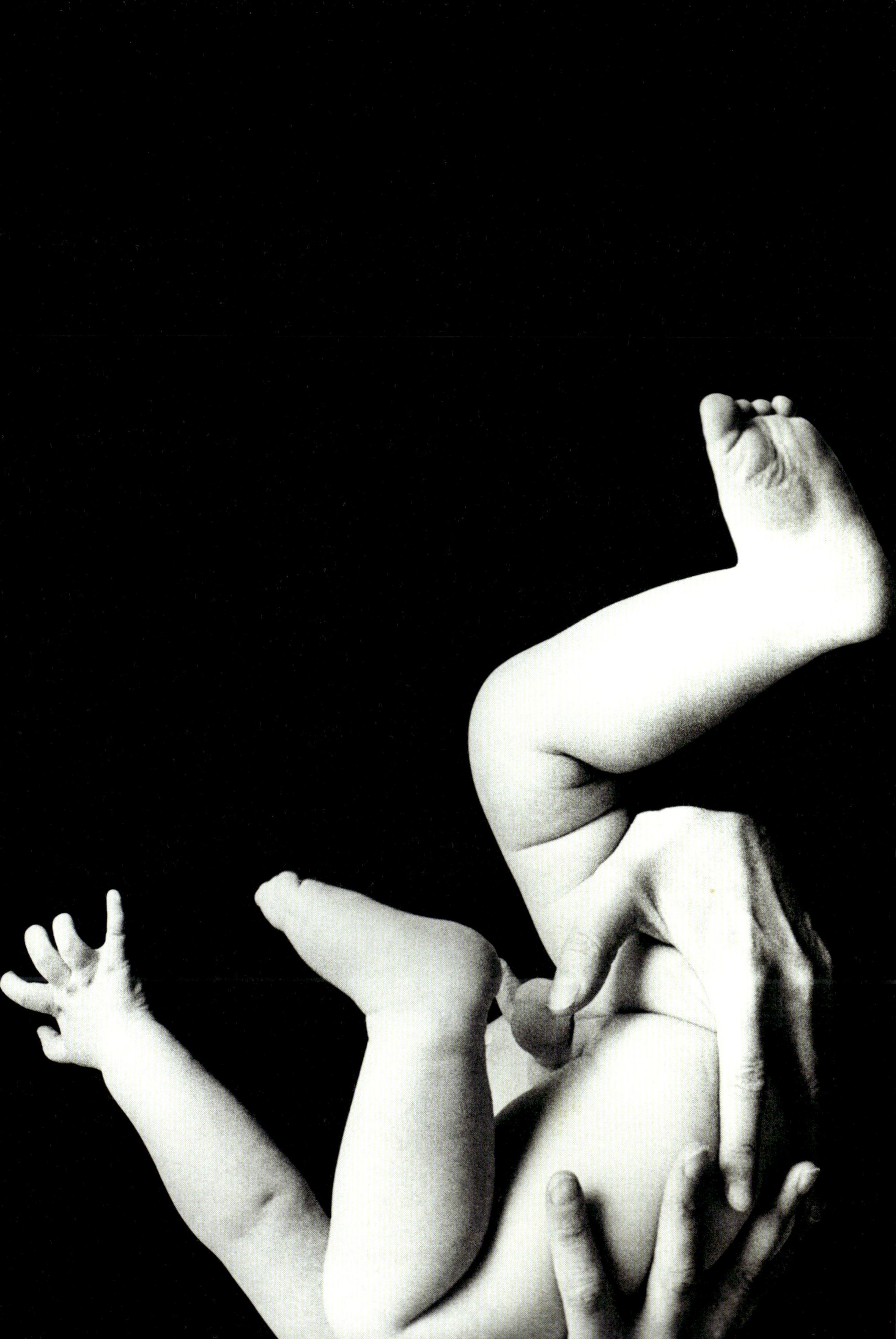

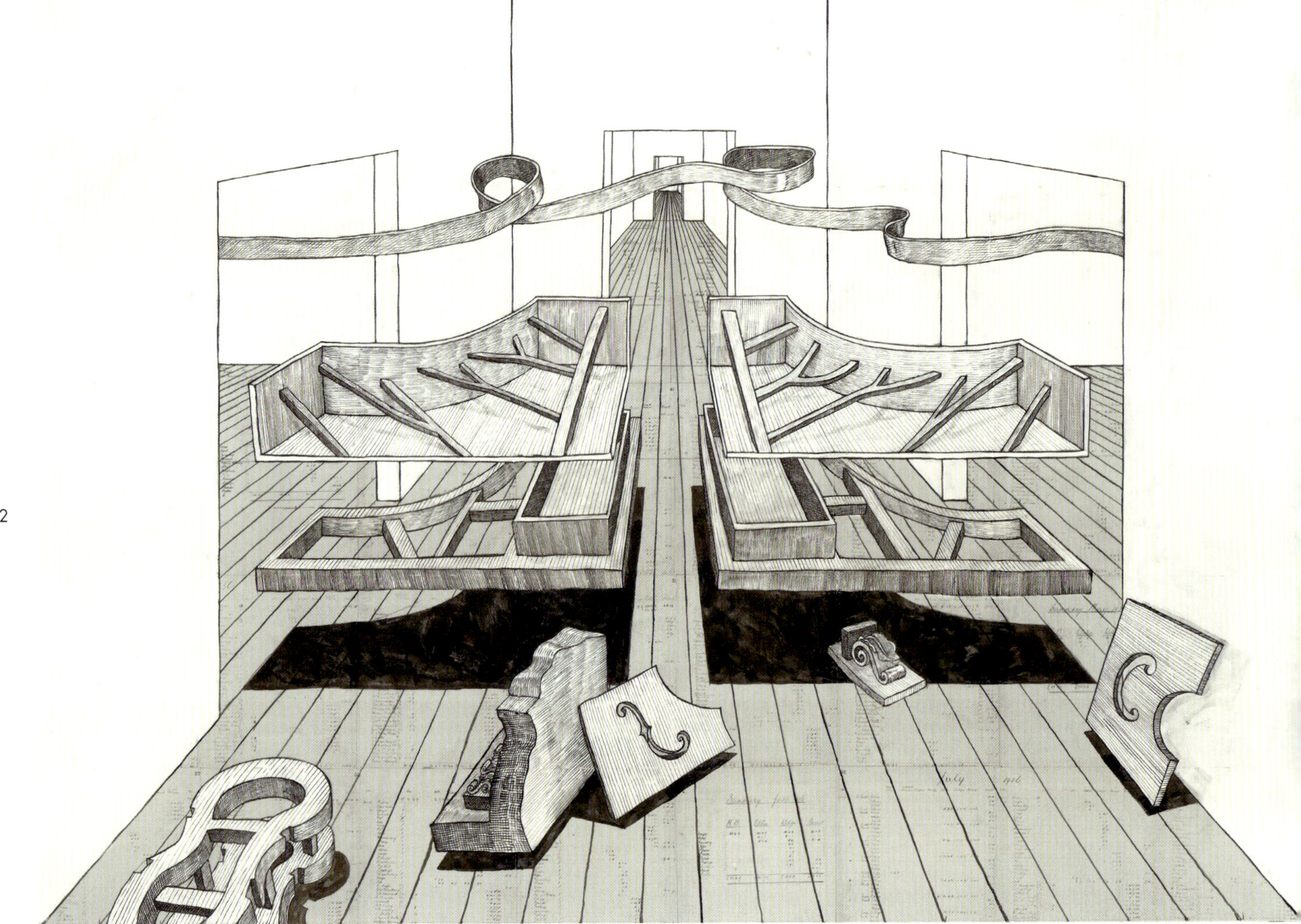

Edward Allington
Unfinished Instruments   1989

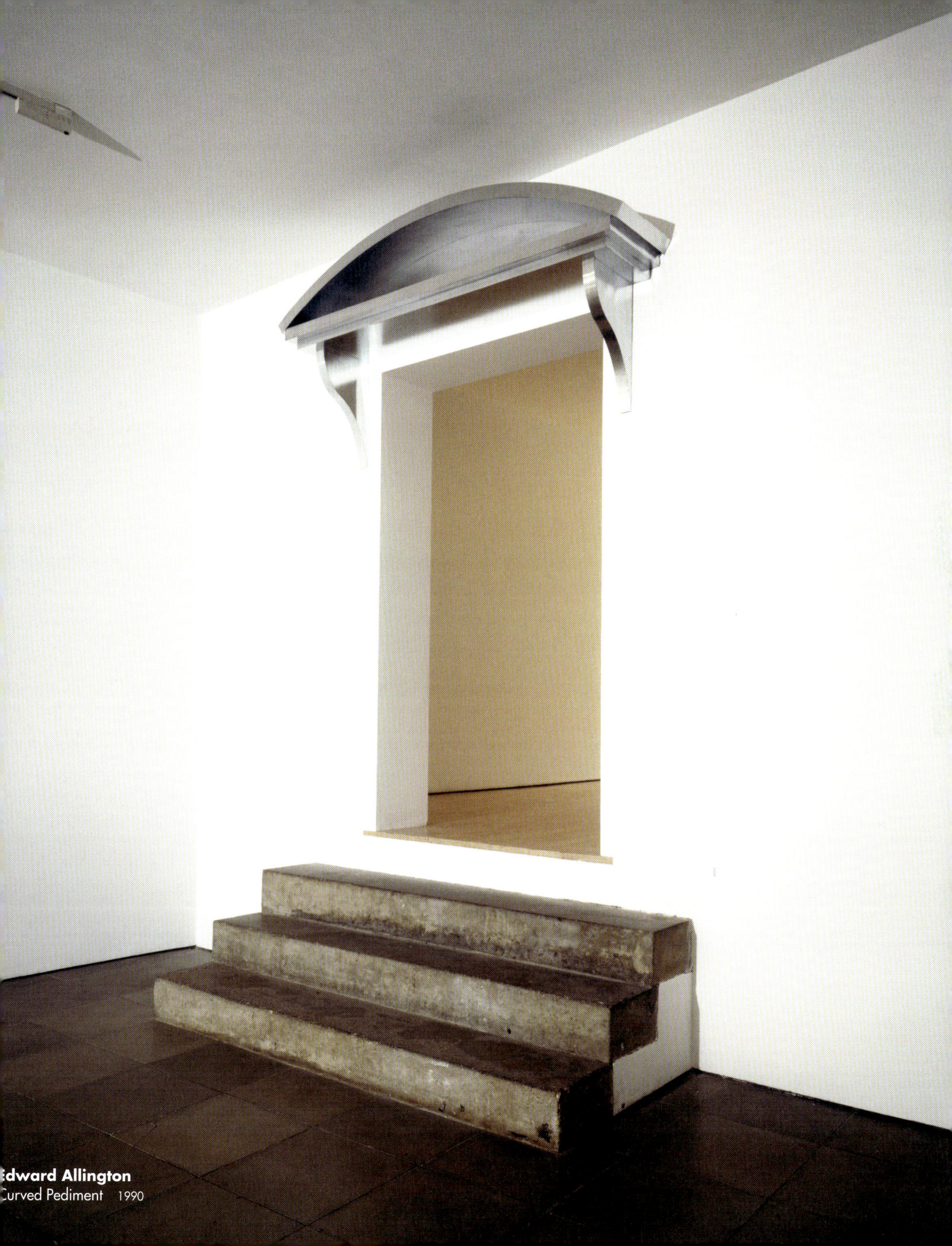

Edward Allington
Curved Pediment 1990

Siah Armajani
Gazebo for Two Anarchists: Emilio Coda and Richard Henry Dana   1991

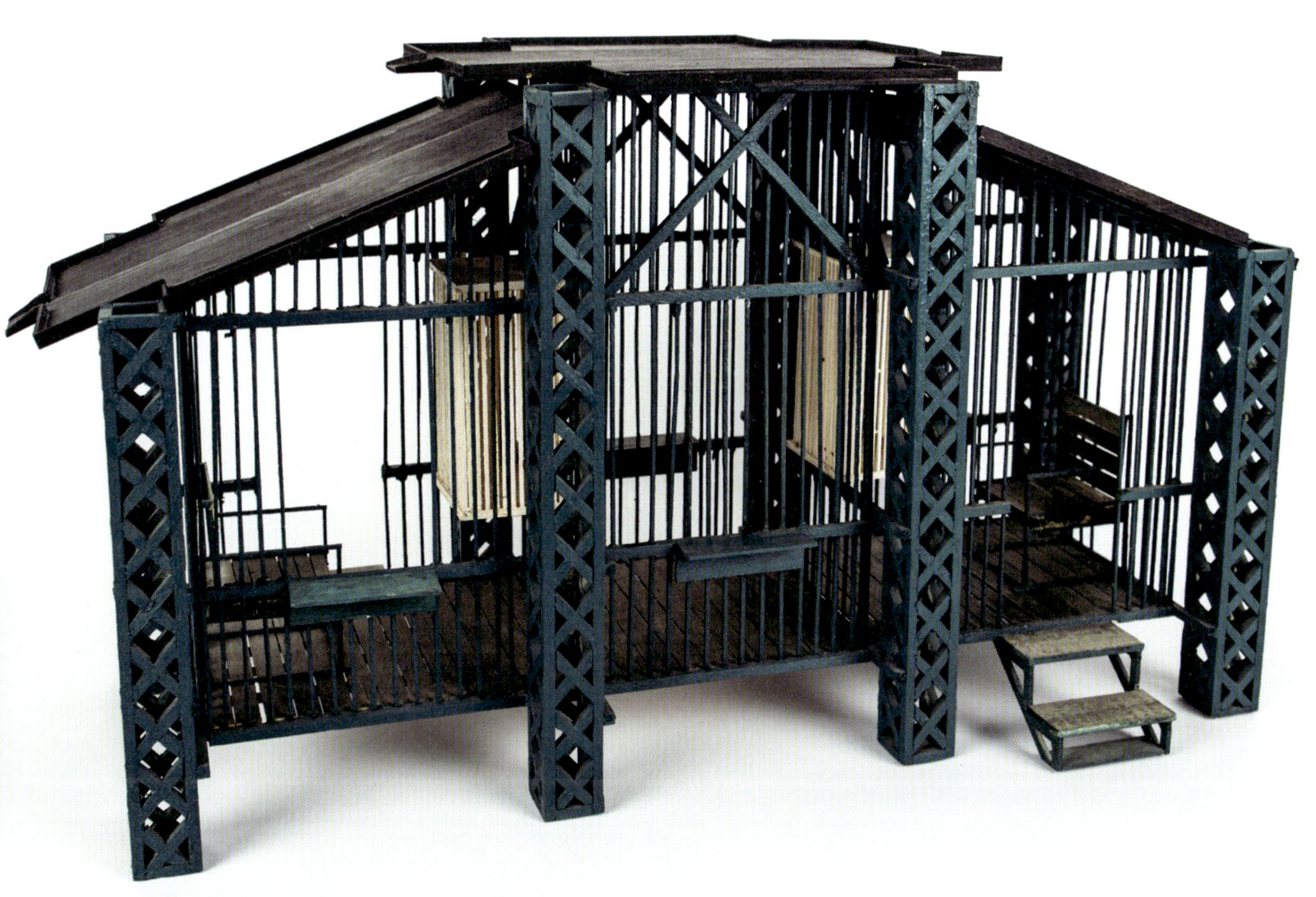

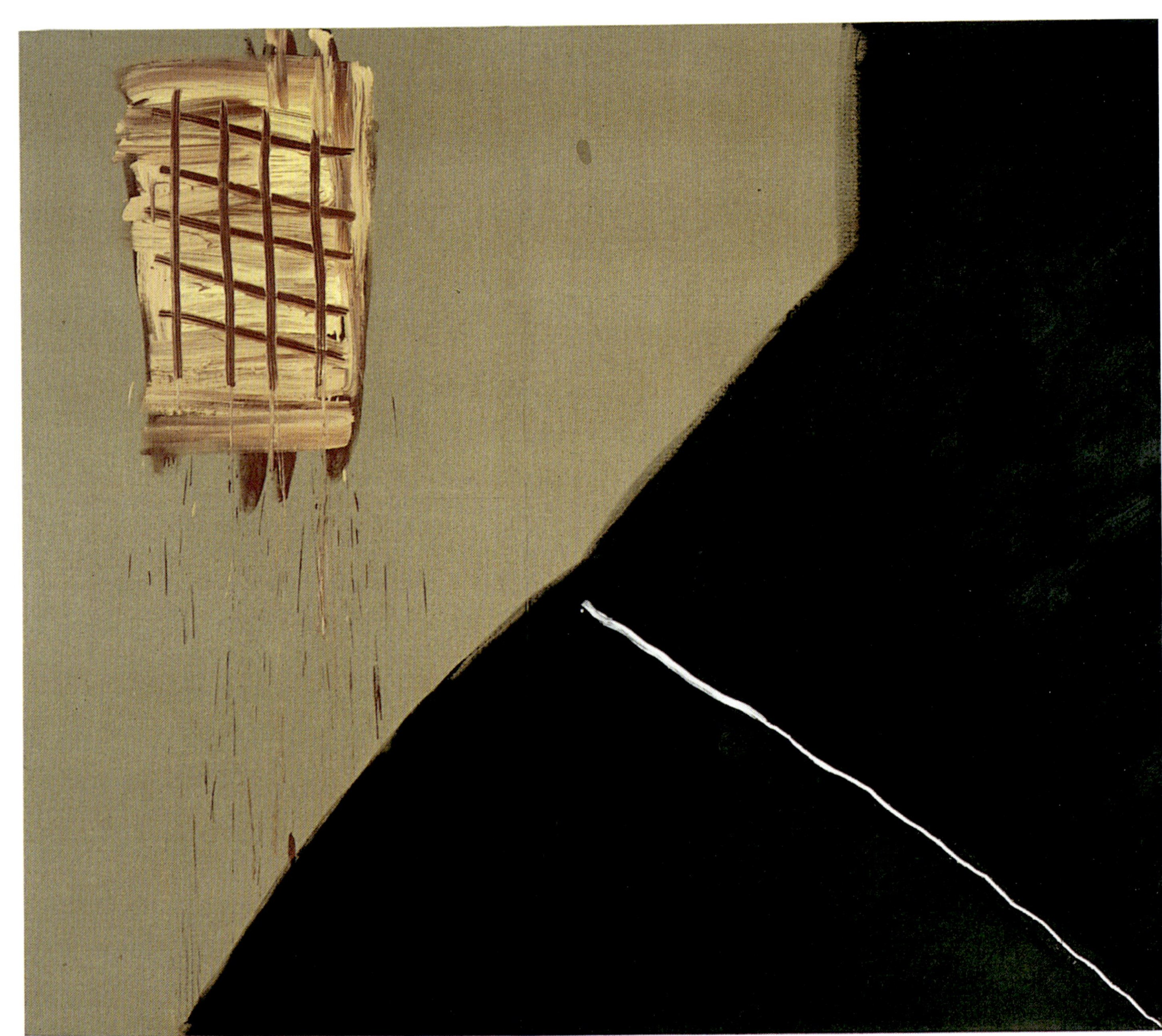

Basil Beattie
Imagine If   1993

Gordon Bennett
Suprematist Painting II (Purity)   1993

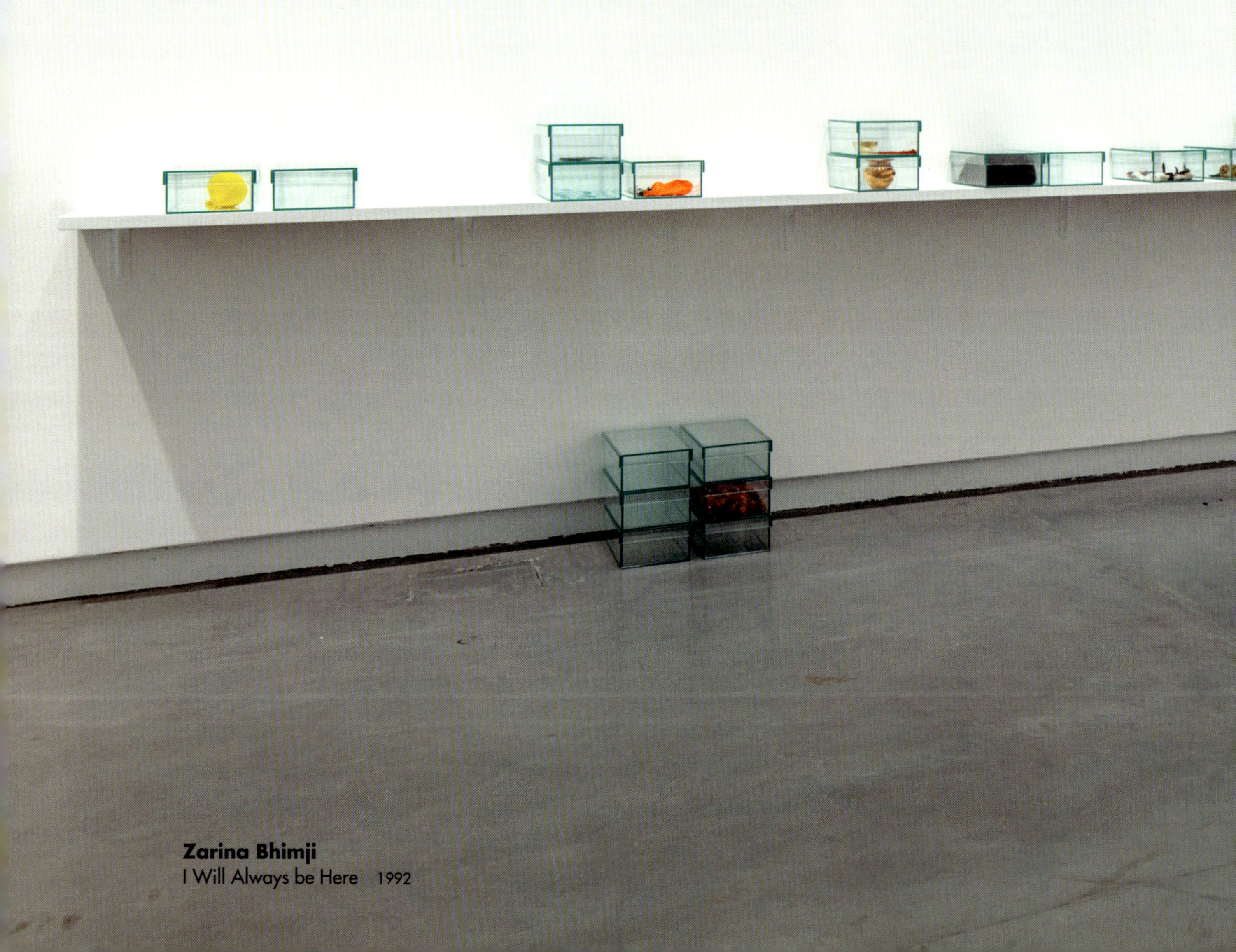

Zarina Bhimji
I Will Always be Here   1992

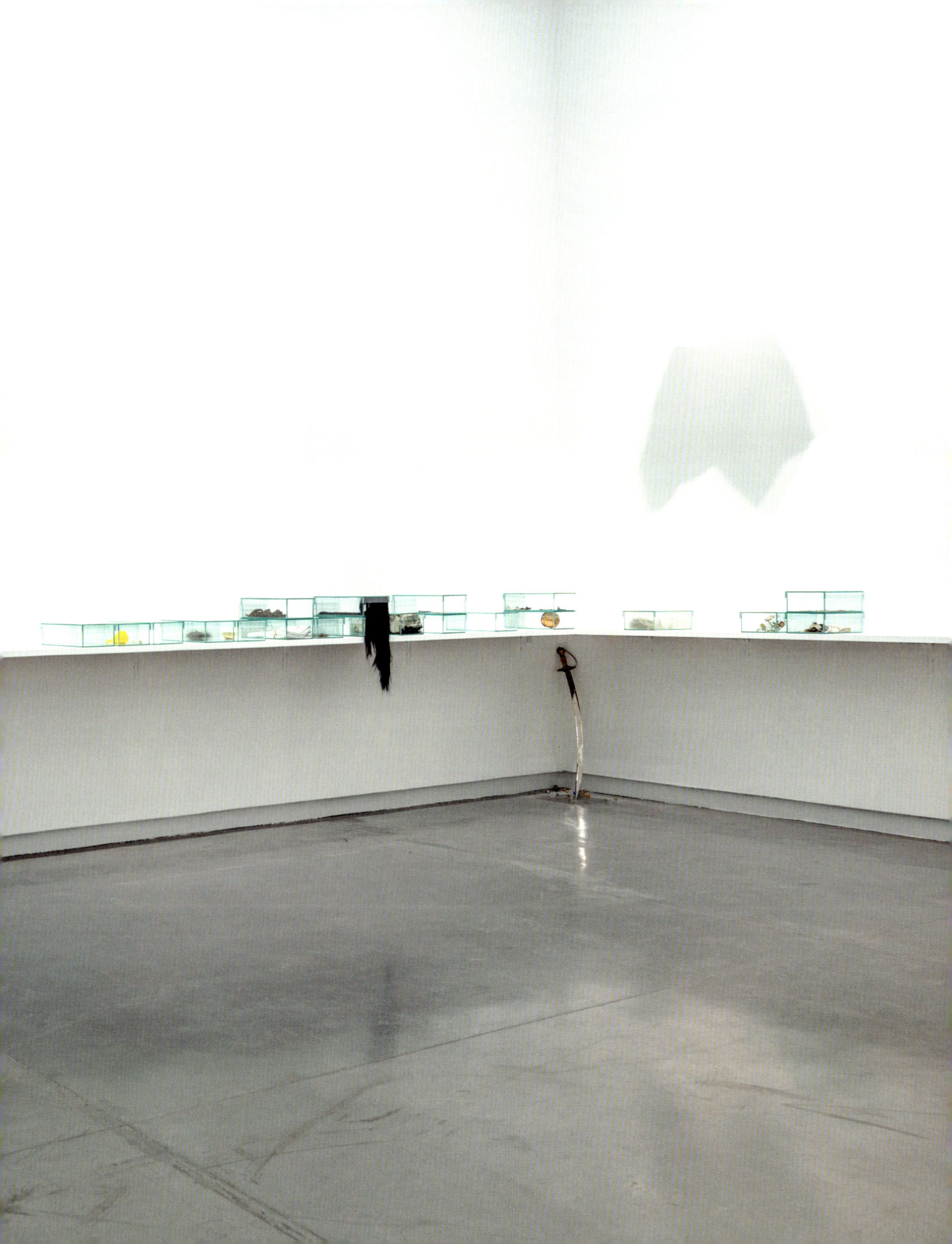

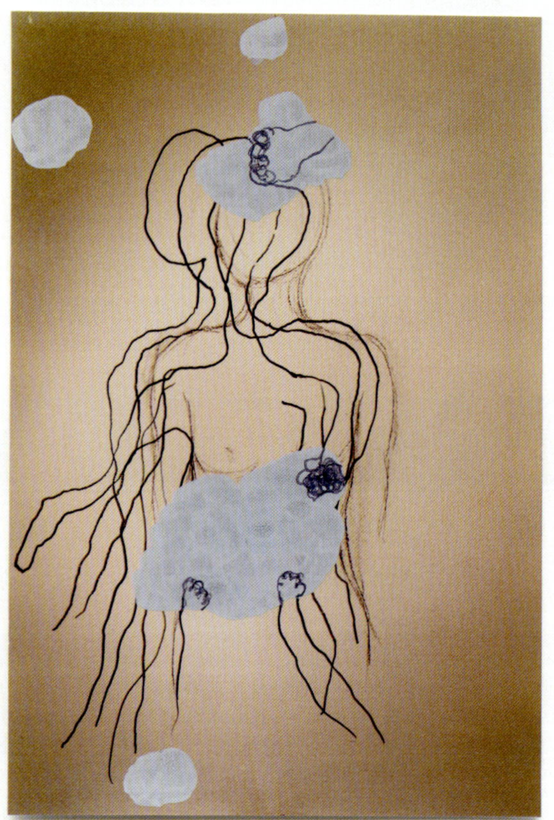

Ansuya Blom
… this human being …   1993–95

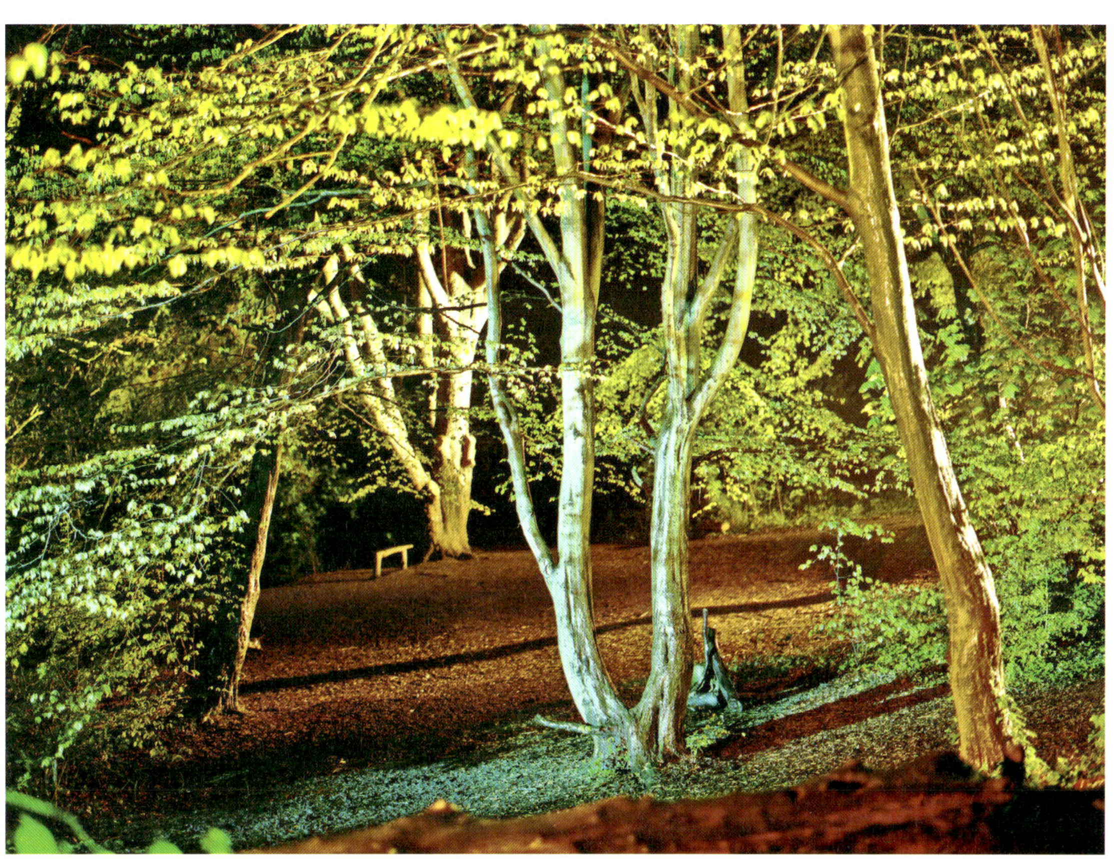

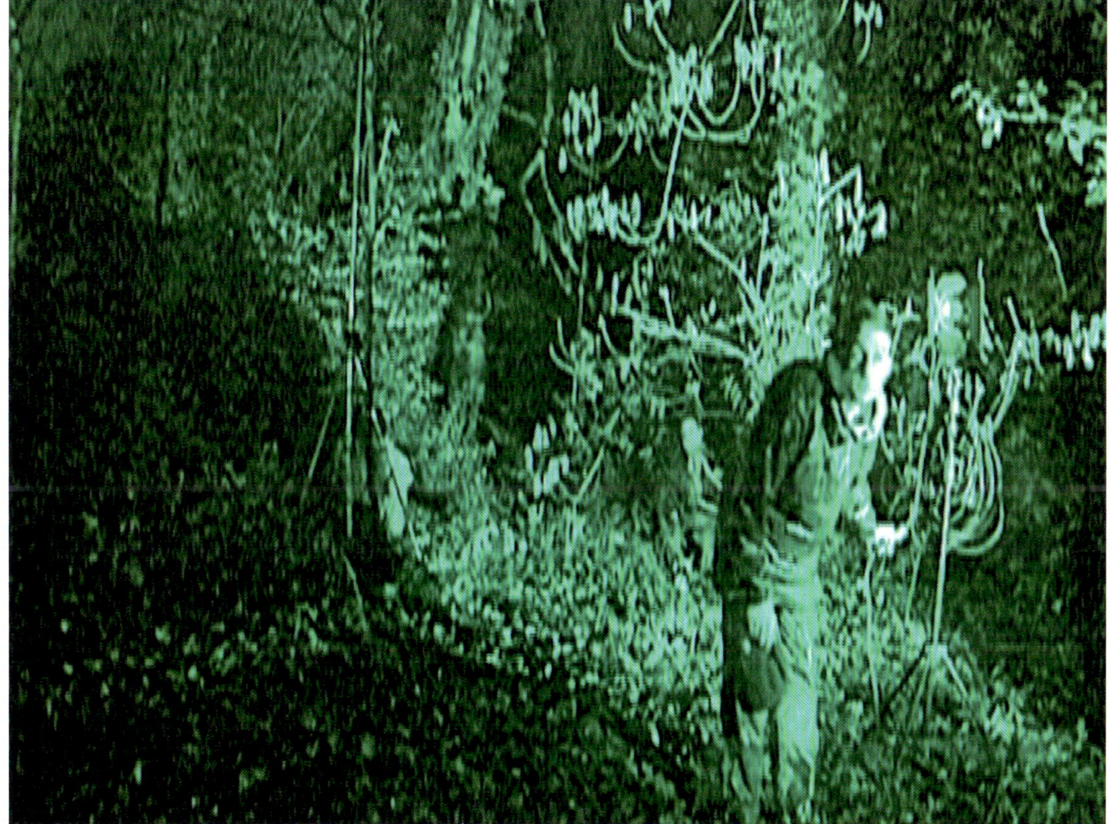

Adam Chodzko
top: Nightvision ['heaven'; production still]   1998
bottom: Nightvision ['image intensifier'; screeen shot]   1998

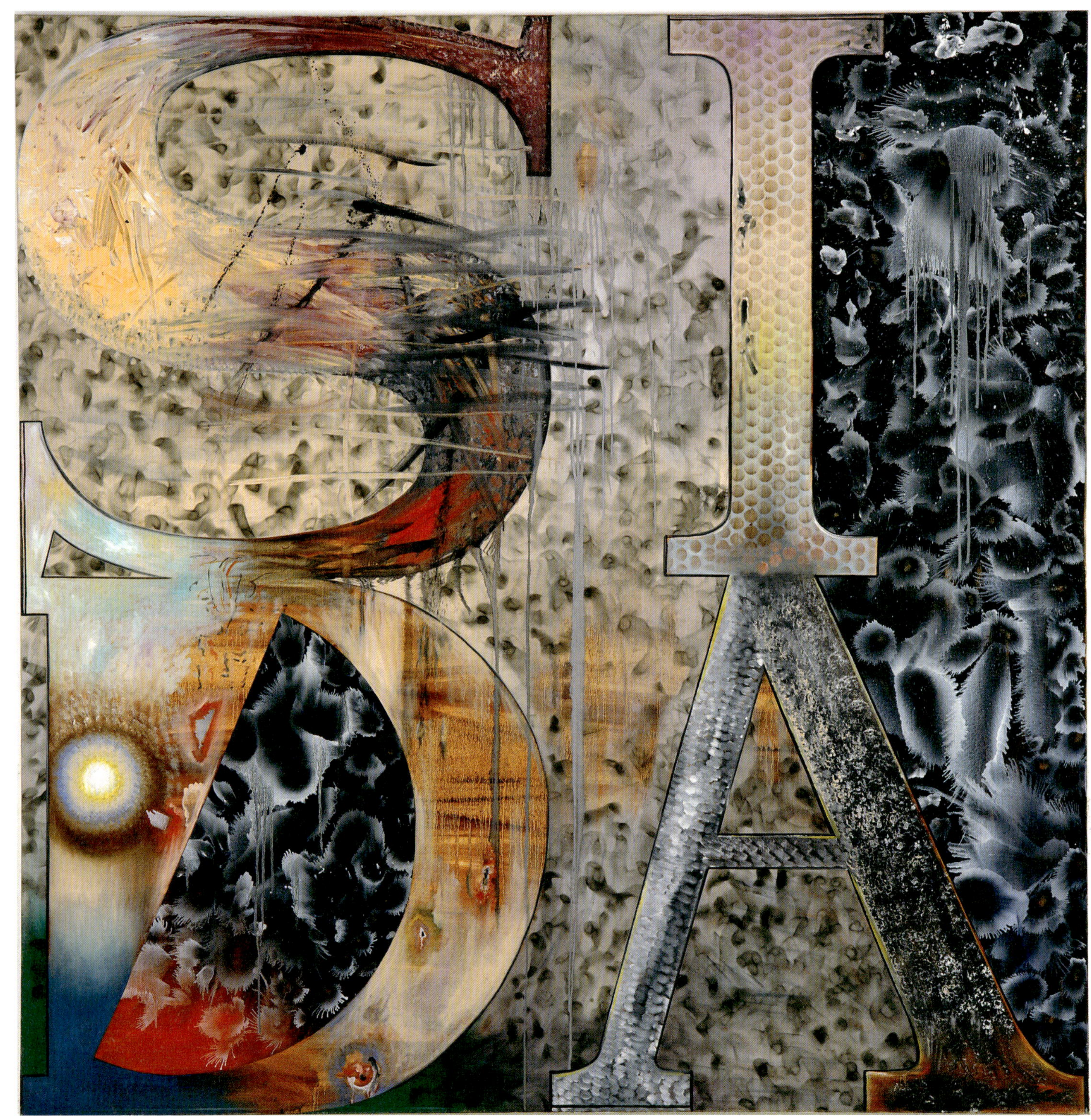

Juan Davila

Love   1988

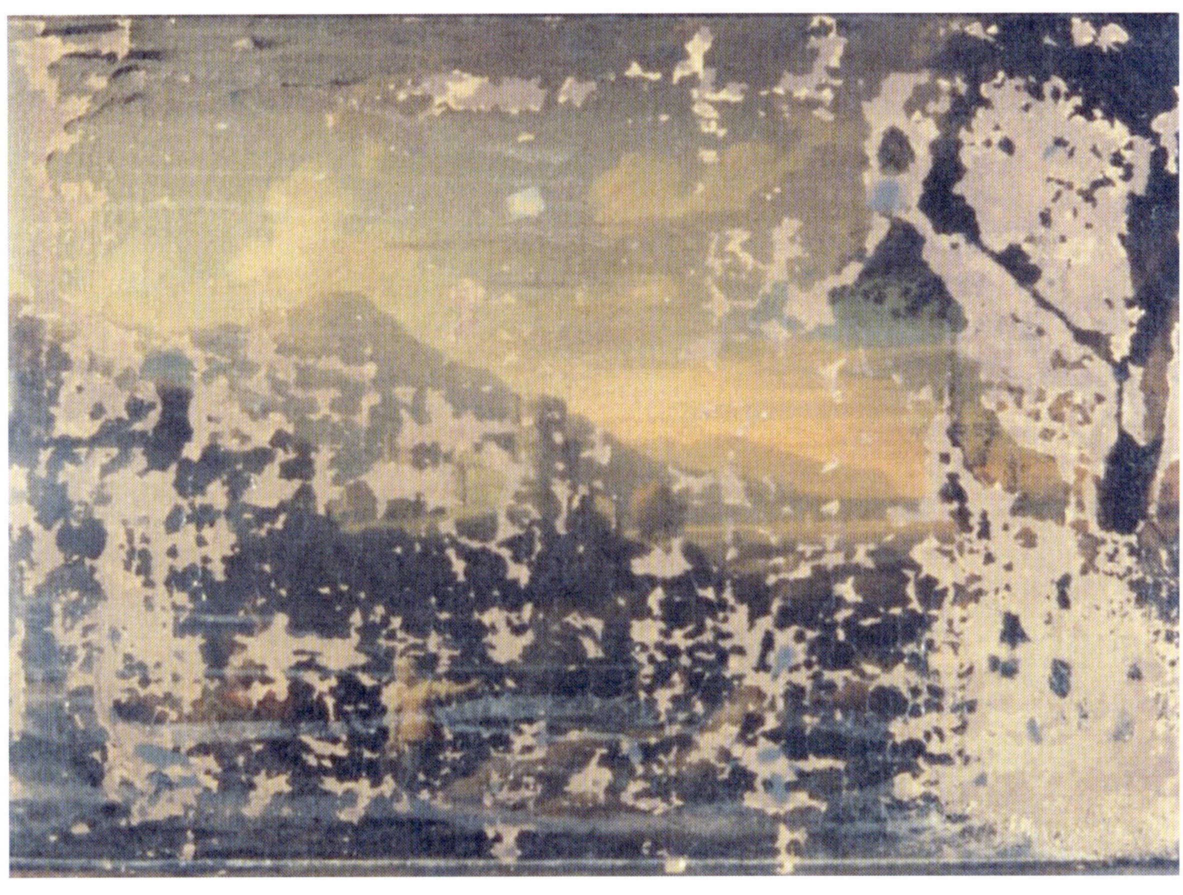

Mark Dion and Jason Simon
Artful History, a Restoration Comedy   1988

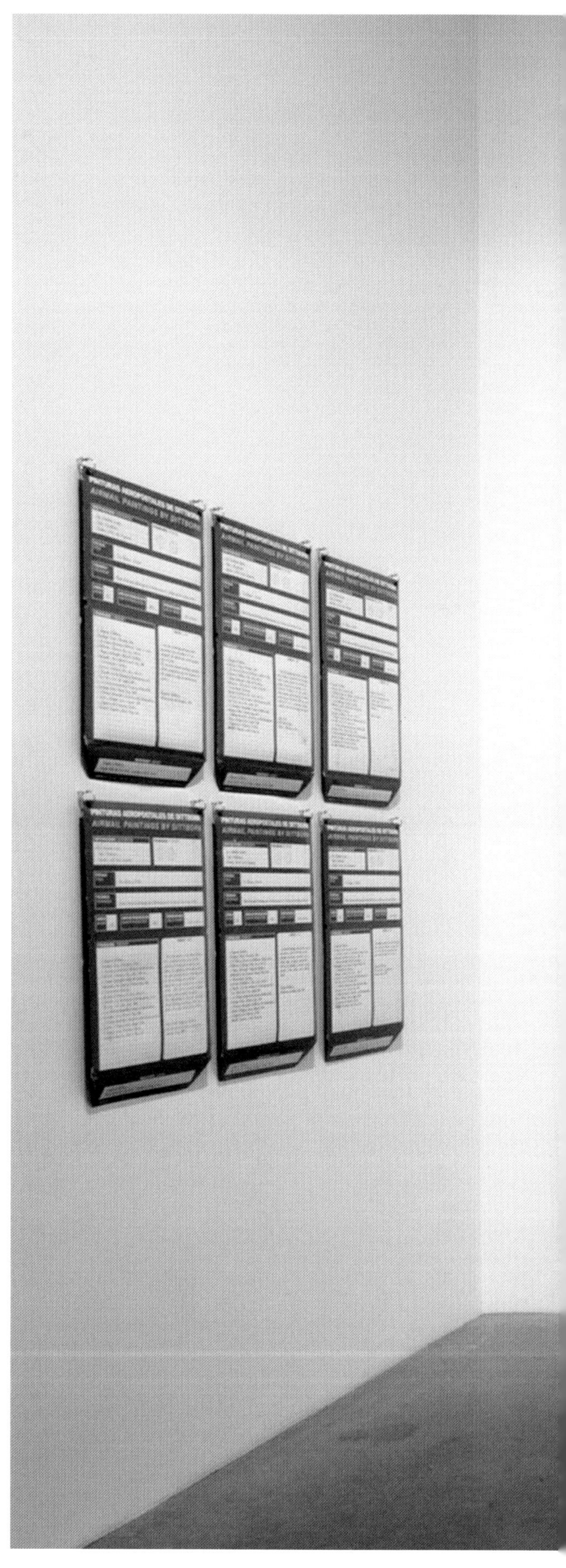

Eugenio Dittborn
To Return (RTM) Airmail Painting No.103   1993

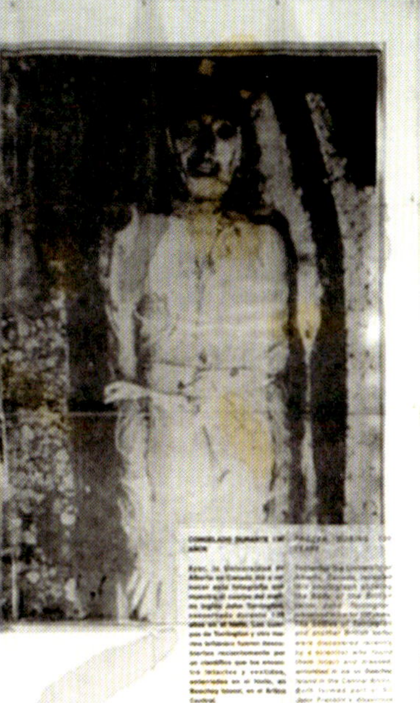

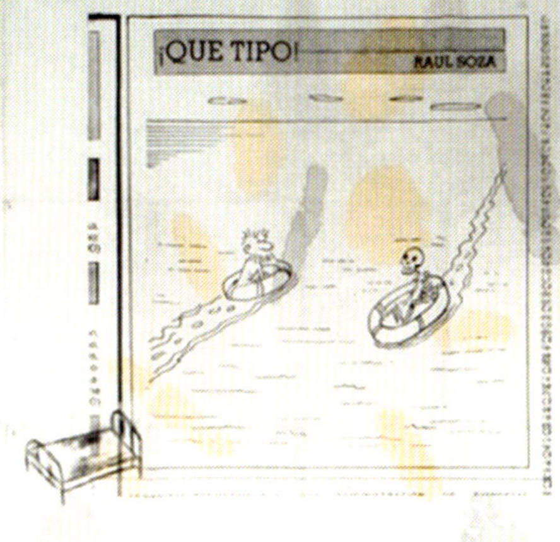

¡QUE TIPO!
RAUL SOZA

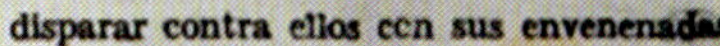

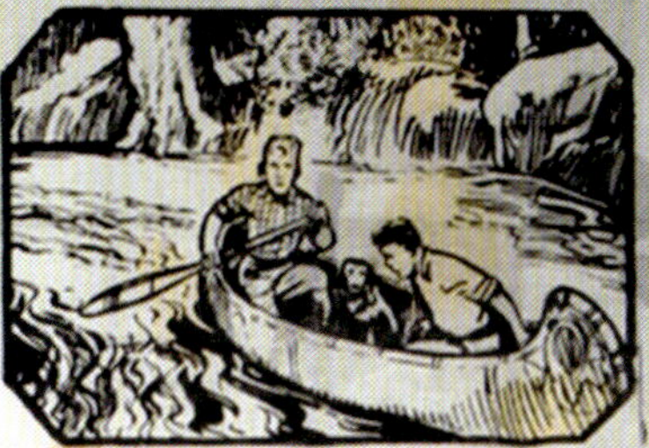

disparar contra ellos con sus envenenadas
la y se dejaron llevar por la corriente, que
clamó de pronto Reno---, se ha roto la pl

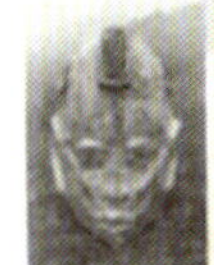

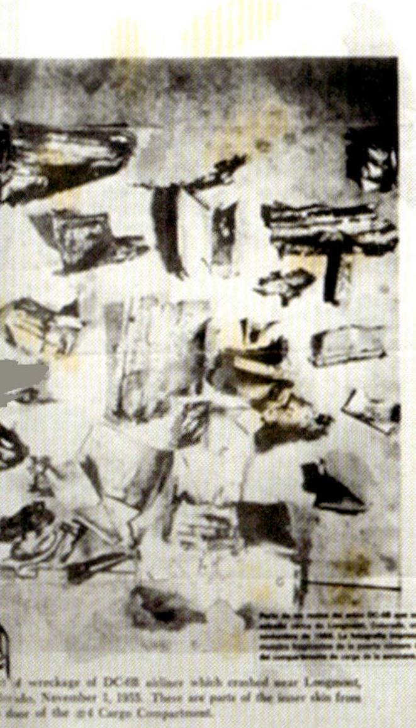

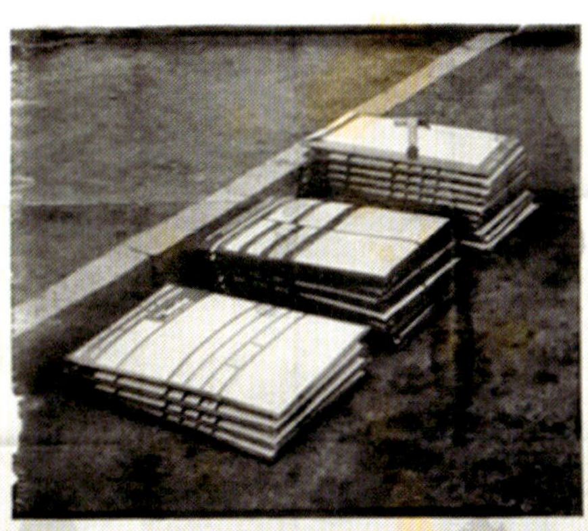

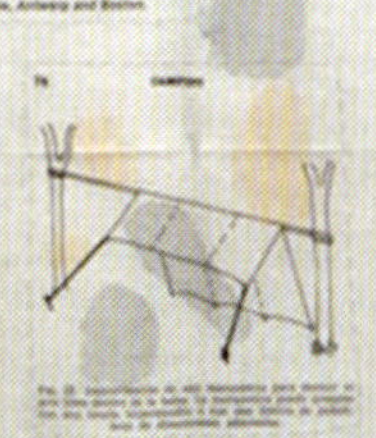

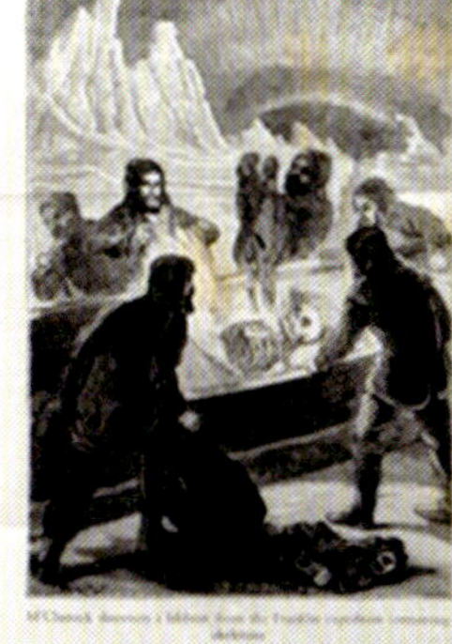

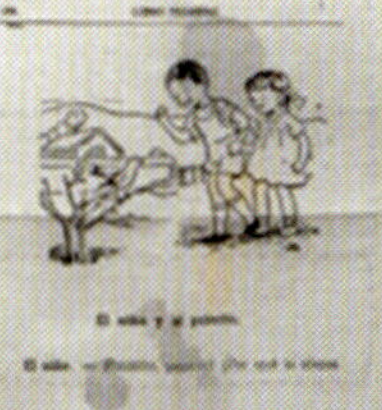

Rose Finn-Kelcey
God Kennel – A Tabernacle – (Model)   1992

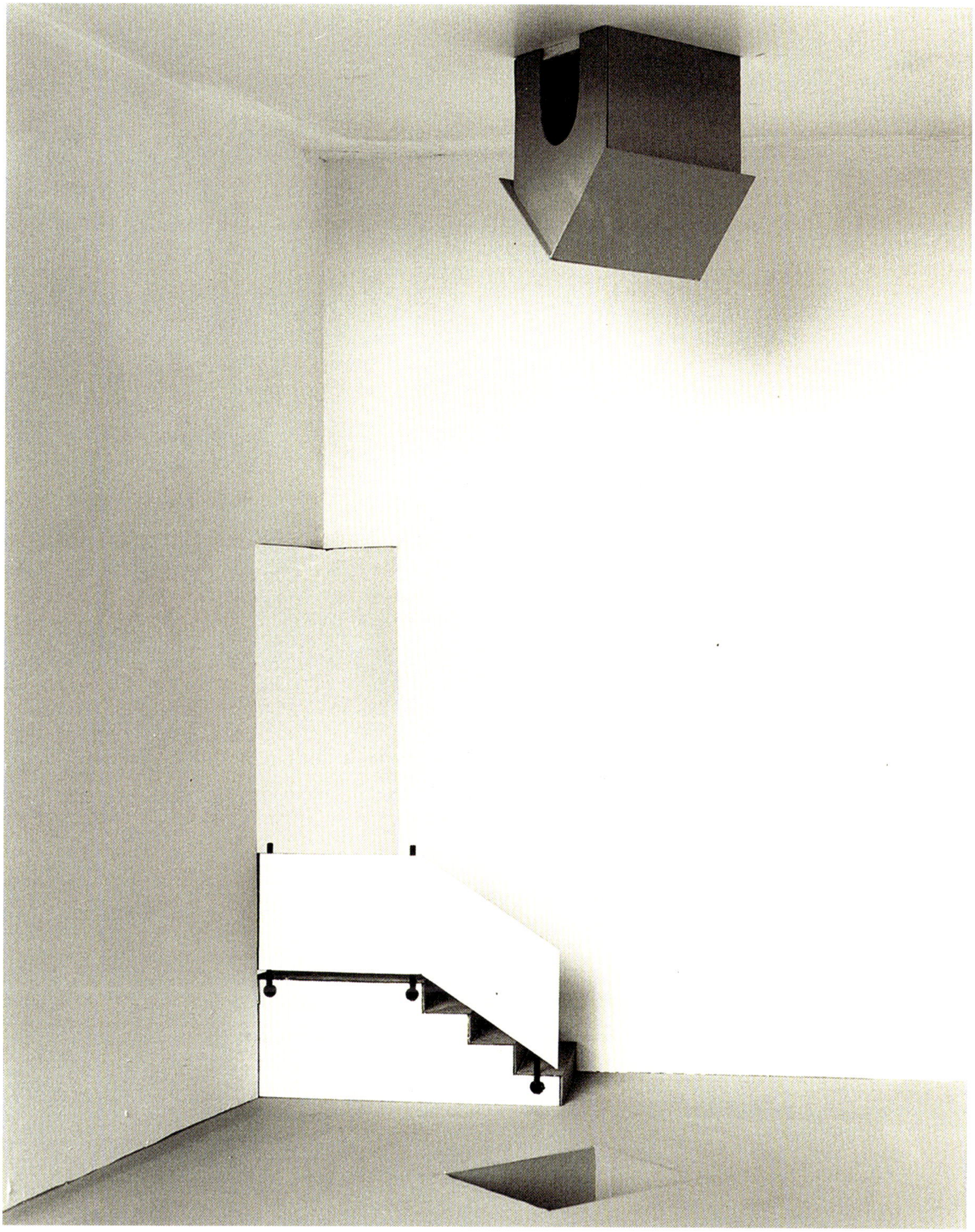

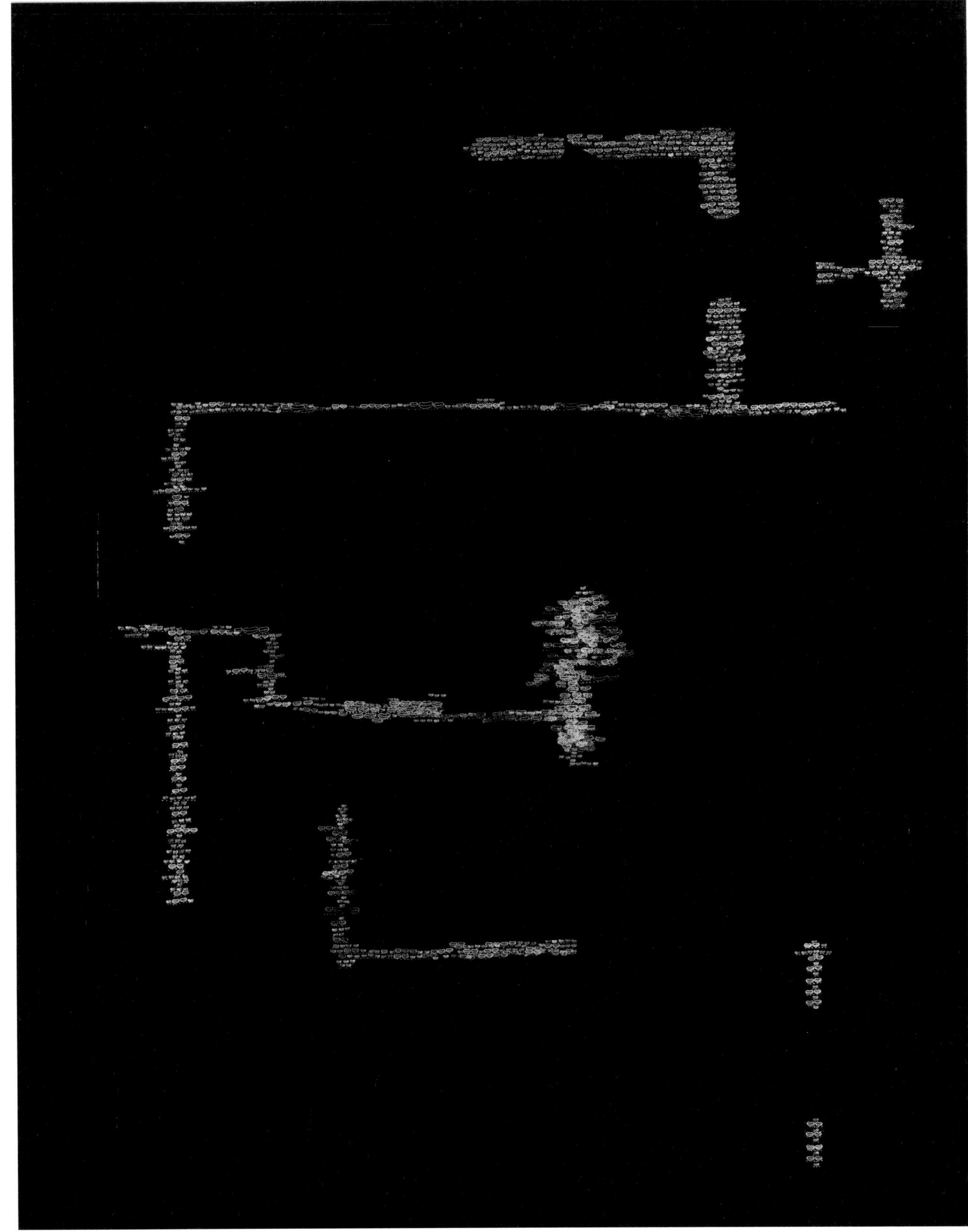

Ellen Gallagher
Untitled   1998

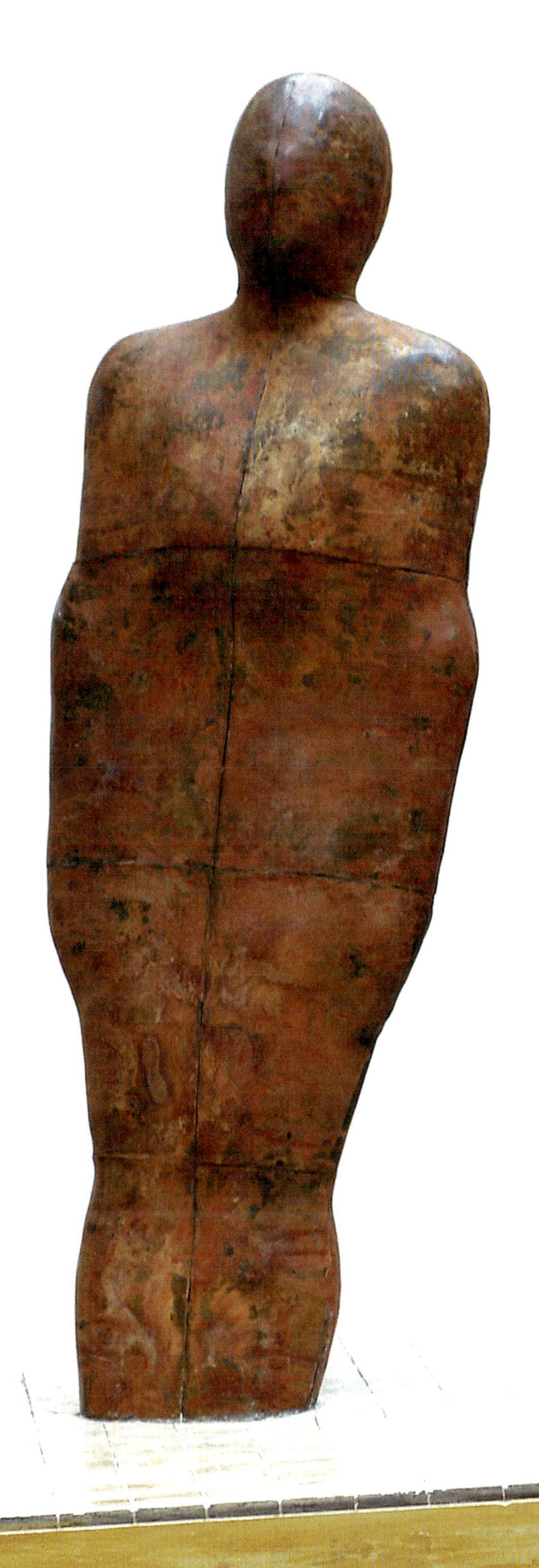

Antony Gormley
Maquette for 'Iron Man'   1991

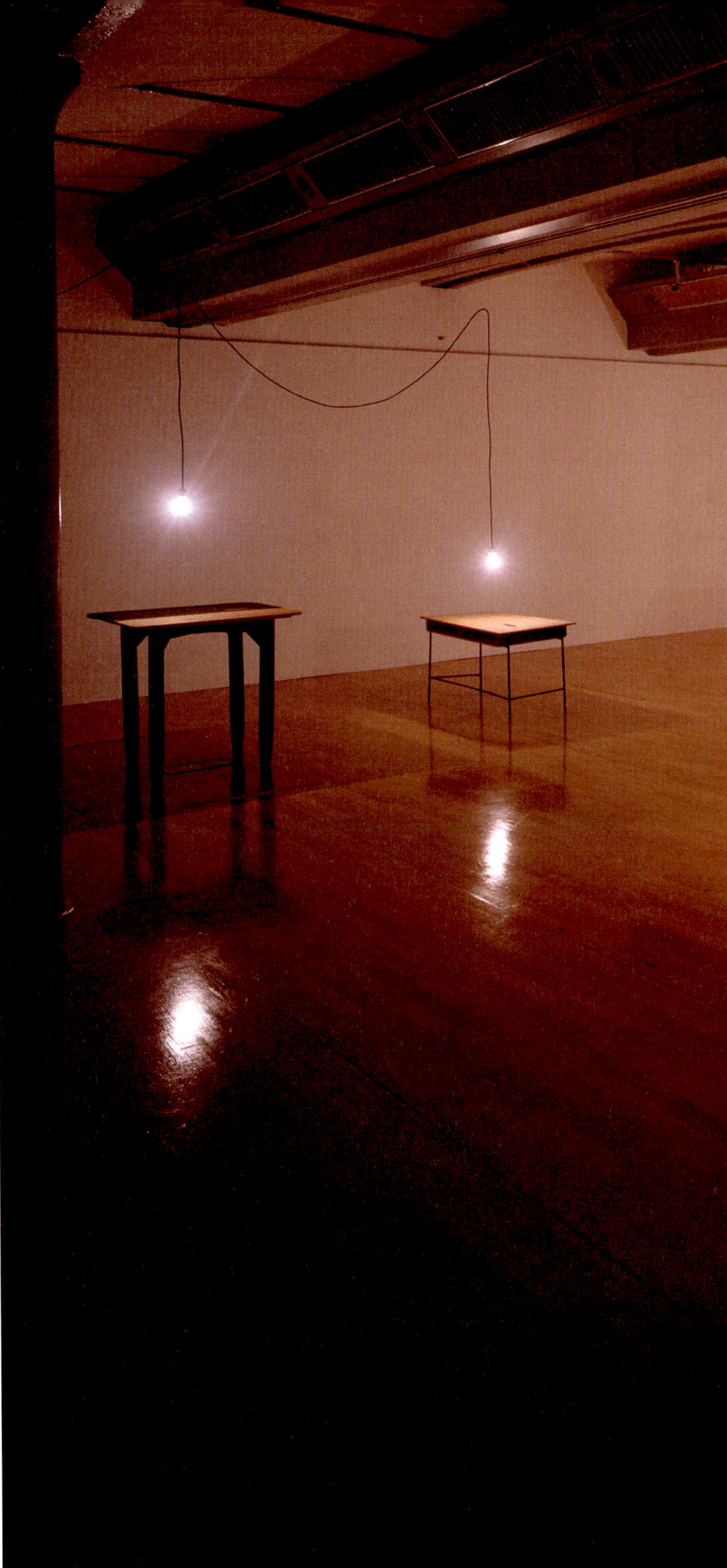

Víctor Grippo
Tables of Work and Reflection   1978–94

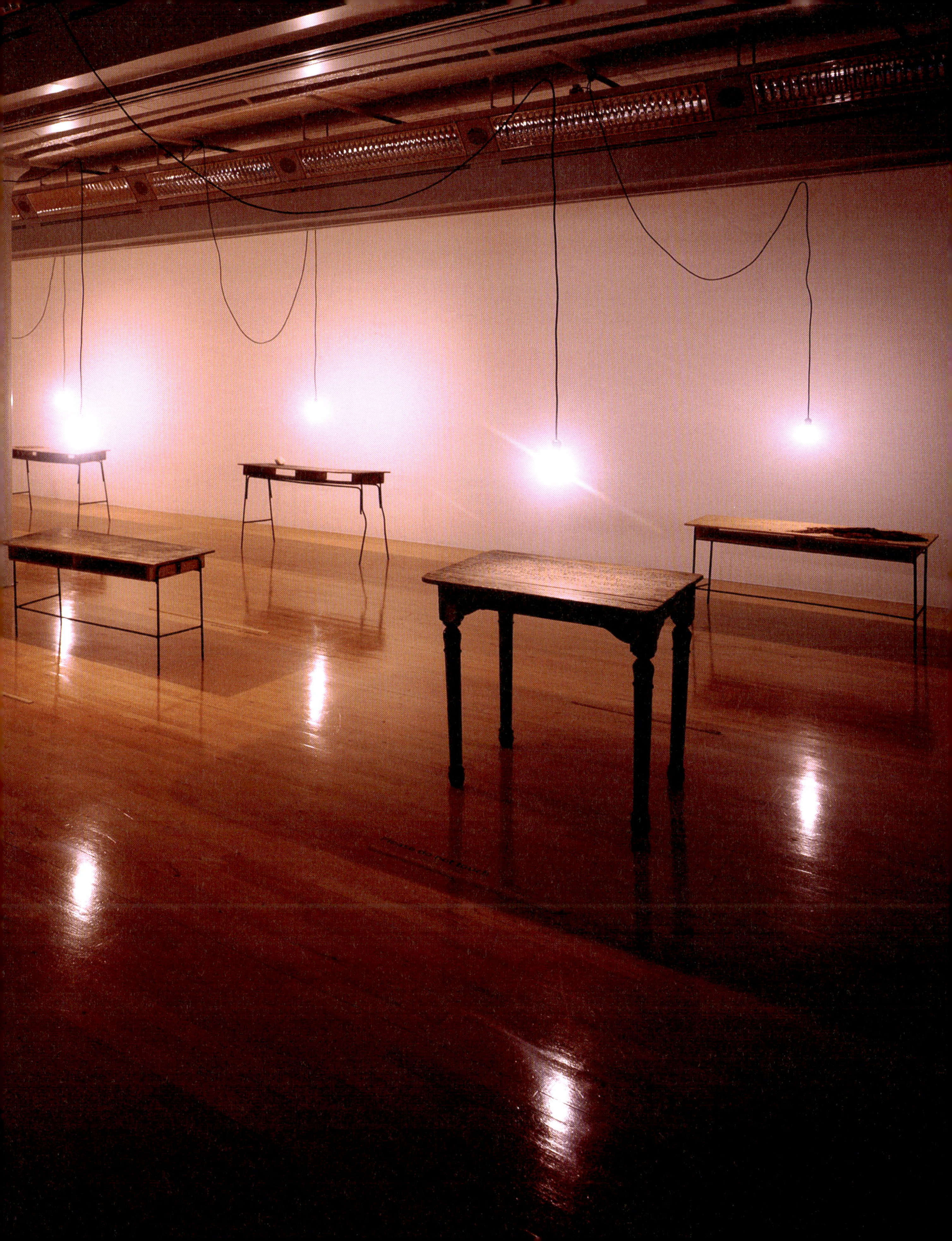

Graham Gussin
Surrendering 2   1994–95

Overleaf
left: Surrendering 3   1994–95
right: Surrendering 1   1994–95

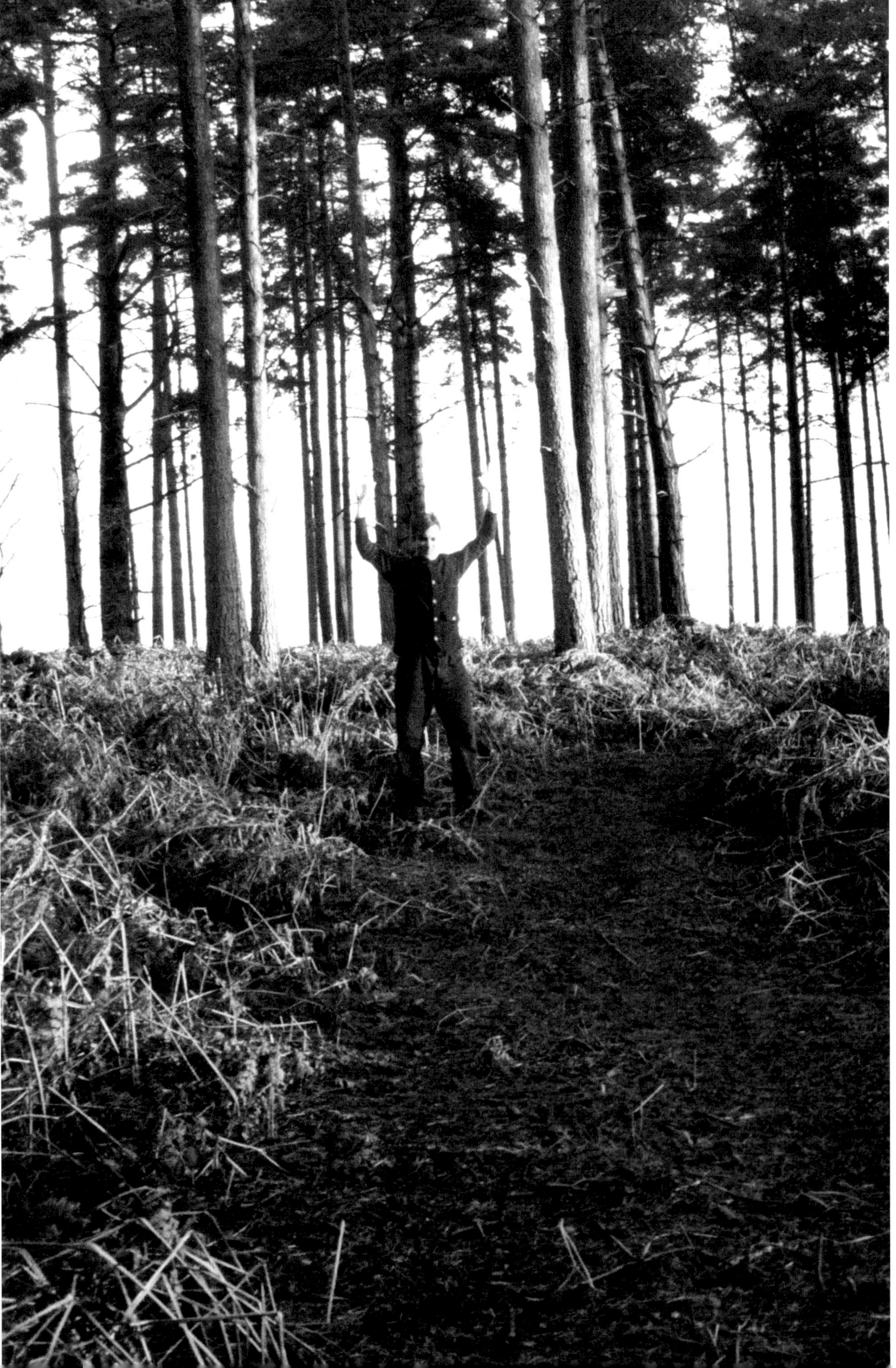

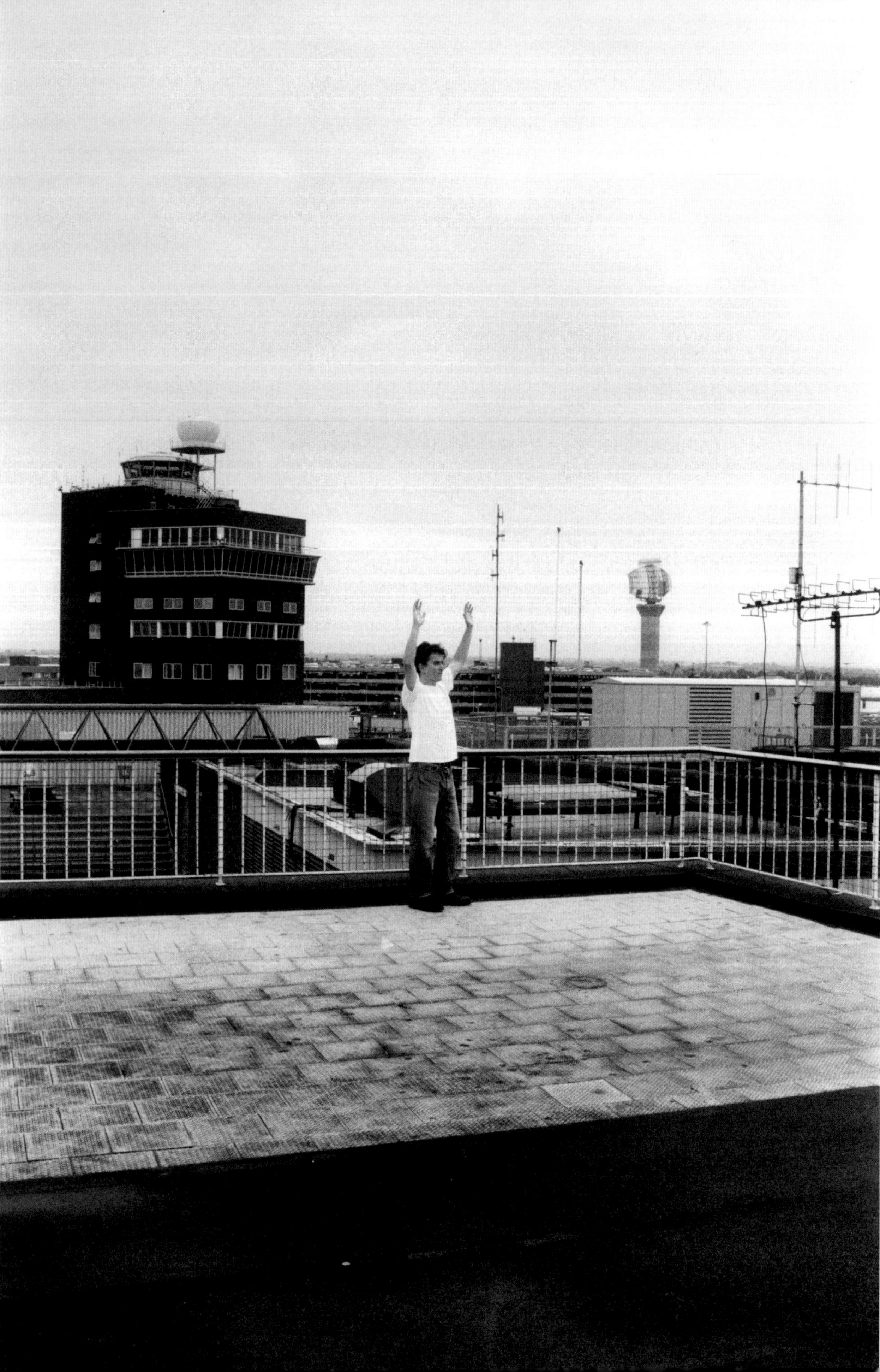

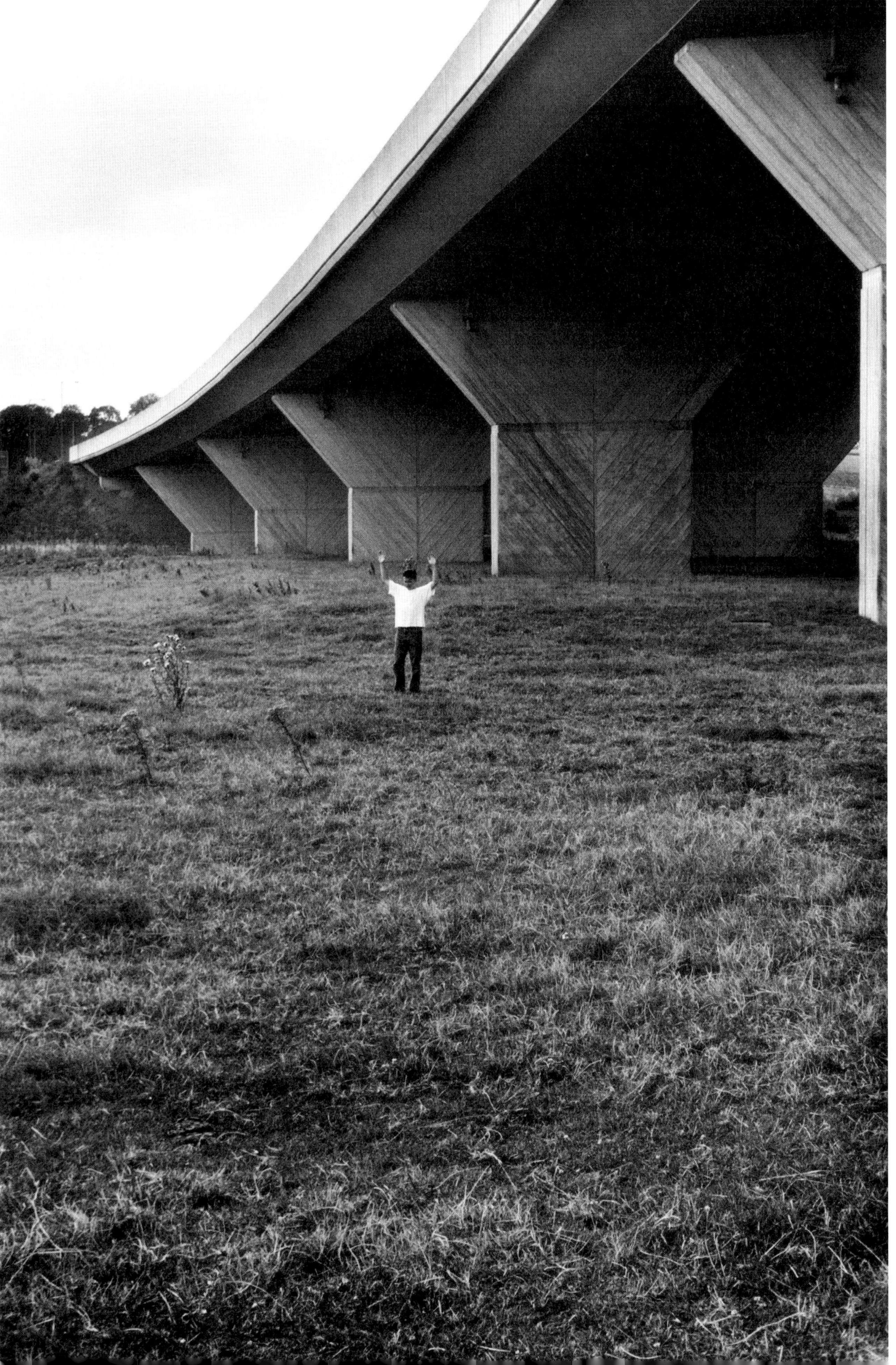

Callum Innes
Exposed Painting Paynes Grey/Yellow Oxide/Red Oxide on White   1999

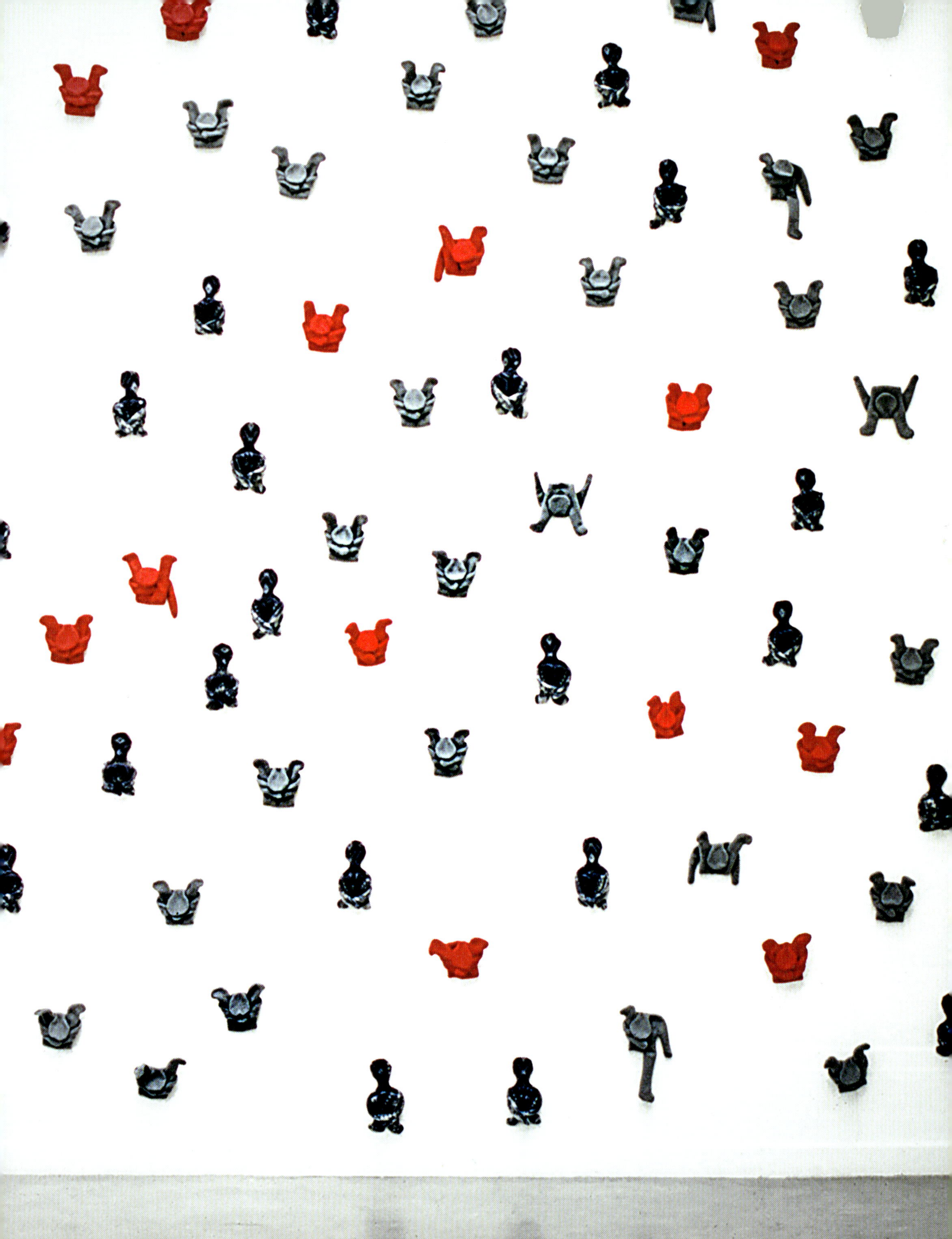

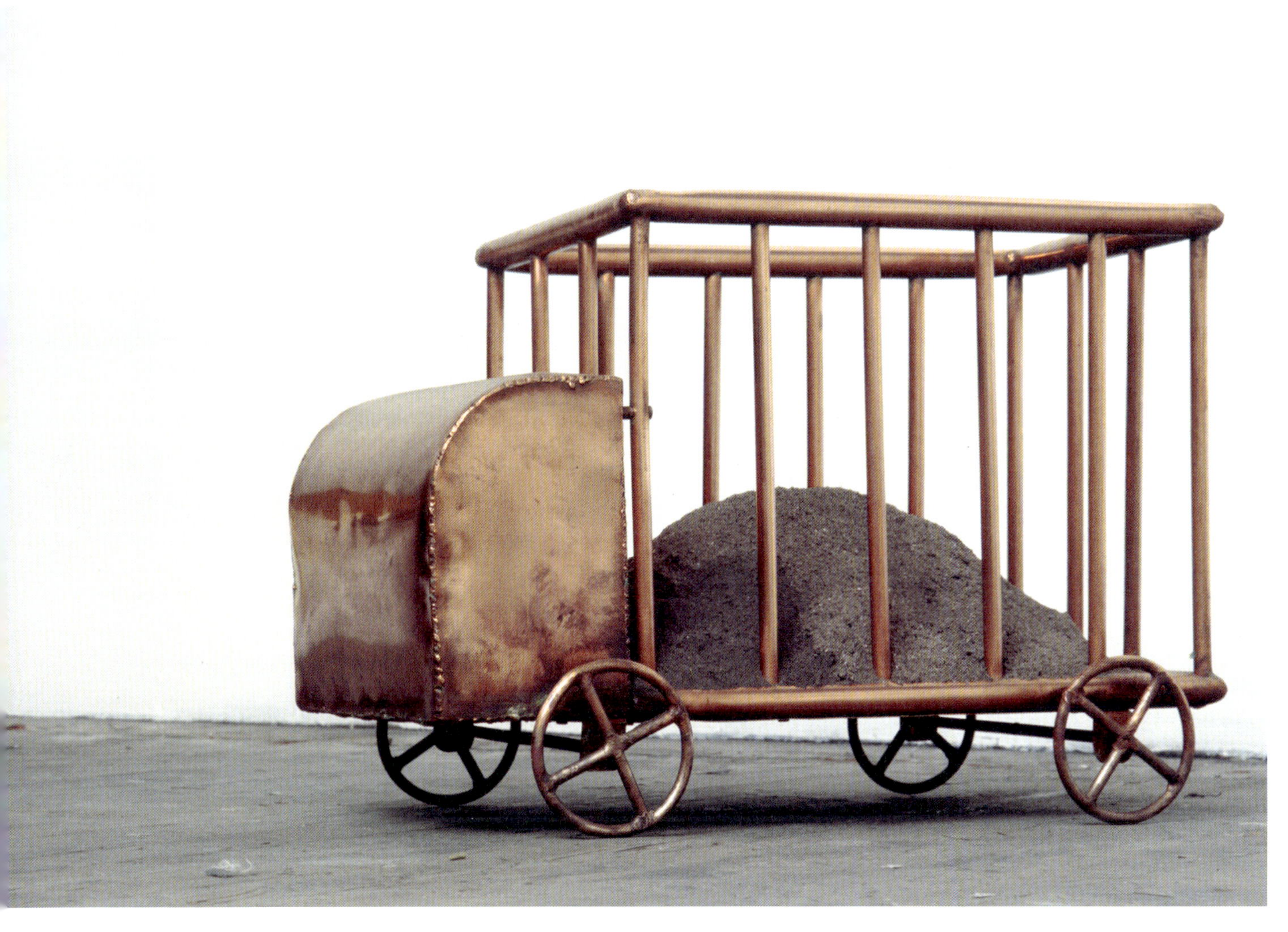

Permindar Kaur
left: Falling   1995
above: Loss   1995

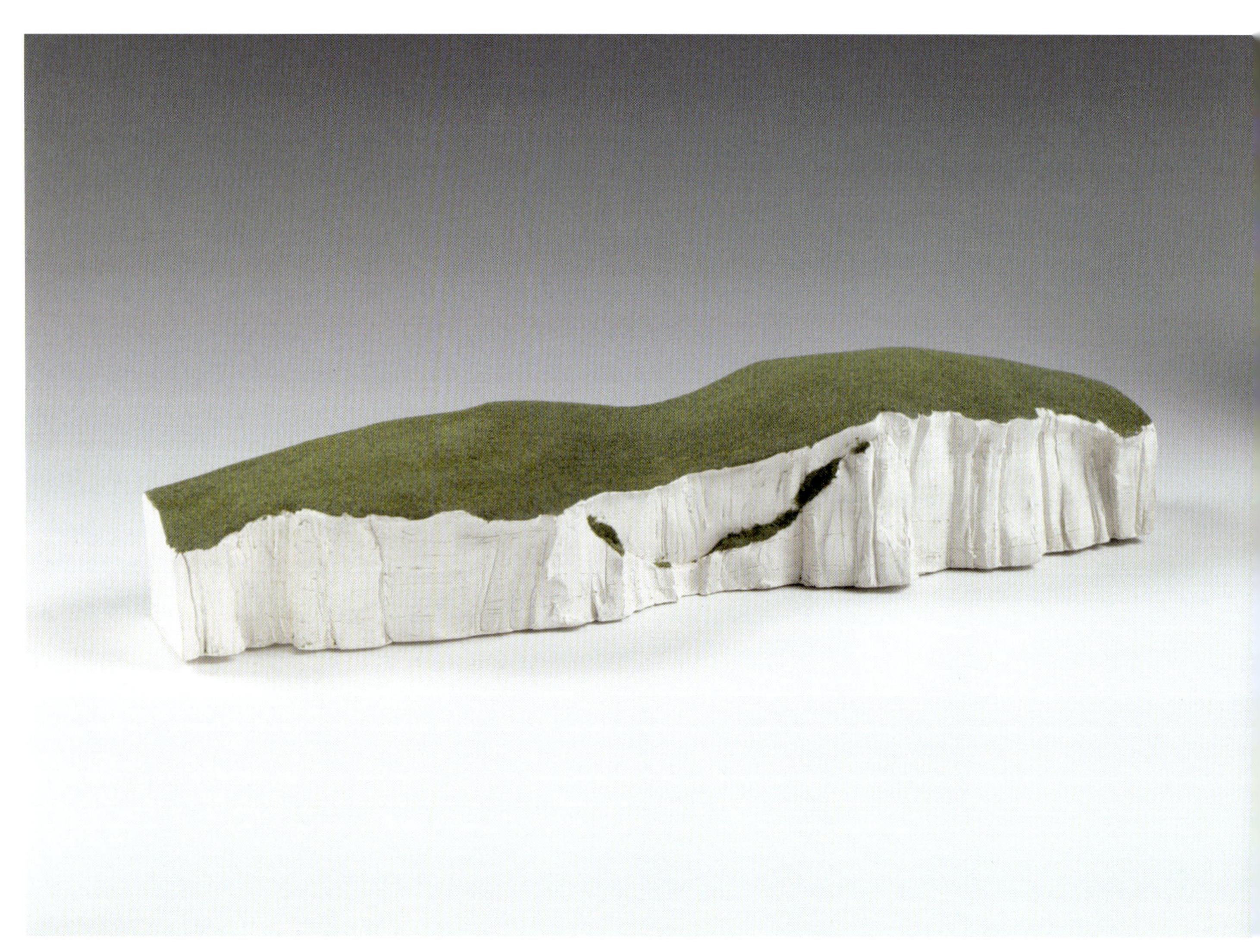

Tania Kovats
Little Vera   1998

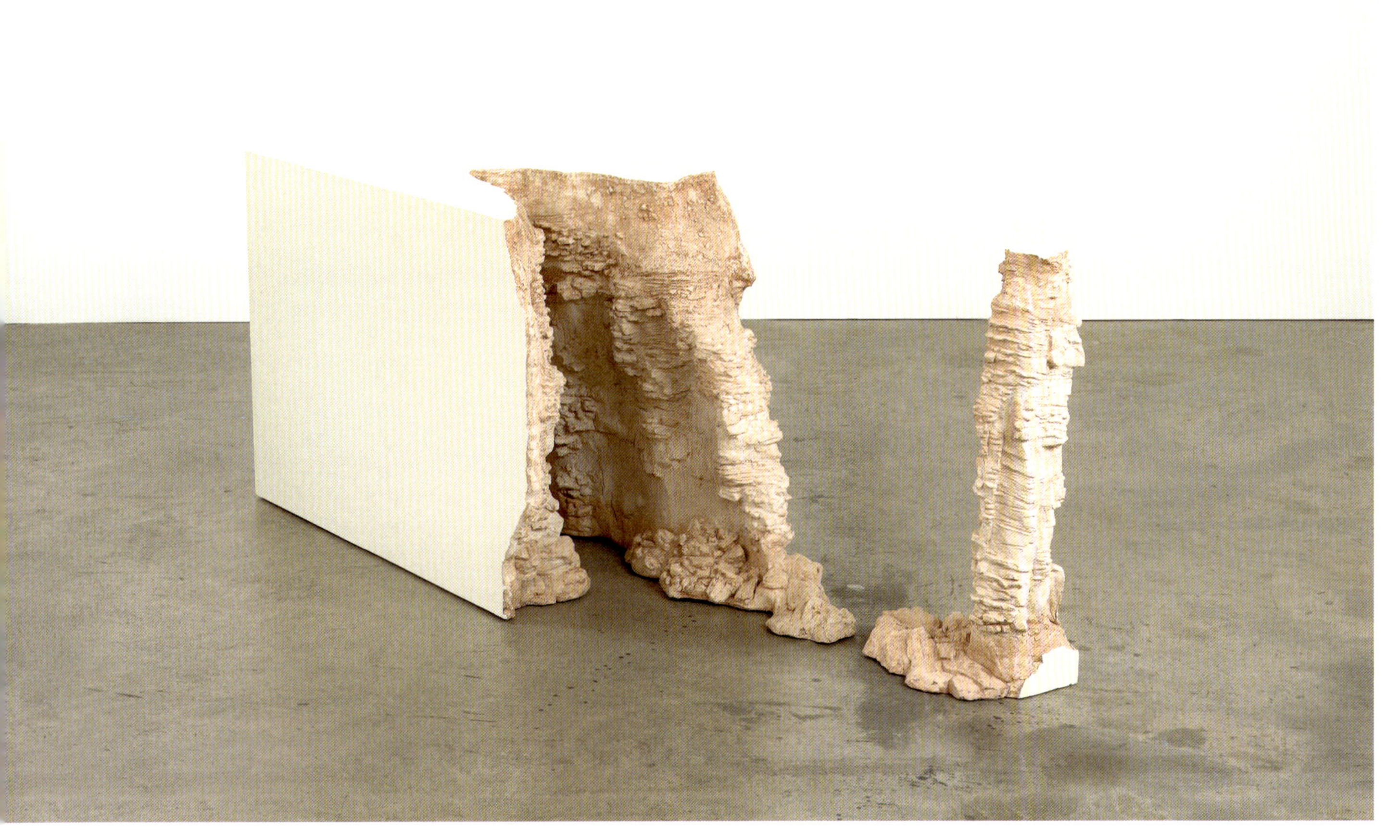

Tania Kovats
Peninsula   1998

Cildo Meireles
Jogo de Velha AX/OP 8B   1993–94

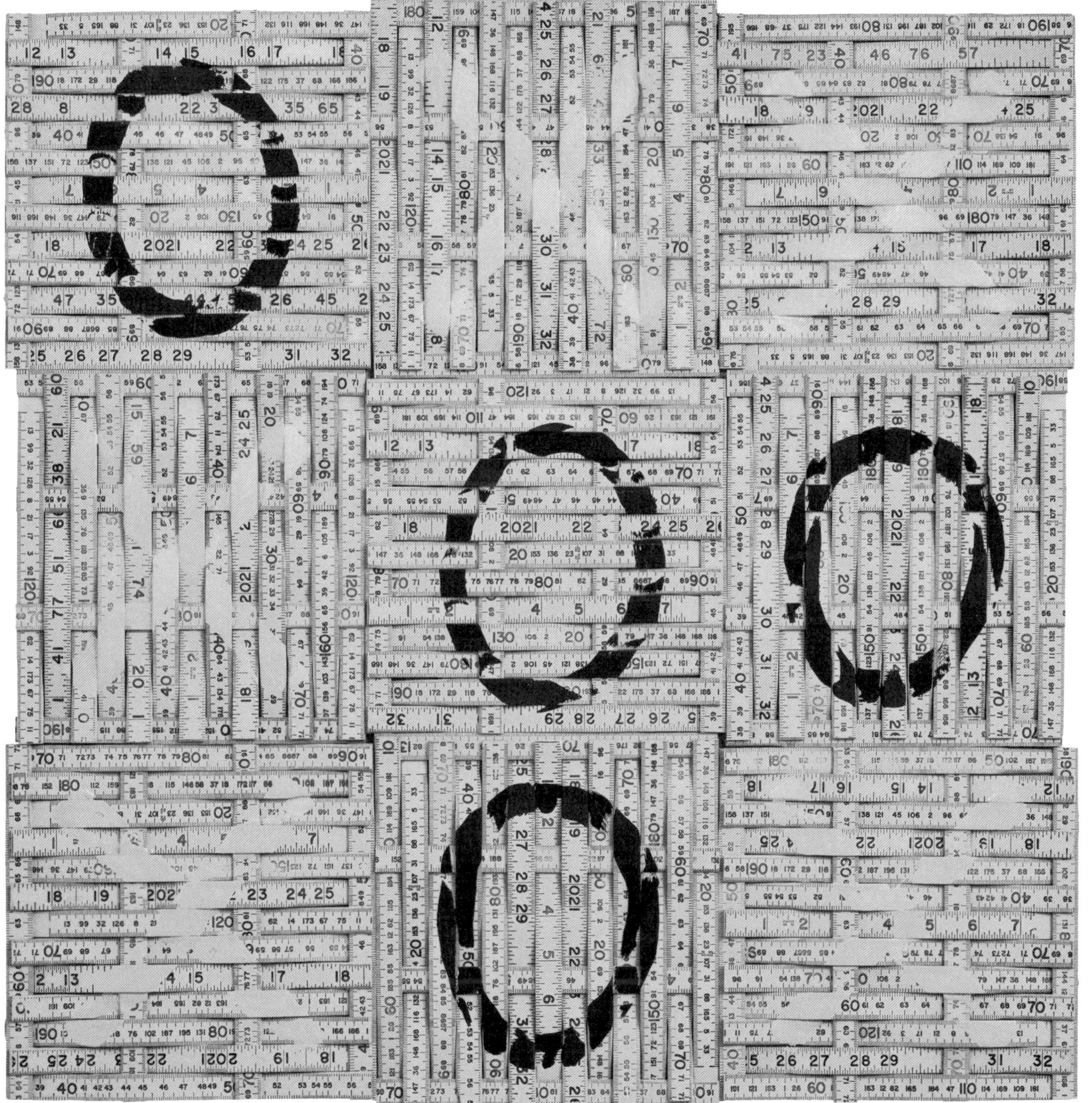

84

Lisa Milroy
Finsbury Square   1995

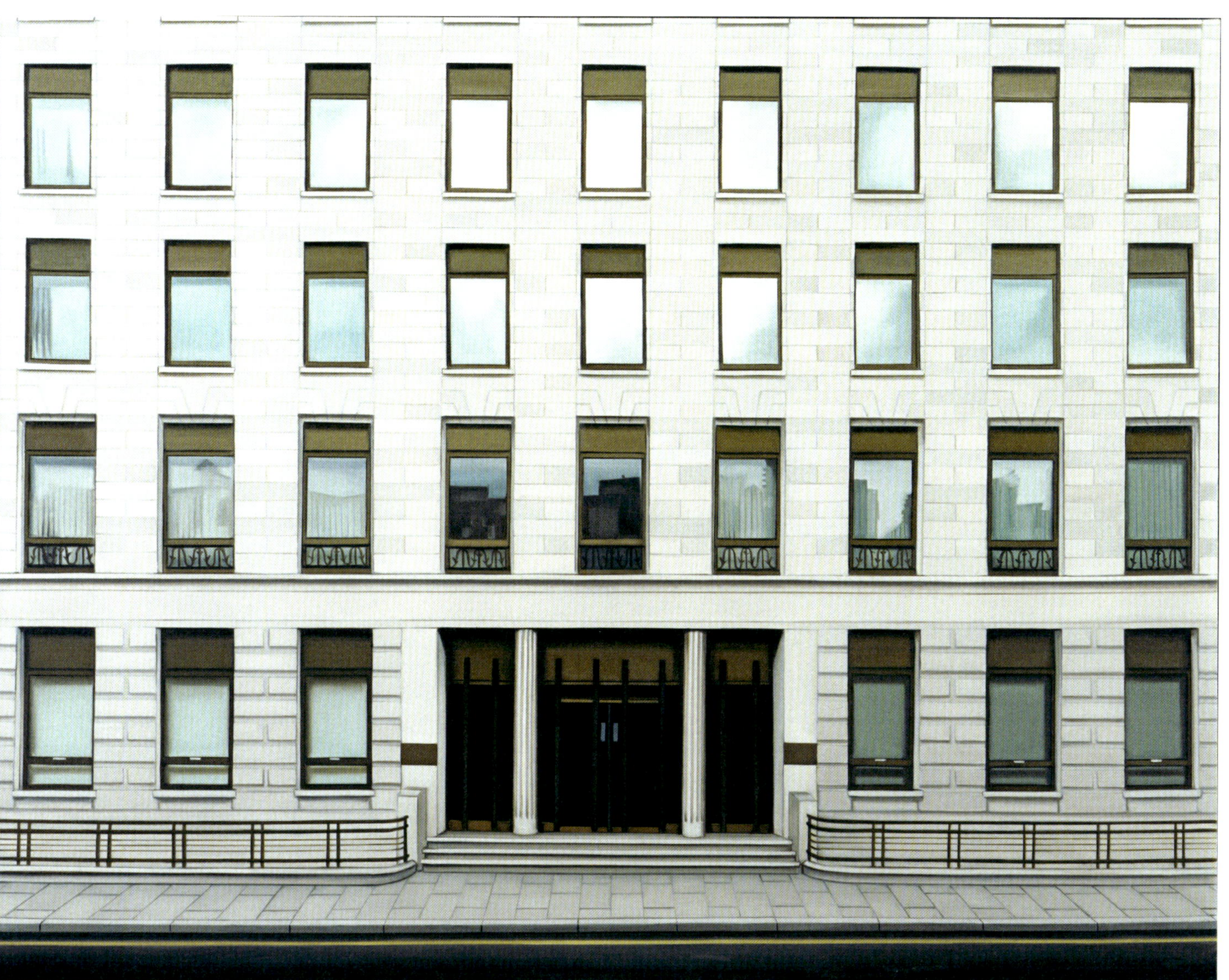

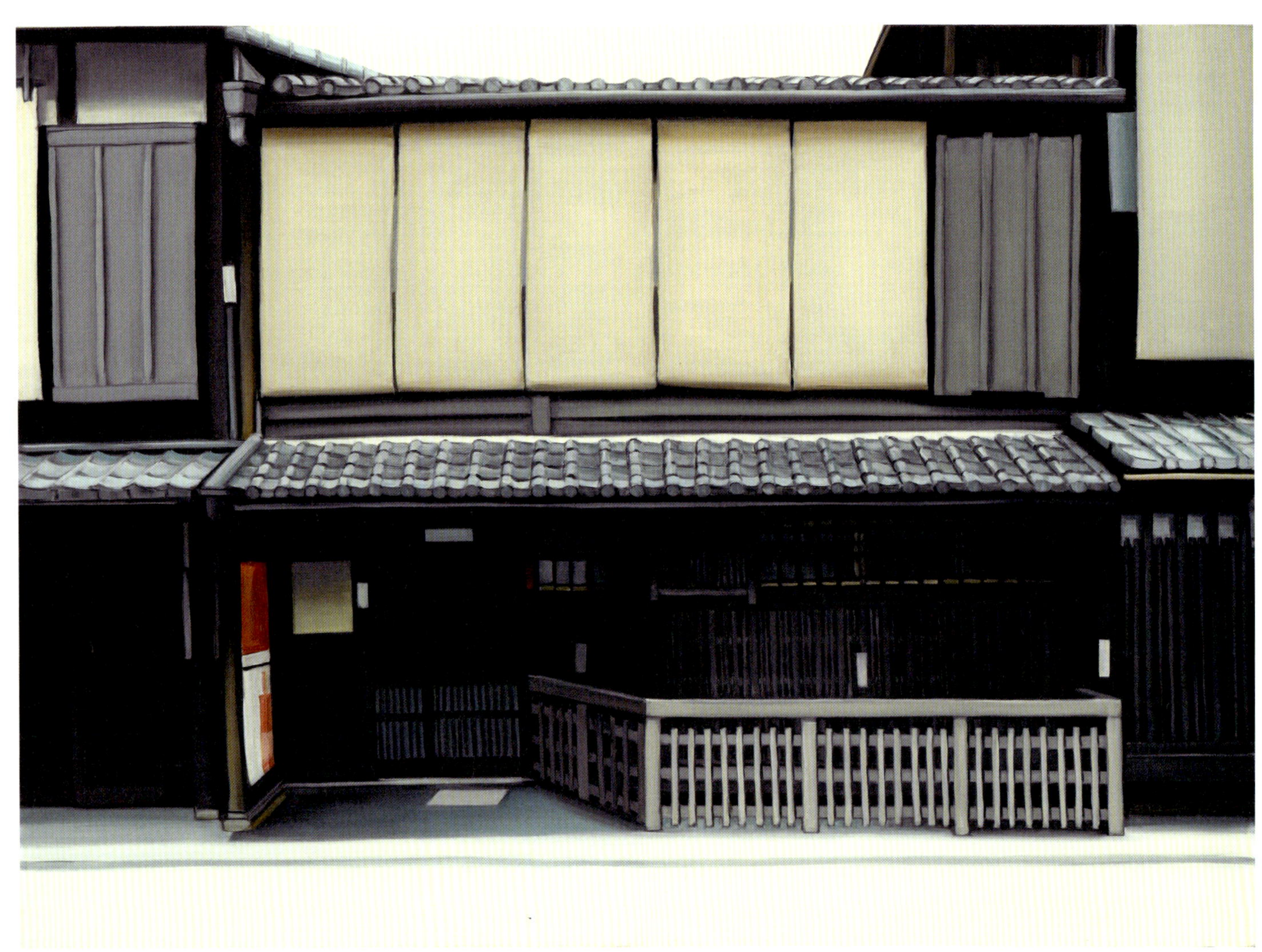

Lisa Milroy
Kyoto House 1994

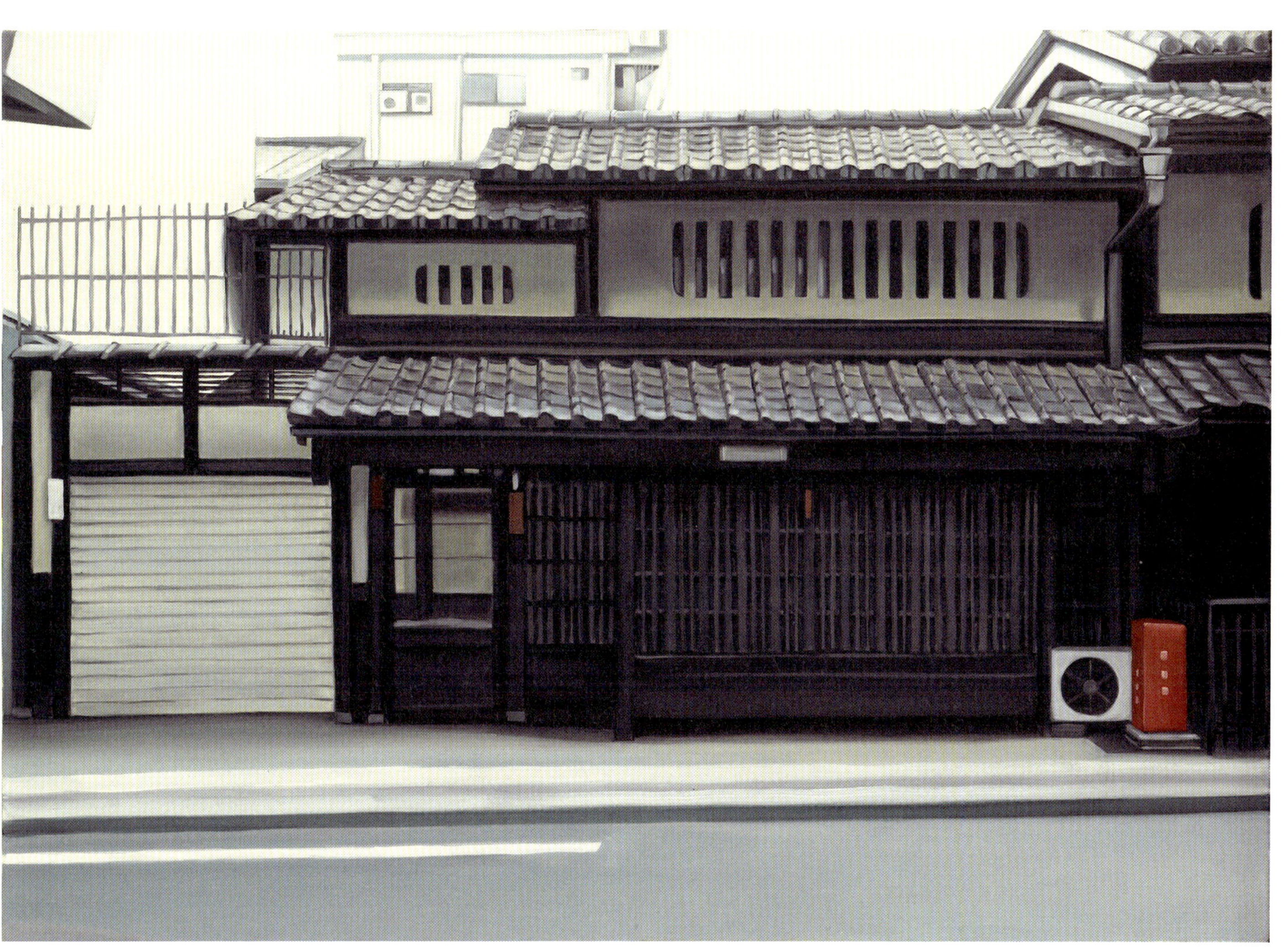

Lisa Milroy
Kyoto House   1994

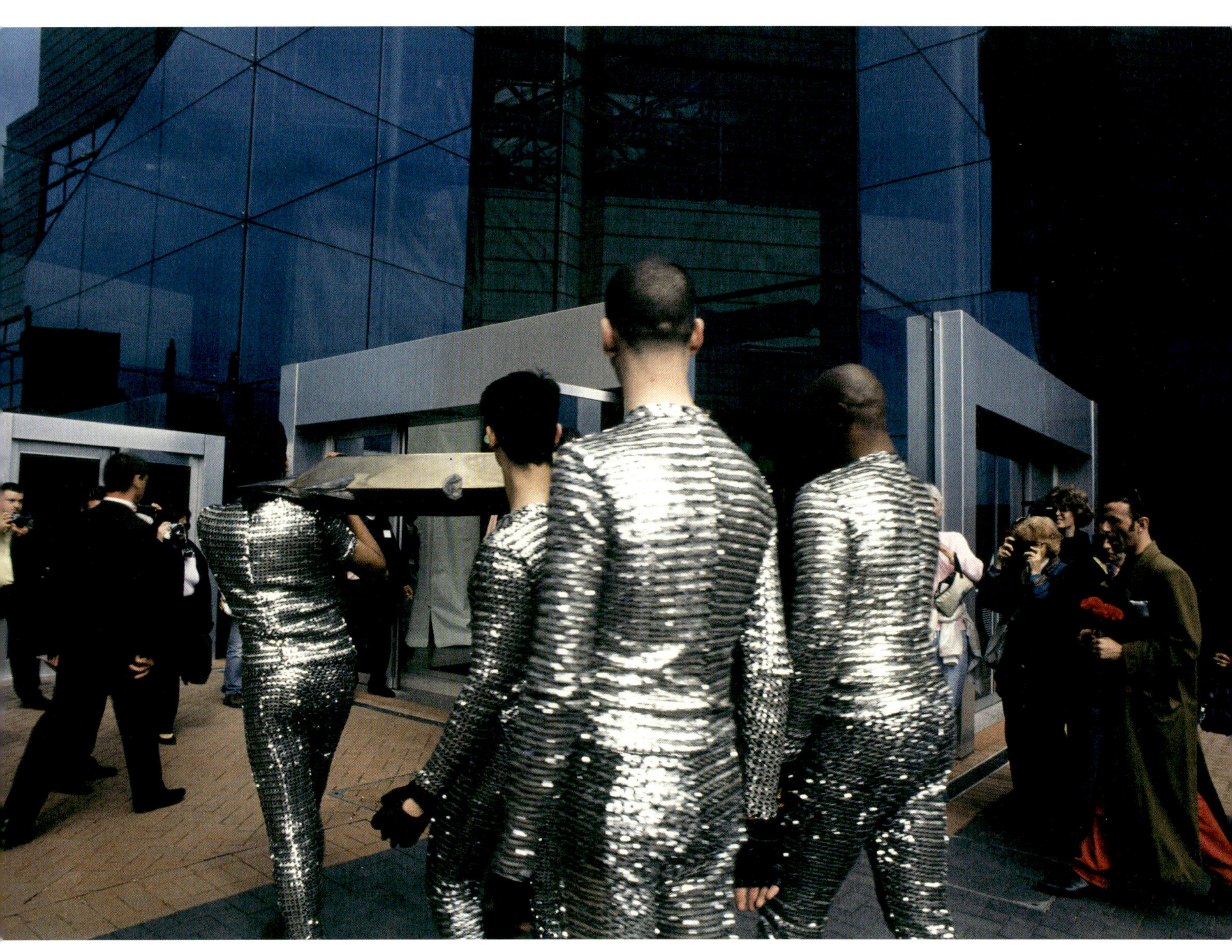

Antoni Miralda
The Miralda Honeymoon Project. Birmingham: The Eternity Ring   1991

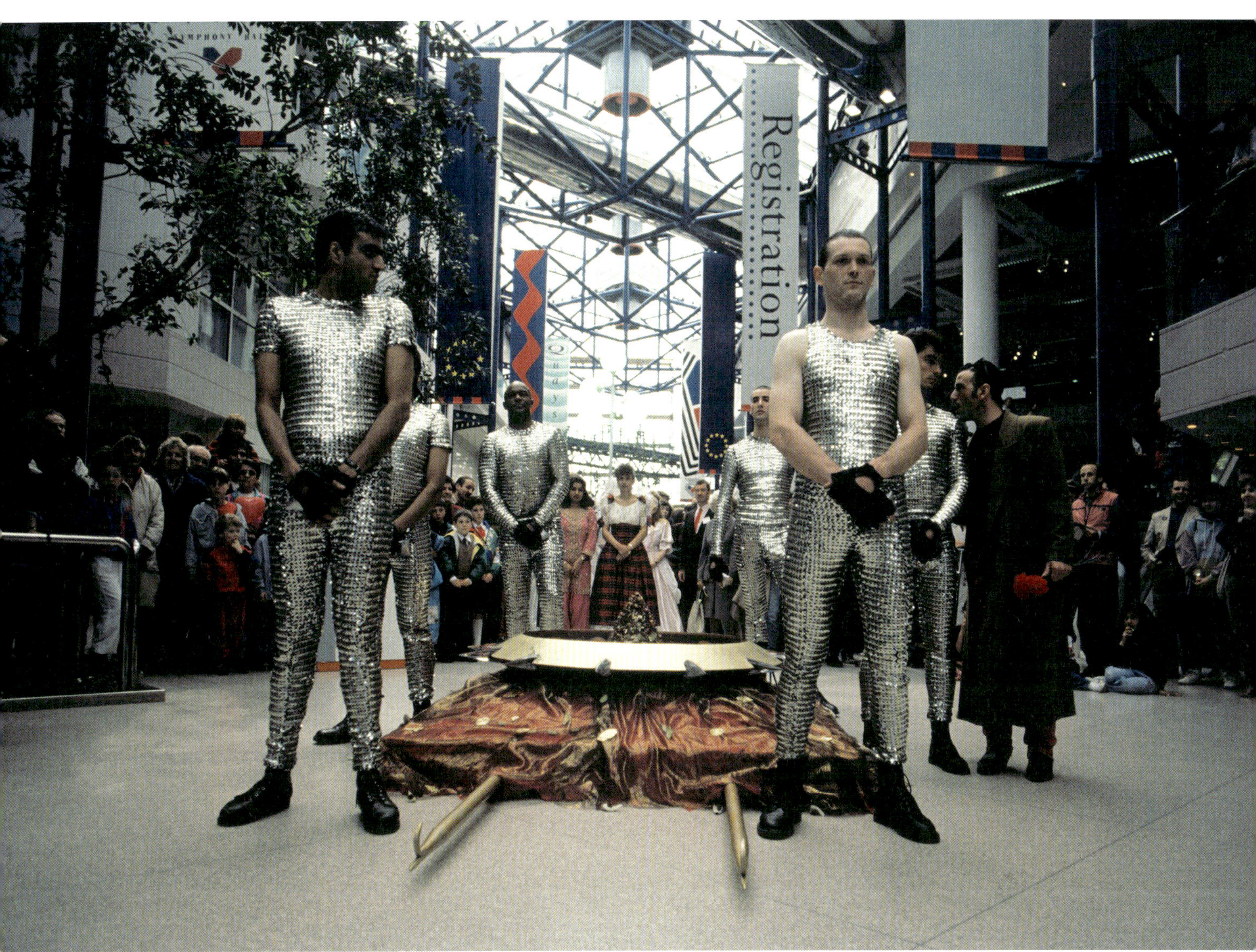
Registration

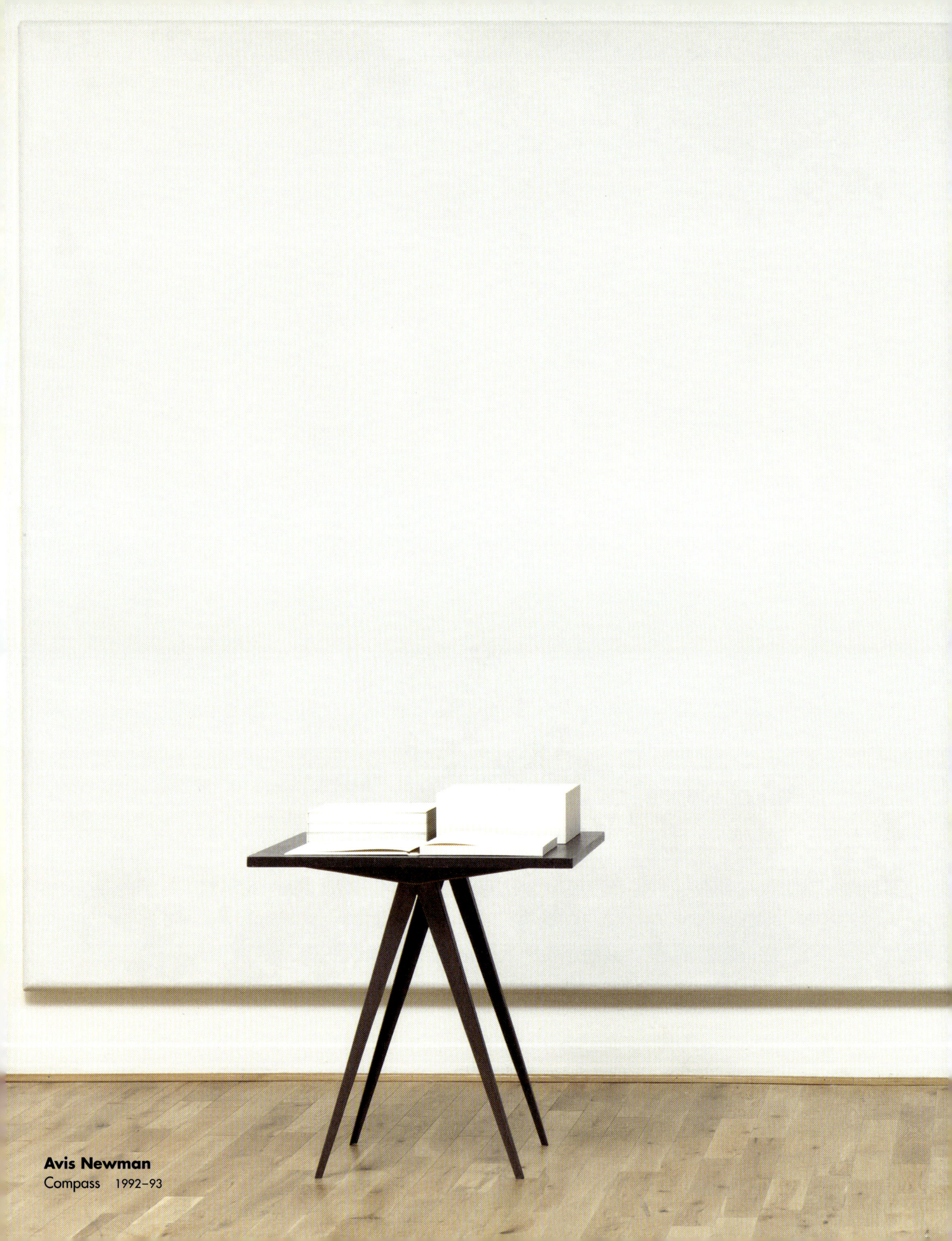

Avis Newman

Compass   1992–93

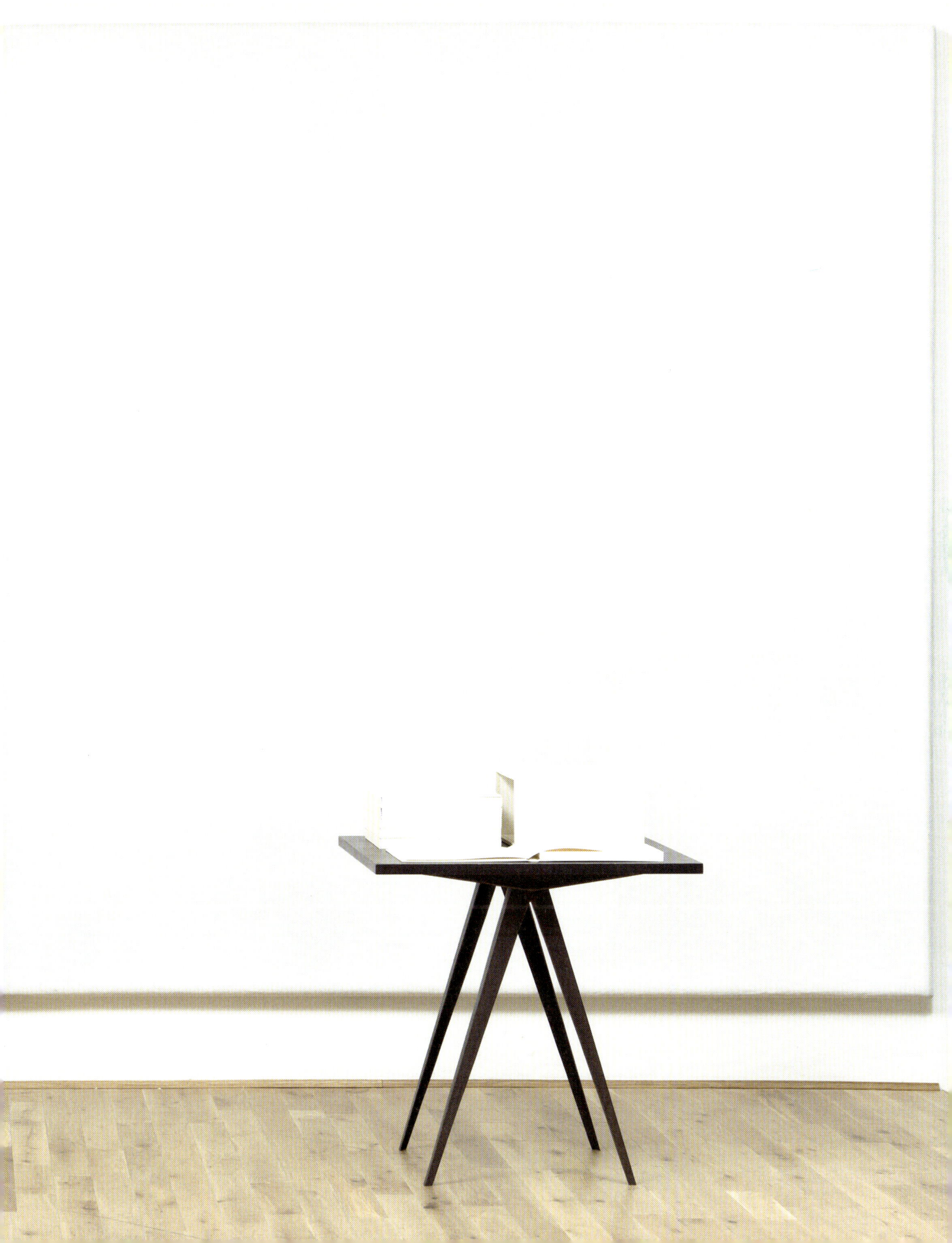

Lucia Nogueira
Untitled   1993

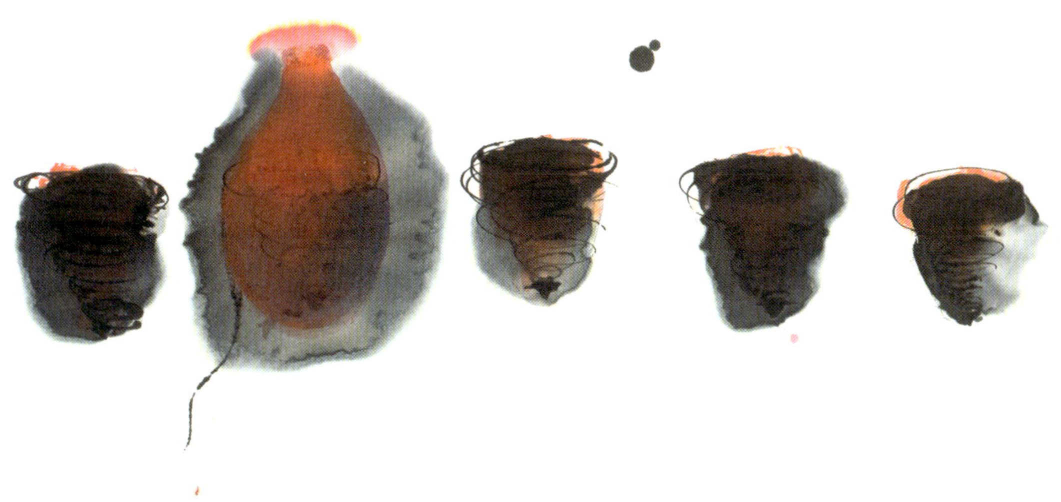

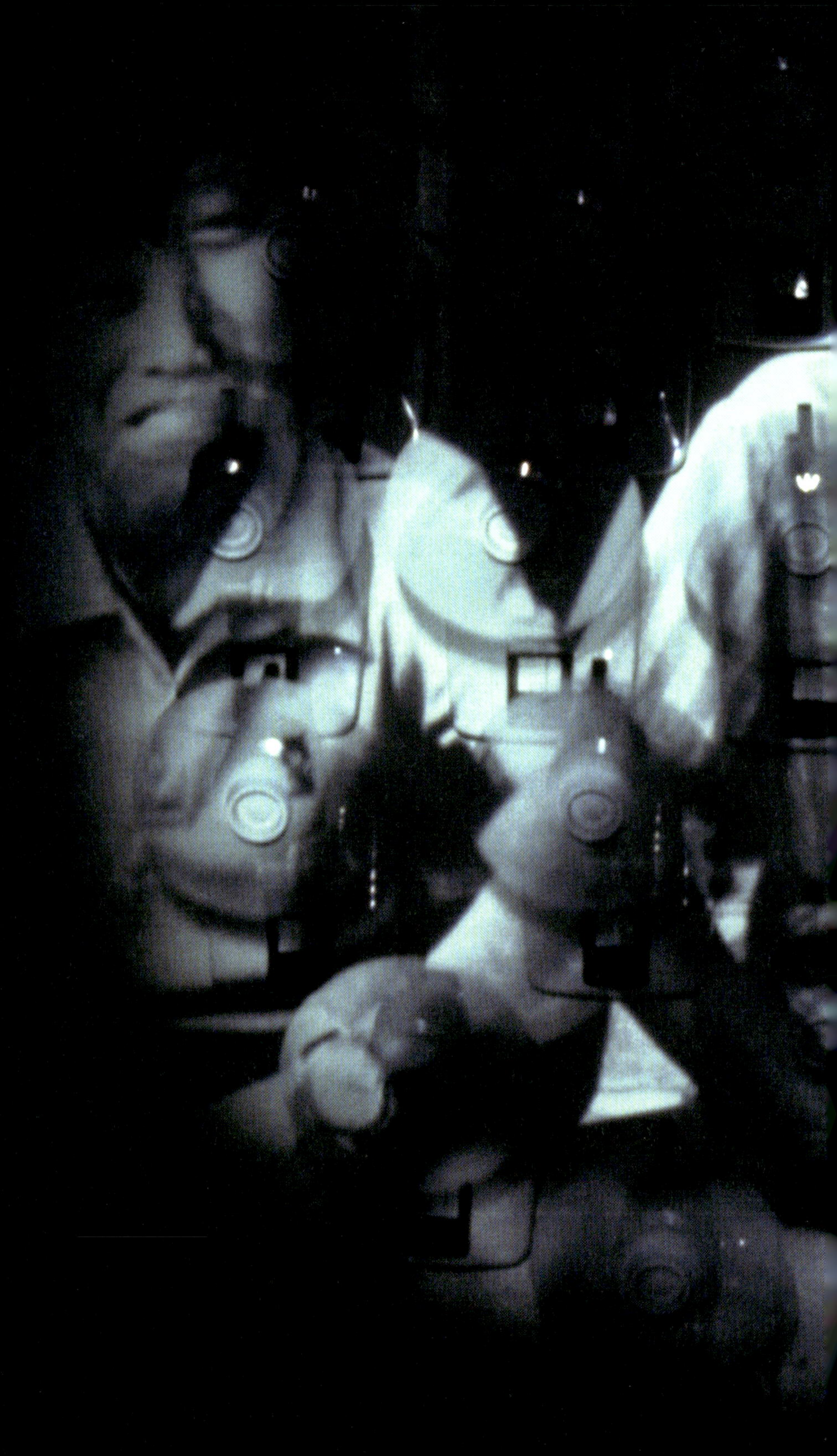

Vong Phaophanit
Fragments   1990

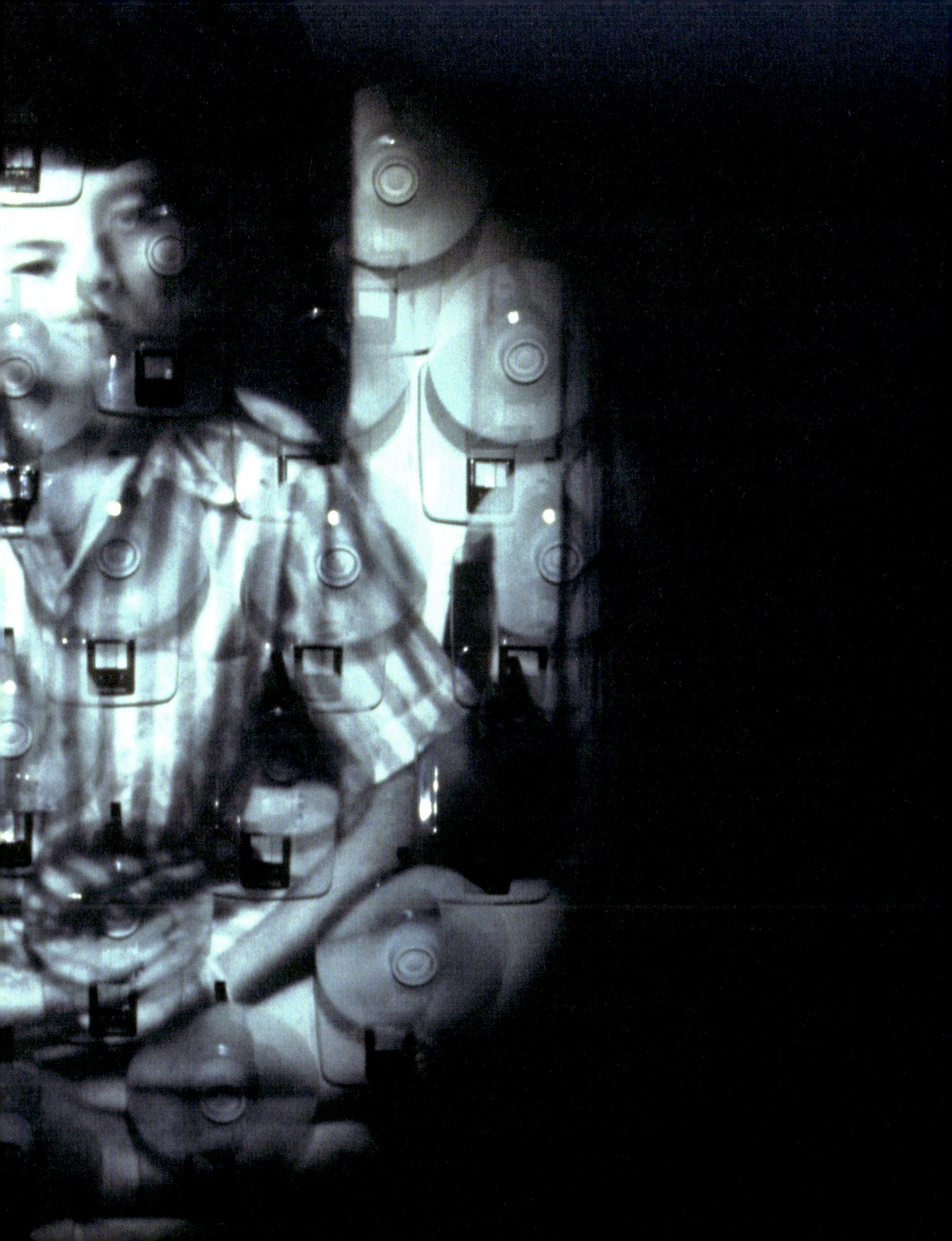

Adrian Piper
Please God   1990

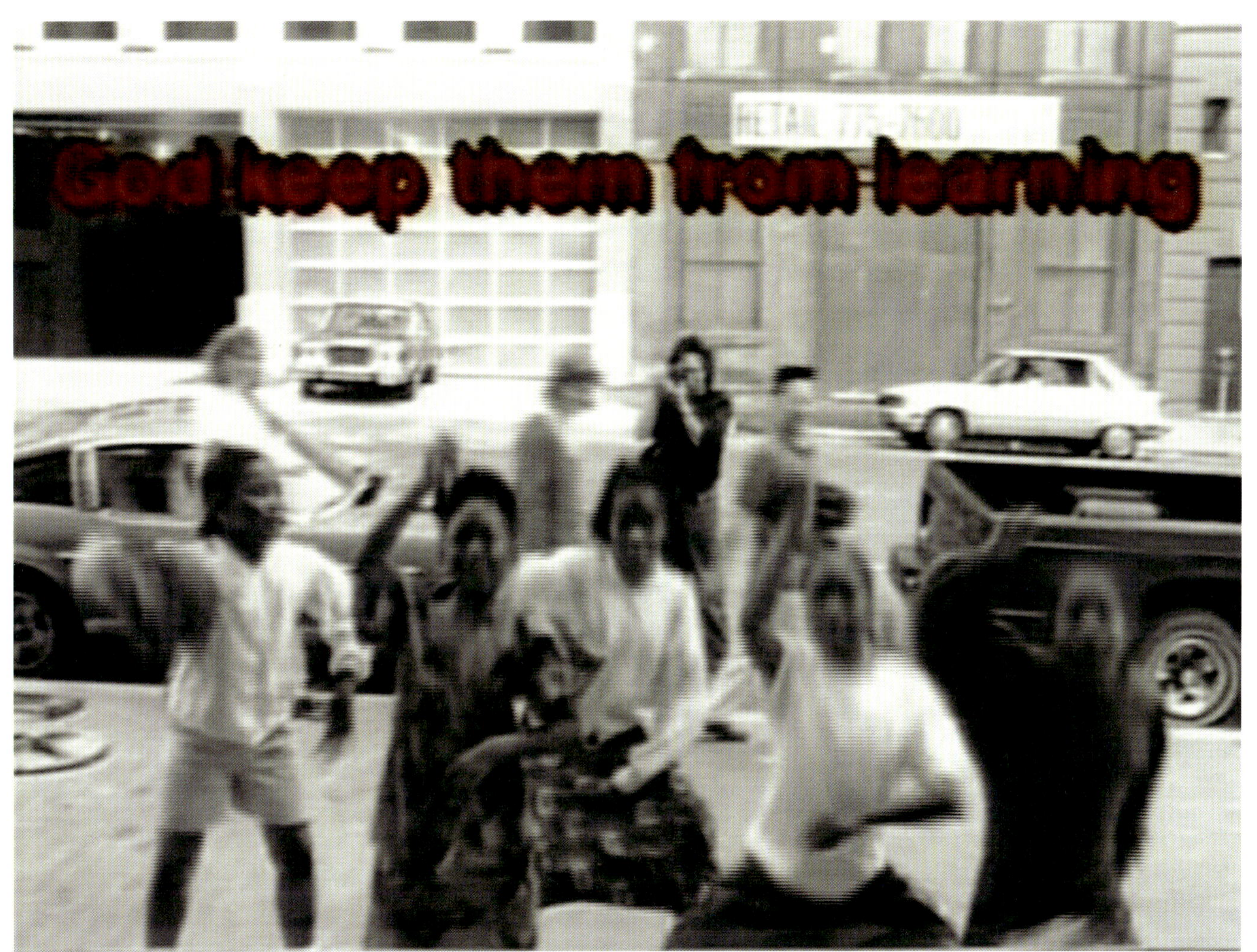
God keep them from learning
RETAIL 775-7500

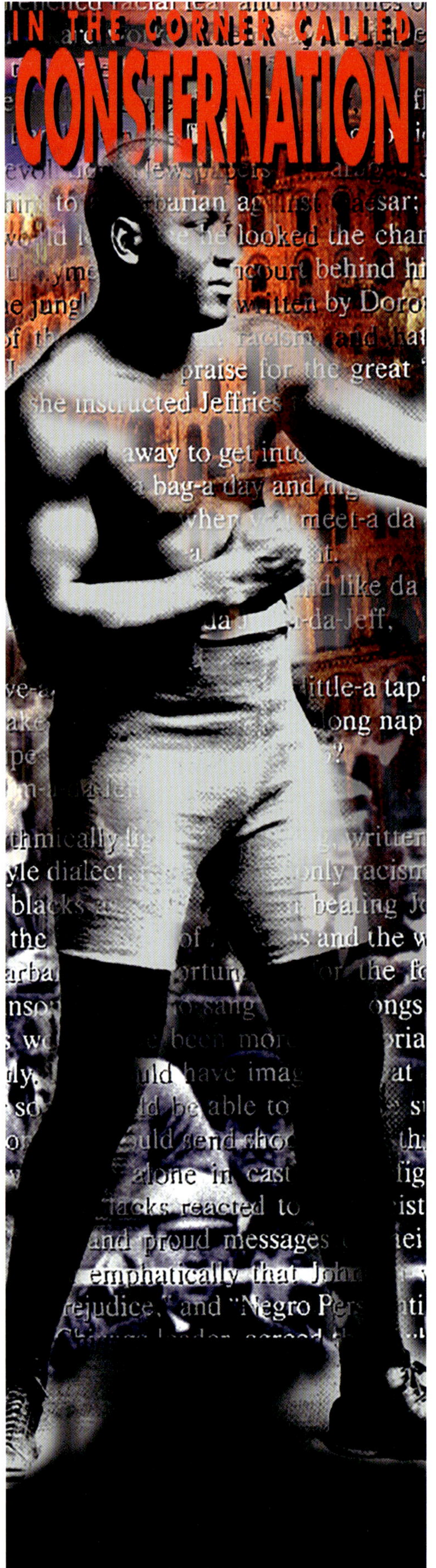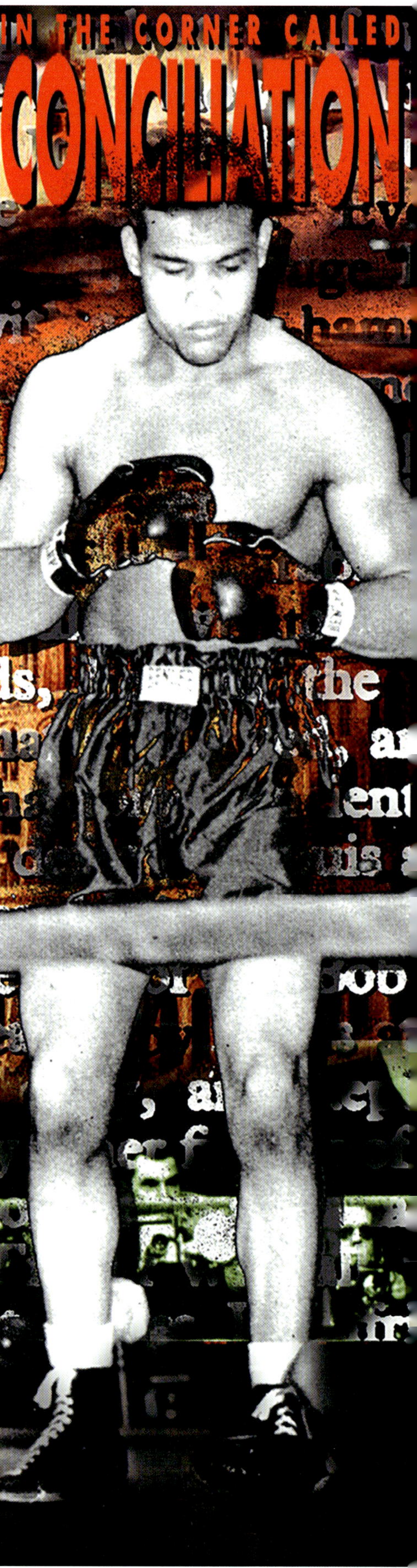

Keith Piper
Four Corners,
a Contest of Opposites   1995

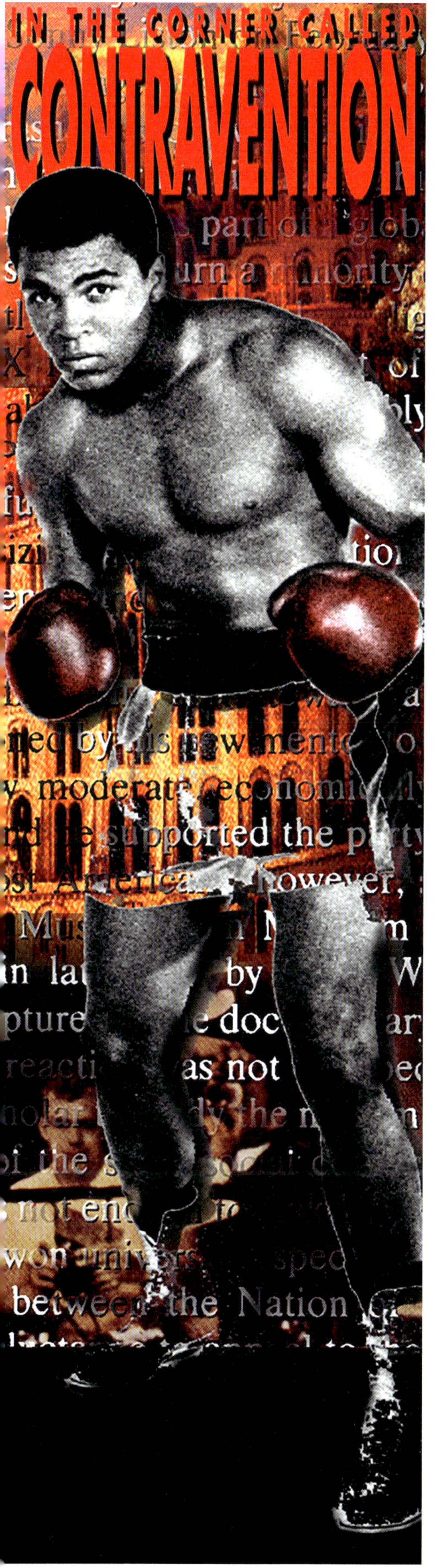

IN THE CORNER CALLED
CONTRAVENTION

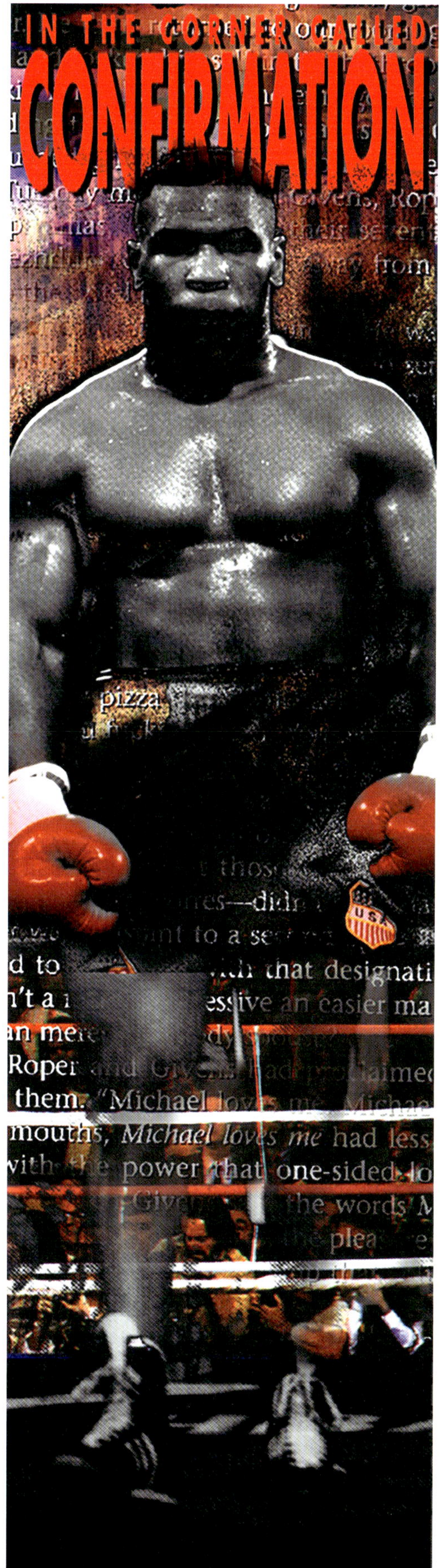

IN THE CORNER CALLED
CONFIRMATION

Donald Rodney
In the House of my Father   1997

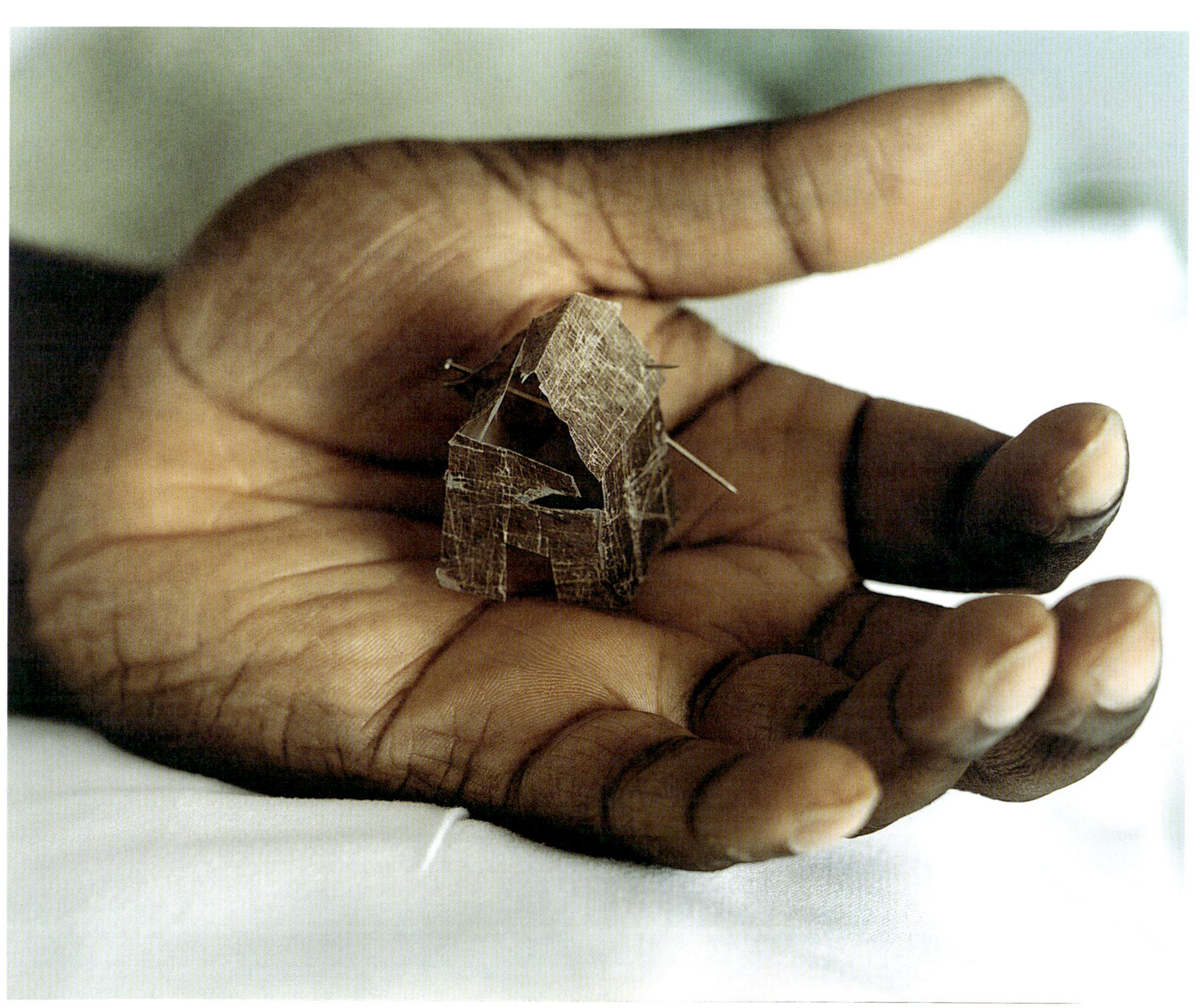

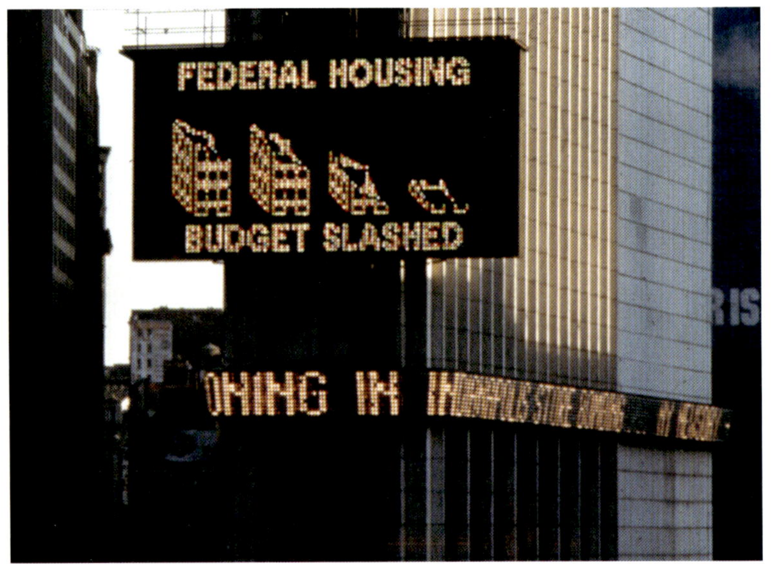

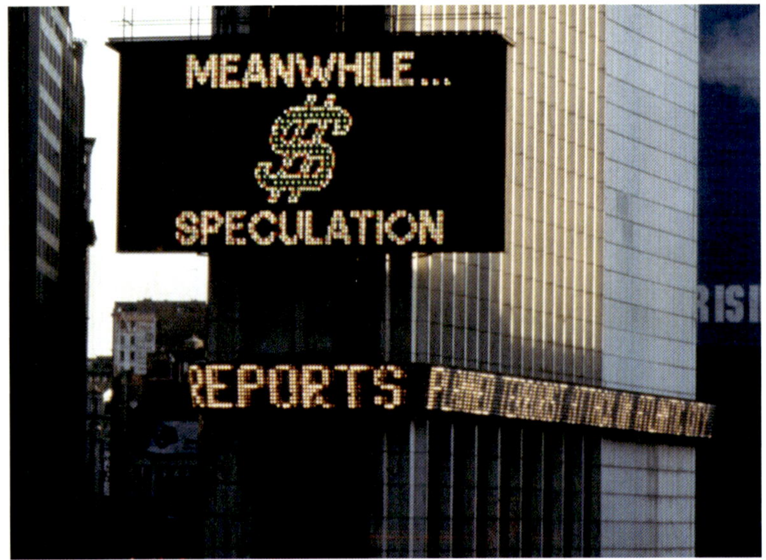

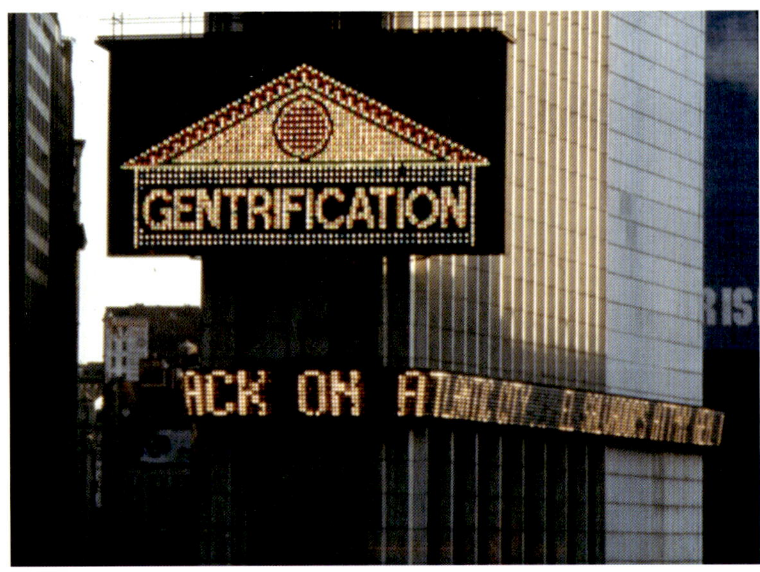

Martha Rosler
Housing is a Human Right   1989

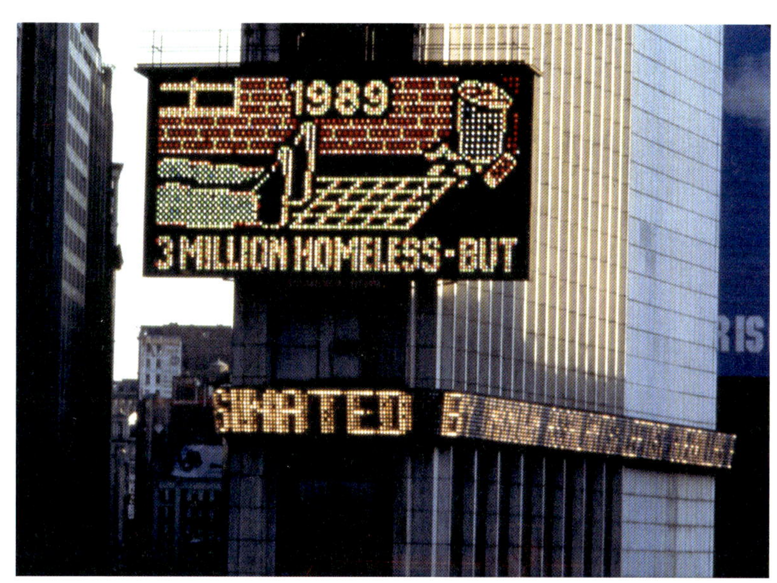

1989
3 MILLION HOMELESS - BUT
S...ATED
R I S

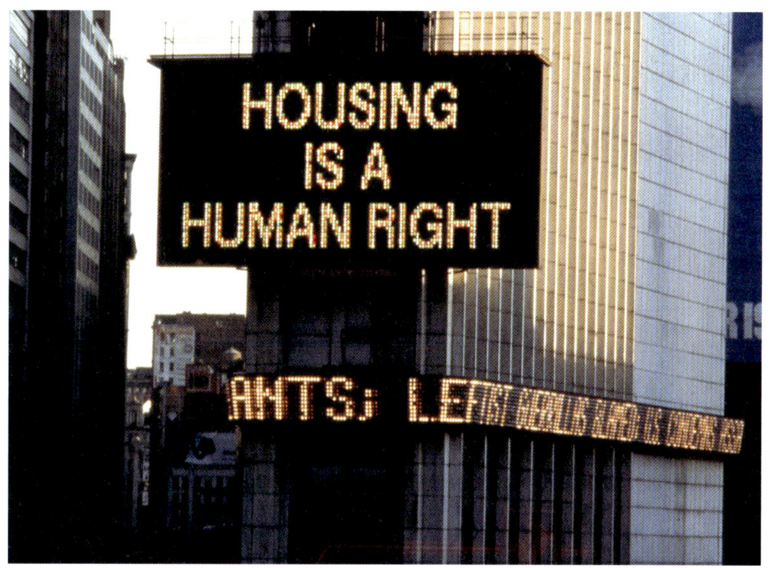

HOUSING
IS A
HUMAN RIGHT
ANTS; LE
R I S

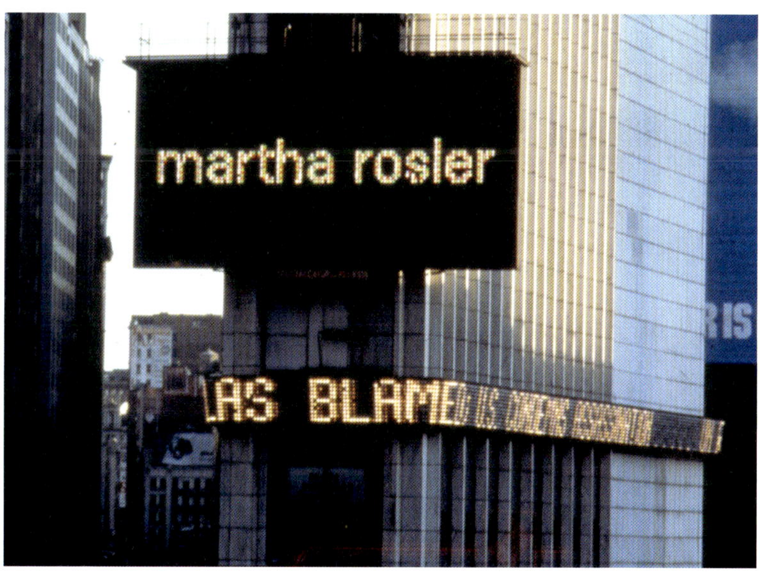

martha rosler
AS BLAME
R I S

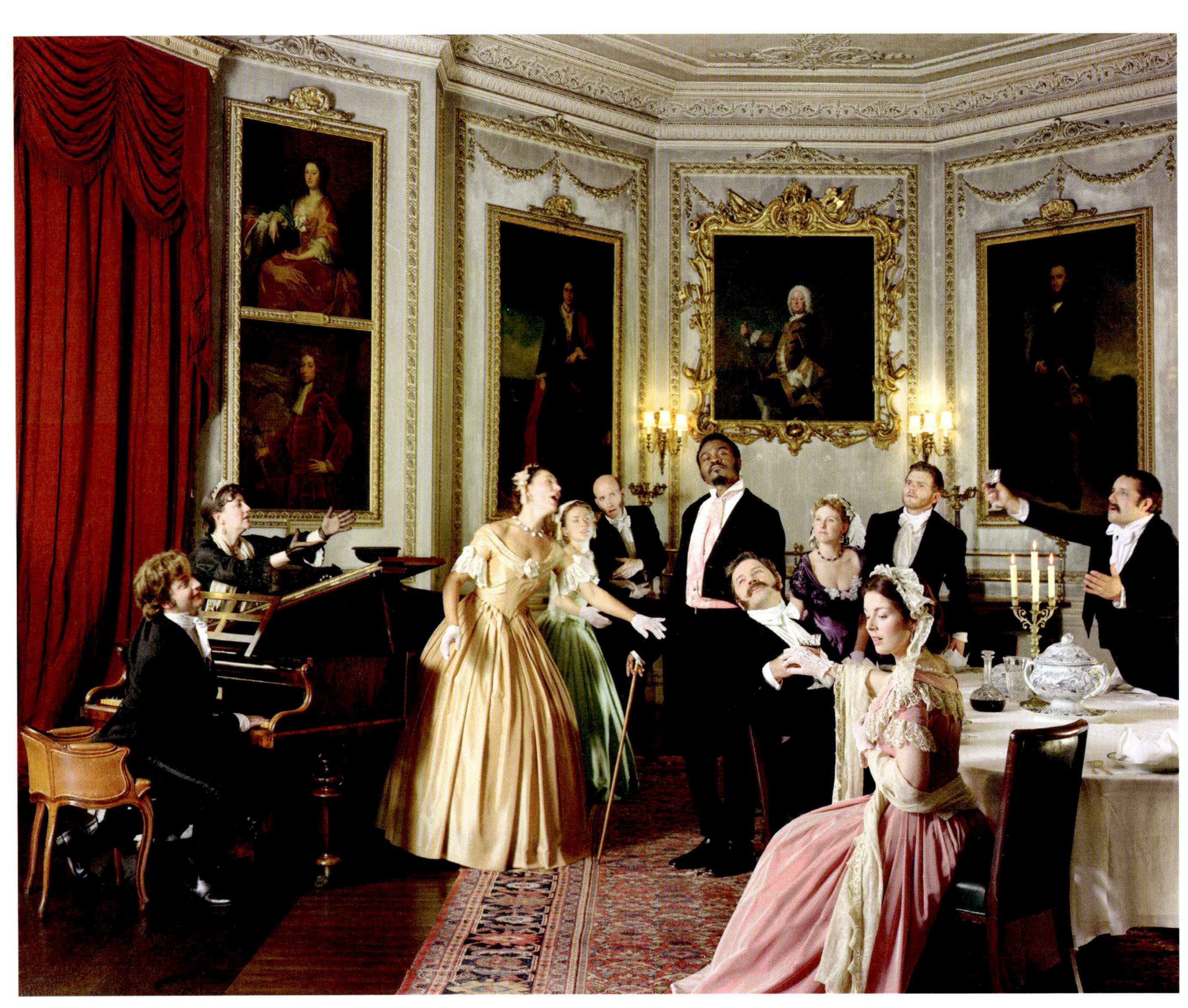

Yinka Shonibare
Diary of a Victorian Dandy 19.00hrs.   1998

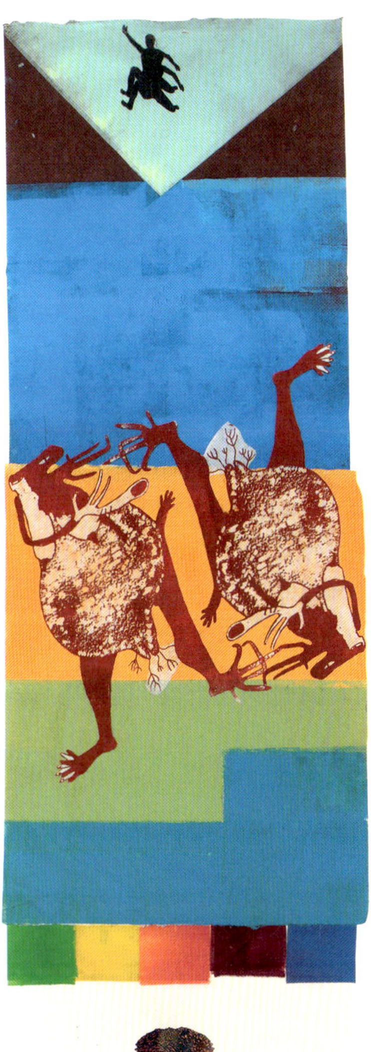

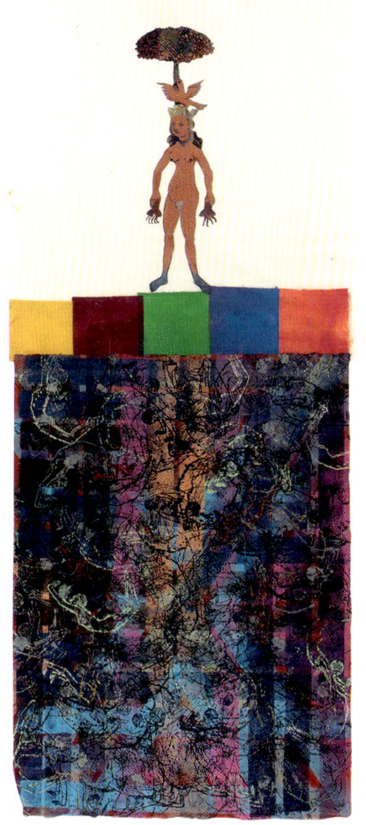

Nancy Spero
Carnival   2000

106

Georgina Starr
The Nine Collection of the 7ᵗʰ Museum   1994

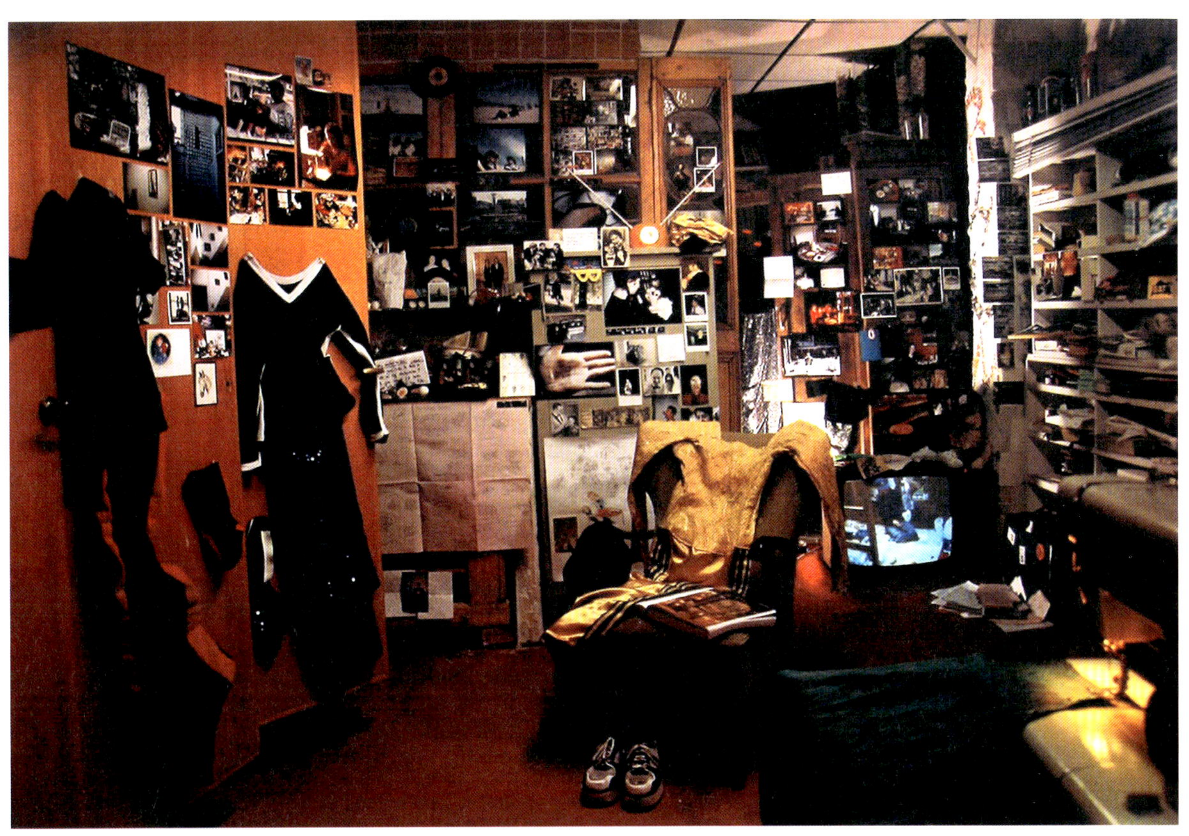

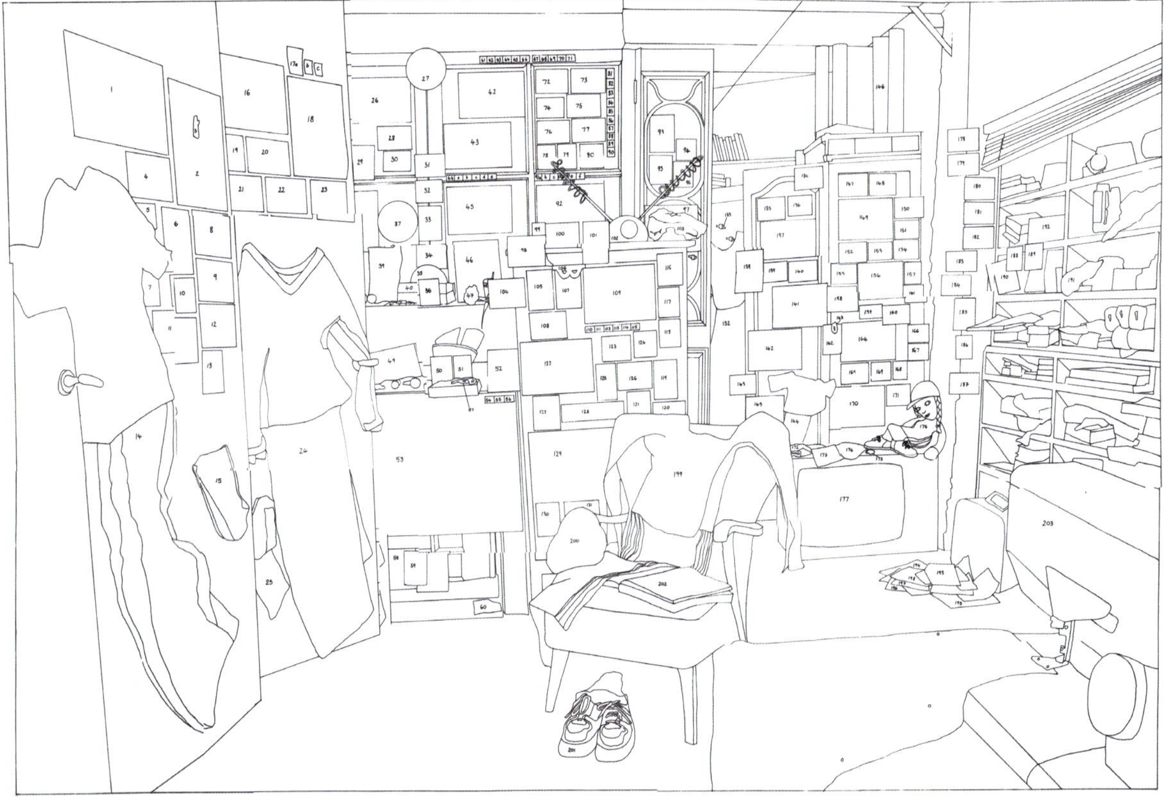

Schematic rendering of The Collection

Side Panel (First section)

1 The Garden at Lahey (Lahey Collection, Den Haag)
2 Patient Luncheon (Lahey Collection, Den Haag)
3 Wooden Sculpture (Lahey Collection, Den Haag)
4 The Narrow Corridor (Lahey Collection, Den Haag)
5 The Guest Room (Lahey Collection, Den Haag)
6 The Secret Closet (Lahey Collection, Den Haag)
7 The Birth of Sculpture (Recollection Collection)
8 Staircase at Lahey (Lahey Collection, Den Haag)
9 Staircase and Mirror (Lahey Collection, D.H.)
10 Statue (location unknown)
11 Aquarius the Water Carrier (Recollection Collection, Den Haag)
12 Escape by Plane (The Seven Sorrows Collection, Depression)
13 Portrait of a Horse (Recollection Collection, Den Haag)
14 Costume for Dining with the Third Storyteller (Costume Collection, Den Haag)
15 Costume for Junior No.1 (Costume Collection, Den Haag)

Side Panel (Second section)

16 Interior Scene in Grey-tone (Costume Collection, Den Haag)
17 x First daughter (Lahey Collection, Den Haag)
x Second daughter (Lahey Collection, Den Haag)
x Third daughter (Lahey Collection, Den Haag)

18 Portrait of Christine Lahey (Portrait Collection, Den Haag)
19 The Making of the Golden Gown Part 1 (Costume Collection, Den Haag)
20 The Making of the Golden Gown Part 2 (Costume Collection, Den Haag)
21 Cleaning the cloth (Costume Collection, Den Haag)
22 The Making of the Golden Gown Part 3 (Costume Collection, Den Haag)
23 The Material Landscape (Lahey Collection, Den Haag)
24 Costume for Dining with the Second Storyteller (Costume Collection, Den Haag)
25 Costume for Junior No.1 (Costume Collection, Den Haag)

26 [illegible]
27 [illegible]
28 [illegible]
29 [illegible]
30 [illegible]
31 [illegible]
32 [illegible]
33 [illegible]
34 [illegible]
35 [illegible]
36 [illegible]
37 [illegible]
38 [illegible]
39 [illegible]
40 [illegible]
41 [illegible]
42 [illegible]
43 [illegible]
44 [illegible]
45 [illegible]
46 [illegible]
47 [illegible]
48 [illegible]
49 [illegible]
50 [illegible]
51 [illegible]
52 [illegible]
53 [illegible]
54 [illegible]
55 [illegible]
56 [illegible]
57 [illegible]
58 [illegible]
59 [illegible]
60 [illegible]
61 [illegible]
62 [illegible]
63 [illegible]
64 [illegible]
65 [illegible]
66 [illegible]
67 [illegible]
68 [illegible]
69 [illegible]
70 [illegible]
71 [illegible]
72 [illegible]
73 [illegible]
74 [illegible]

75 Street collection (The Seven Sorrows Collection, Depression)
76 Interior with Hidden Statues (Lahey Collection, Den Haag)
77 National Pictures (2) (Recollection Collection)
78 Christmas Collection (Recollection Collection)
79 Bubble gum Collection (Recollection Collection)
80 Magic (Recollection Collection)
81 Kitchen Interior with Flower Tiles (Lahey Collection, Den Haag)
82 Corridor Interior with Light (Lahey Collection, Den Haag)
83 Portrait with Round Spectacles (Lahey Collection, Den Haag)
84 Portrait with Cranial Back (Lahey Collection, Den Haag)
85 The Three Fearless Graces (Lahey Collection, Den Haag)
86 a,86 b Interior with Plate Collection (Lahey Collection, Den Haag)
87 Interior Painting Corridor (Lahey Collection, Den Haag)
88 The First Painting (Lahey Collection, Den Haag)
89 Plated Exterior (Lahey Collection, Den Haag)
90 Breakfast for One (Lahey Collection, Den Haag)
91 a,b,c,d,e,f The Garden at Lahey (Lahey Collection)
92 New Shoes (The Seven Sorrows Collection, New Shoes)

Middle Panel (Fourth Upper Section)

93 Farewell Collector (Recollection Collection)
94 Portrait of Joanna Hargreaves (Recollection Collection)
95 Portrait of Jorn de Coulery (Runciar and Margaret Oakes Collection and Portrait Collection)
96 Portrait of a Young Man (Portrait Collection)
97 Easter Parade (Recollection Collection)

Middle Panel (Second Lower Section)

98 The Trick with due Hermann-Janssen (Notes for Junior Collection)
99 Virgin Mary (Recollection Collection)
100 Card for Lahey (Lahey Collection)
101 Portrait with Flowerettes (Notes for Junior Collection)
102 Helmet of Invisibility (Borrowed from Visit to a Small Planet Collection)
103 Gloriously Gifted Shirt (Costume Collection)
104 Balloons (The Seven Sorrows Collection, Depression)
105 The Departure (The Seven Sorrows Collection, Depression)
106 X-Ray Specs (Visit to a Small Planet Collection)
107 Wearing X-Ray Specs (Visit to a Small Planet Collection)
108 Luggage for Den Haag (Seven Sorrows Collection, Depression)
109 The Trick (From Hermann-Janssen) (Junior Collection)
110,111,112,113,114,115 Entertaining Junior (Junior Collection)
116 Side Portrait (Mauritshuis Collection)
117 Side Portrait of Mr Wheely (Portrait Collection)
118 Side Portrait of Short Haired Boy (Portrait Collection)
119 In Disguise (Allegory of Happiness Collection, Joker)
120 Shell Face (Allegory of Happiness Collection, Joker)
121 Gregory de Bergerac (Allegory of Happiness Collection, Joker)
122 Den Haag Daywork (The Seven Sorrows Collection, Depression)
123 Anonymous Luggage (Seven Sorrows Collection, Depression)
124 Message from Lahey (Lahey Collection)
125 Performance (Notes for Junior Collection)
126 Portrait of Hauk van Overluys (Notes for Junior Collection)
127 Portrait of Charlie Renault (Notes for Junior Collection)
128 Landscape with Shepherds (Recollection Collection)
129 Notes on Second Storyteller (Storyteller Collection)
130 Genealogy with Saints Humbertine (Storyteller Collection)
131 Notes on First Storyteller (Storyteller Collection)

Back Panel (Mirror Section)

132 Costume for Dining with First Storyteller (Costume Collection)
133 Discovery of Arrows (The Seven Sorrows Collection, Anger)

Back Panel (Second Section)

134 Letter from First Storyteller (Storyteller Collection)
135 Still Life for a Woman (Lahey Collection)
136 Cat Conversation (Visit to a Small Planet Collection)
137 Breakfast for One (Lahey Collection)
138 Letter from Second Storyteller (Storyteller Collection)
139 Dining Alone (1) (The Seven Sorrows Collection)
140 Dining Alone Invisible (2) (Visit to a Small Planet Collection)
141 Dining Alone (3) (The Seven Sorrows Collection)
142,143 The Adorned Couple and Matching Letter (Portrait Collection)
144 First Costume for Junior (Junior Collection)
145 Letter from Unknown Storyteller (Storyteller Collection)

Back Panel (Third Section)

146 Craft Tube (Lahey Collection, Den Haag)
147 Cupids Feast (Allegory of Happiness Collection, Dining Together)
148 Breakfast for One (Lahey Collection, Den Haag)
149 Beautiful Breakfast for One (Lahey Collection)
150 Frenchy (Allegory of Happiness Collection, Song)
151 Allegory of Celebration (Allegory of Happiness Collection, Holidays)
152 Still Life for a Man (Lahey Collection, Den Haag)
153 Three Graces (Allegory of Happiness Collection, Dining Together)
154 La Seine (Allegory of Happiness, Dining Together)
155 Maid of Seam (Allegory of Happiness Collection, Dining Together)
156 Feast of the Gods (Allegory of Happiness Collection, Dining Together)
157 Moments Like This (Allegory of Happiness Collection, Joker)
158 The Boathouse Banquet (Allegory of Happiness Collection, Dining Together)
159 The Last Supper (Allegory of Happiness Collection, Dining Together)
160 Bar-b-que (Allegory of Happiness Collection, Dining Together)
161 Rabbit Dress (Recollection Collection)
162 Letter from the Third Storyteller (Storyteller Collection)
163 Scent of the Storyteller (Storyteller Collection)
164 Dining Alone (4) (The Seven Sorrows Collection, Loneliness)
165 Dining Alone 5 (The Seven Sorrows Collection, Loneliness)
166,167,168,169 Parties (Allegory of Happiness Collection, Dining Together)
170 Dining Alone (6) (The Seven Sorrows Collection, Loneliness)
171 A Corner Lack (Recollection Collection)
172 The Grave Gun (The Seven Sorrows Collection, Anger)
173 Peter Pan Kids (Recollection Collection)
174 Notes on Apollos Painting (Recollection Collection)
175 Bandage for a Sliced Finger (The Seven Sorrows Collection, Pain)
176 Junior in her Golden Gown (Lahey Collection)
177 The Making of Junior (The Junior Collection)

178 [illegible]
179 [illegible]
180 [illegible]
181 [illegible]
182 [illegible]
183 [illegible]
184 [illegible]
185 [illegible]
186 [illegible]
187 [illegible]
188 [illegible]
189 [illegible]
190 [illegible]
191 [illegible]
192 [illegible]
193 [illegible]
194 [illegible]
195 [illegible]
196 [illegible]
197 [illegible]
198 [illegible]
199 [illegible]
200 [illegible]
201 [illegible]
202 [illegible]
203 Sewing Machine (Lahey Collection, Den Haag)

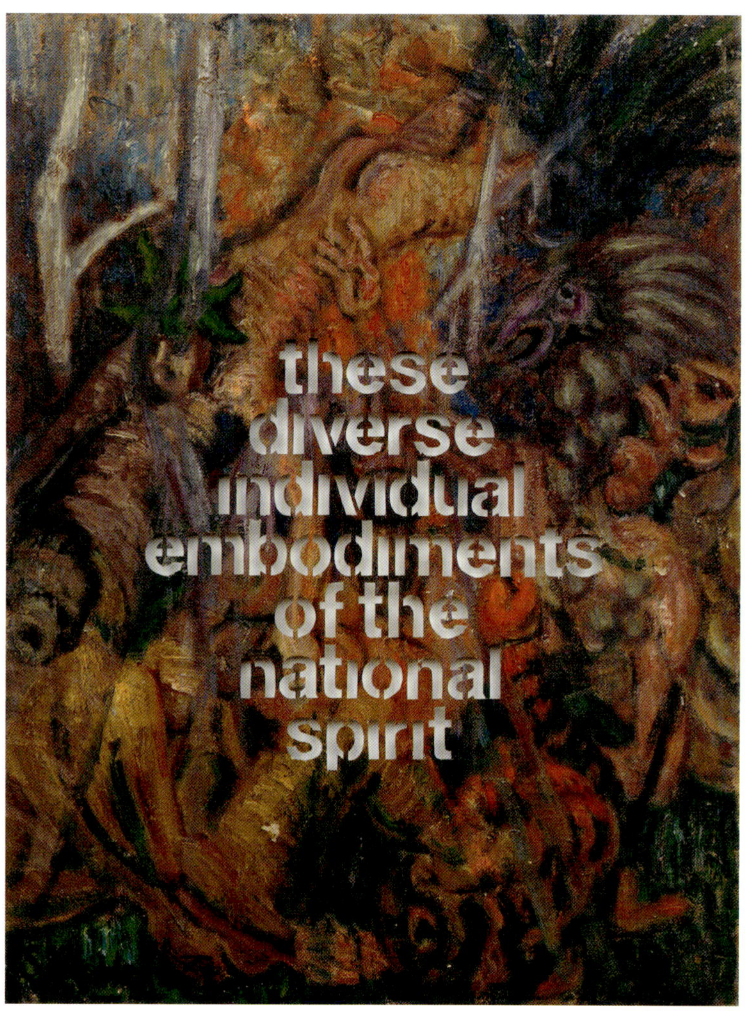

Amikam Toren
Armchair Painting Untitled (these diverse individual embodiments of the national spirit)   1991

Amikam Toren
Of the Times Monday March 19th   1990

Suzanne Treister
Picassoids Video Game   1989

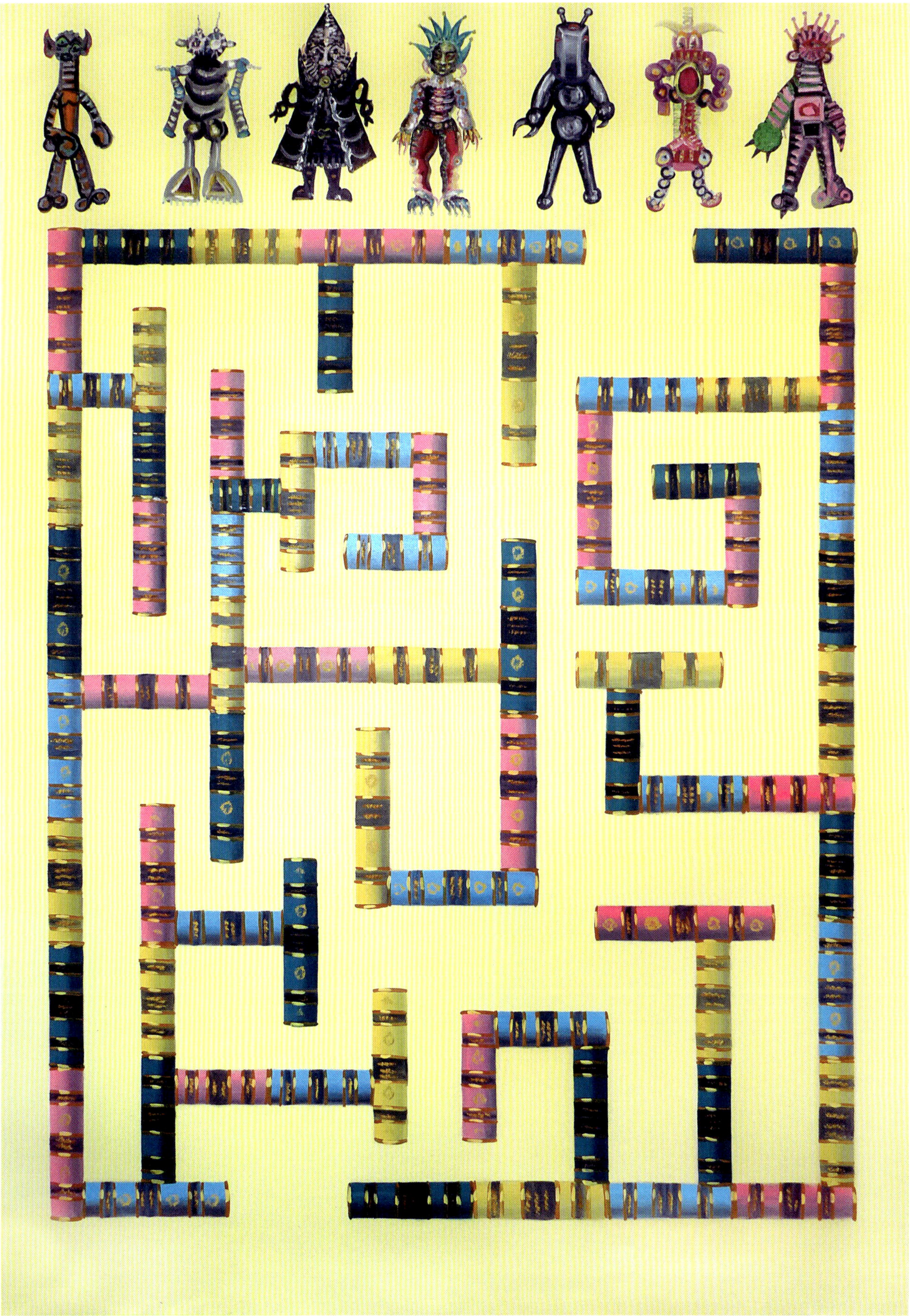

Alison Turnbull
The Echoing Green   1990

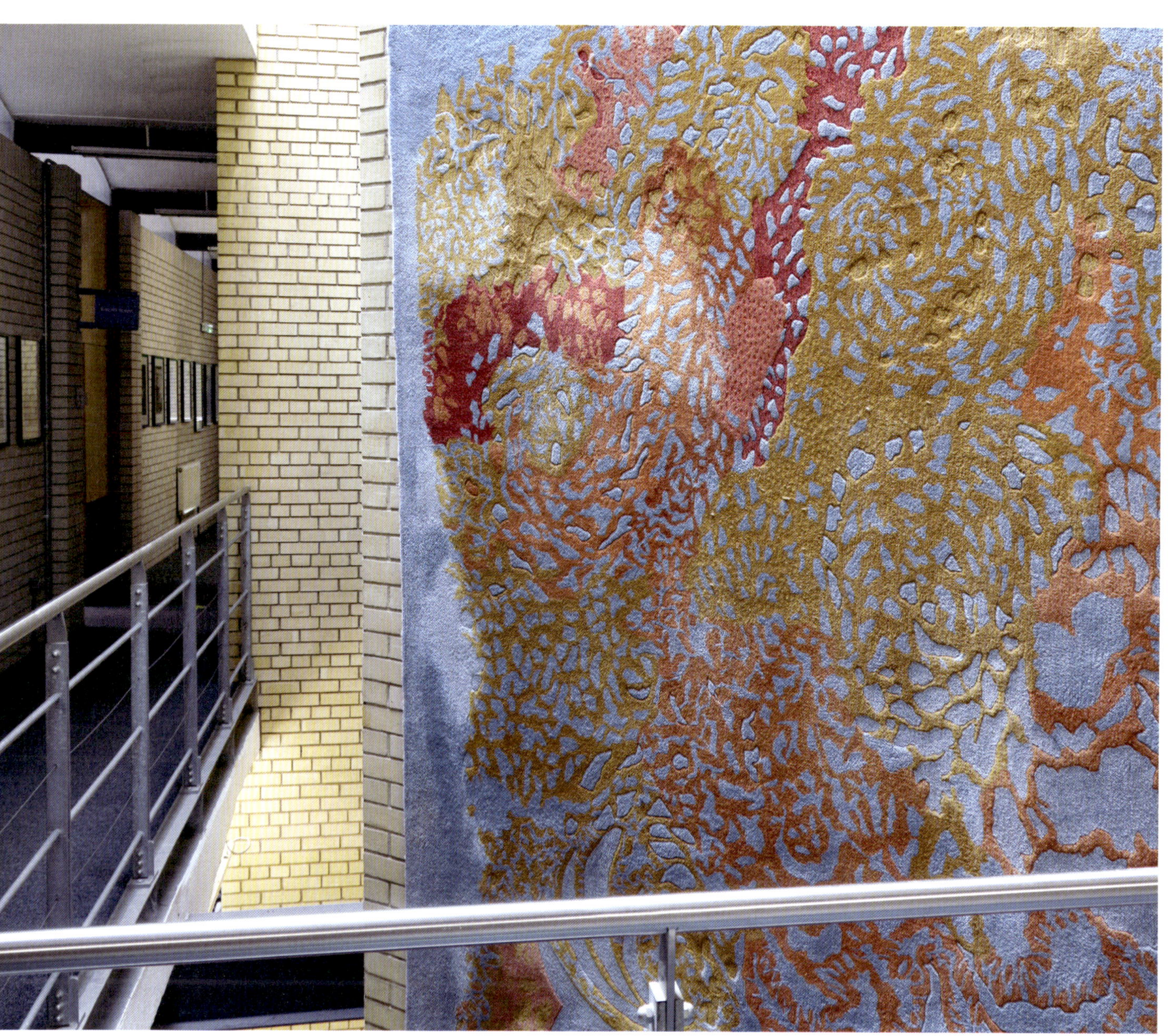

Shelagh Wakely
Rug for CBSO Centre   date unknown

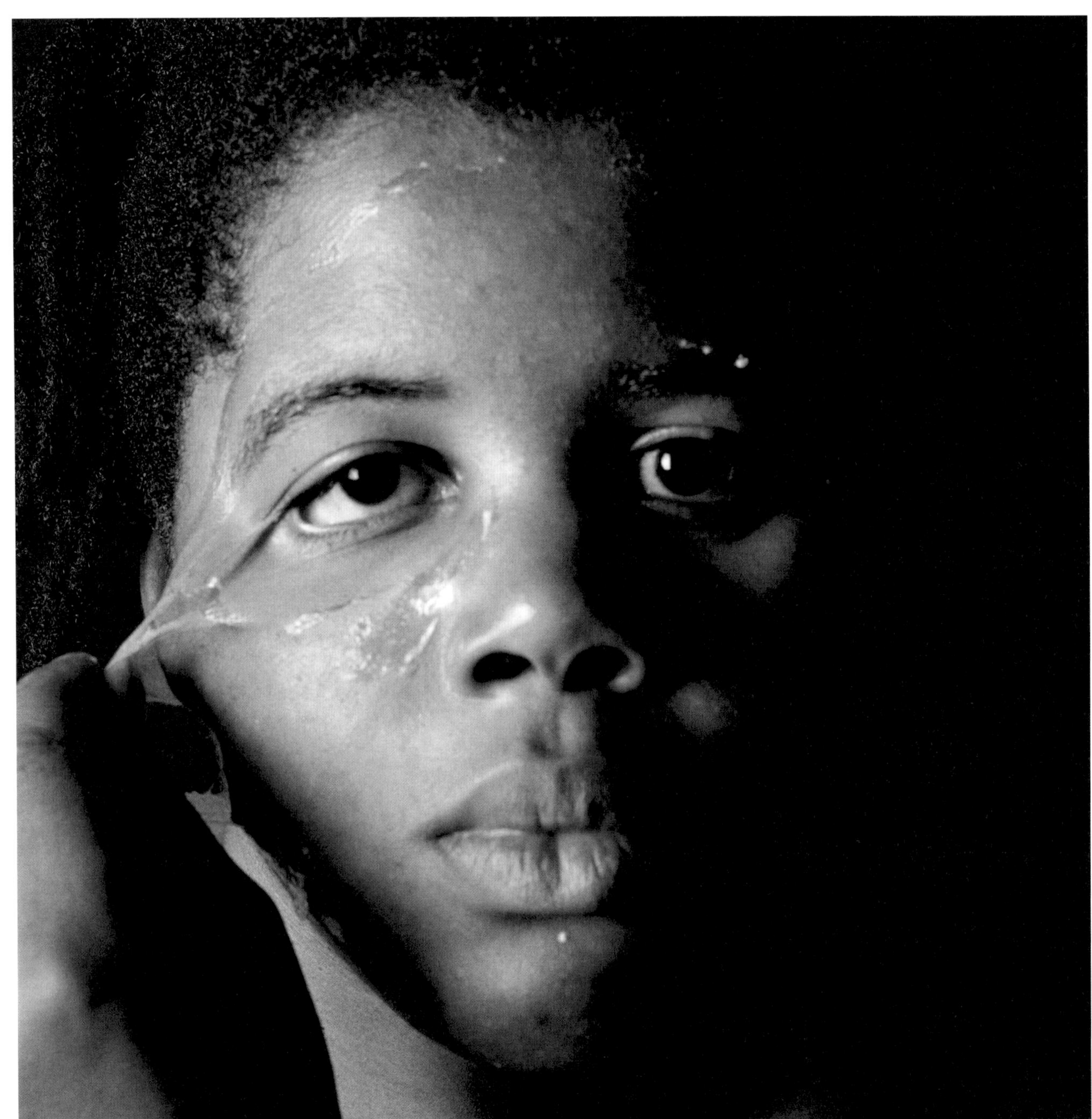

114

Maxine Walker
Untitled   1997

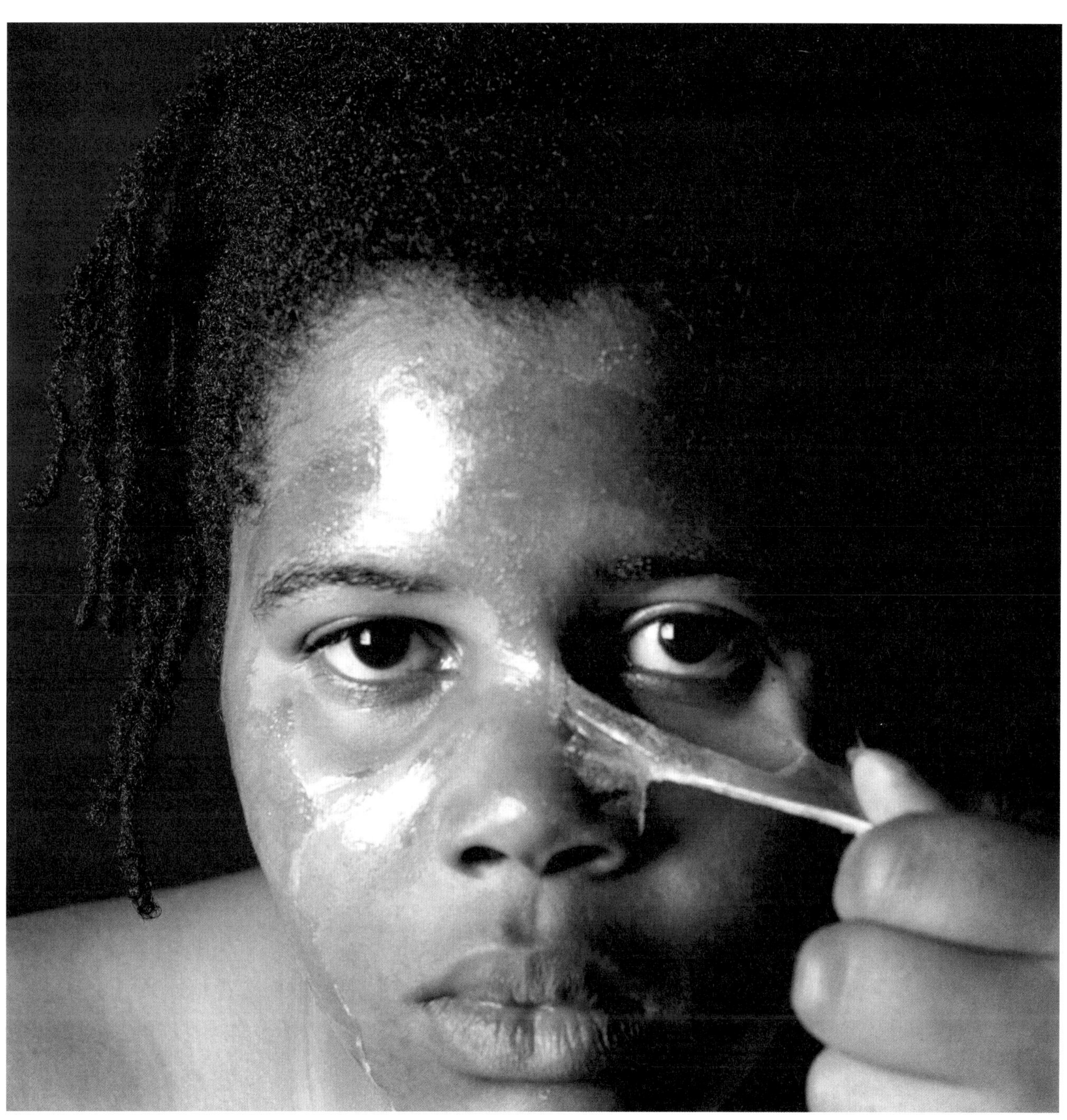

Maxine Walker
Untitled   1997

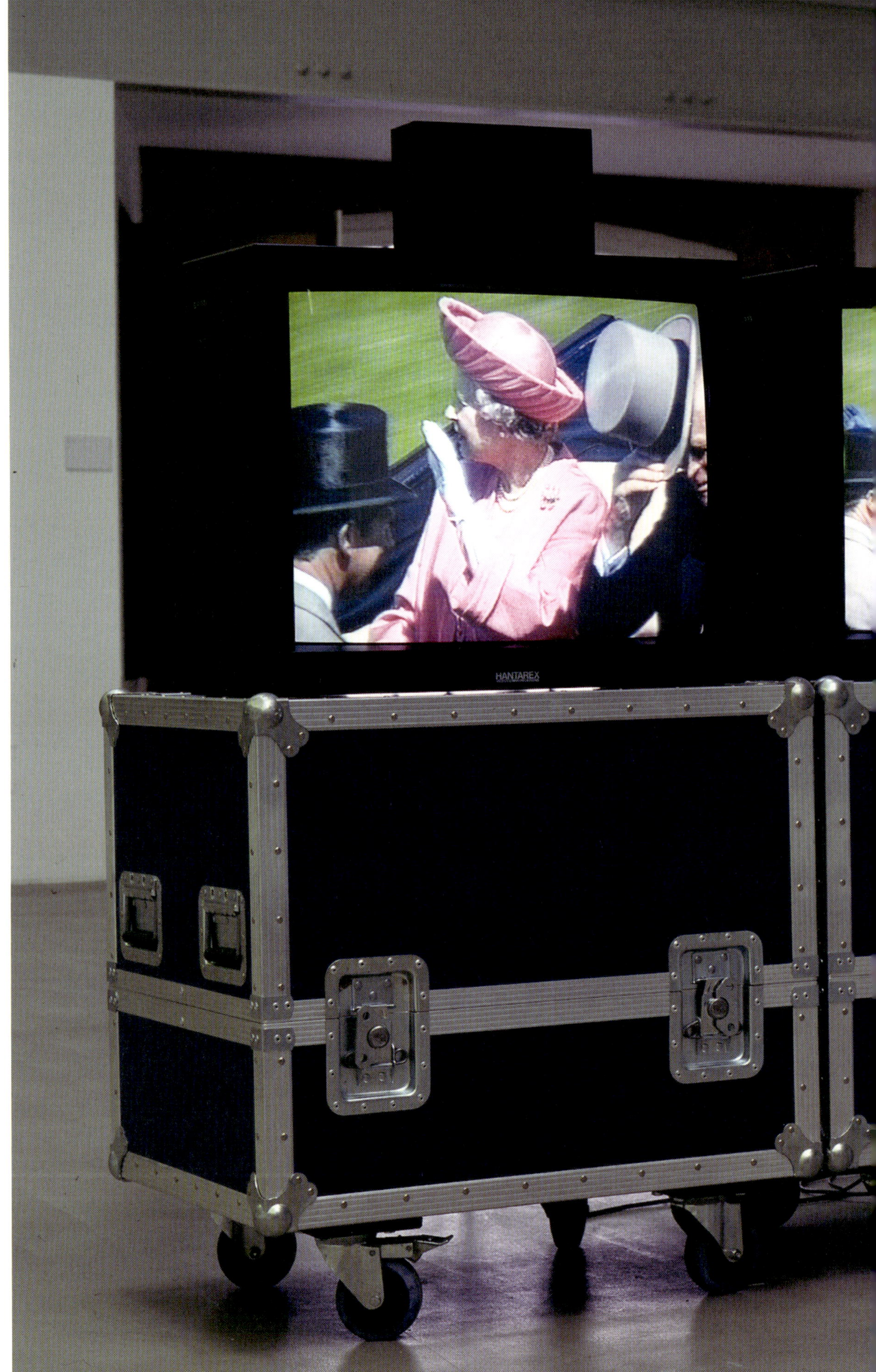

Mark Wallinger
Royal Ascot   1994

116

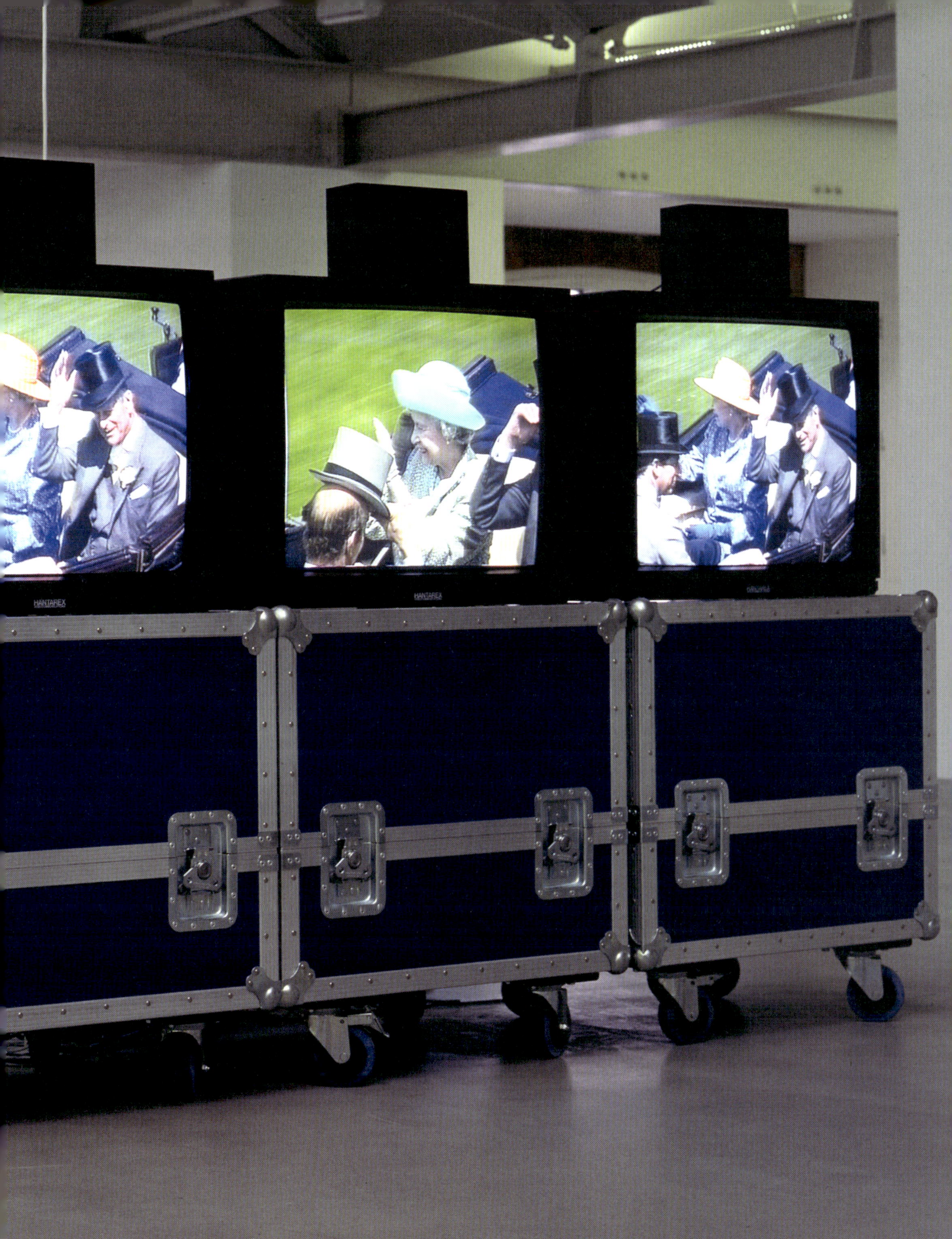
HANTAREX

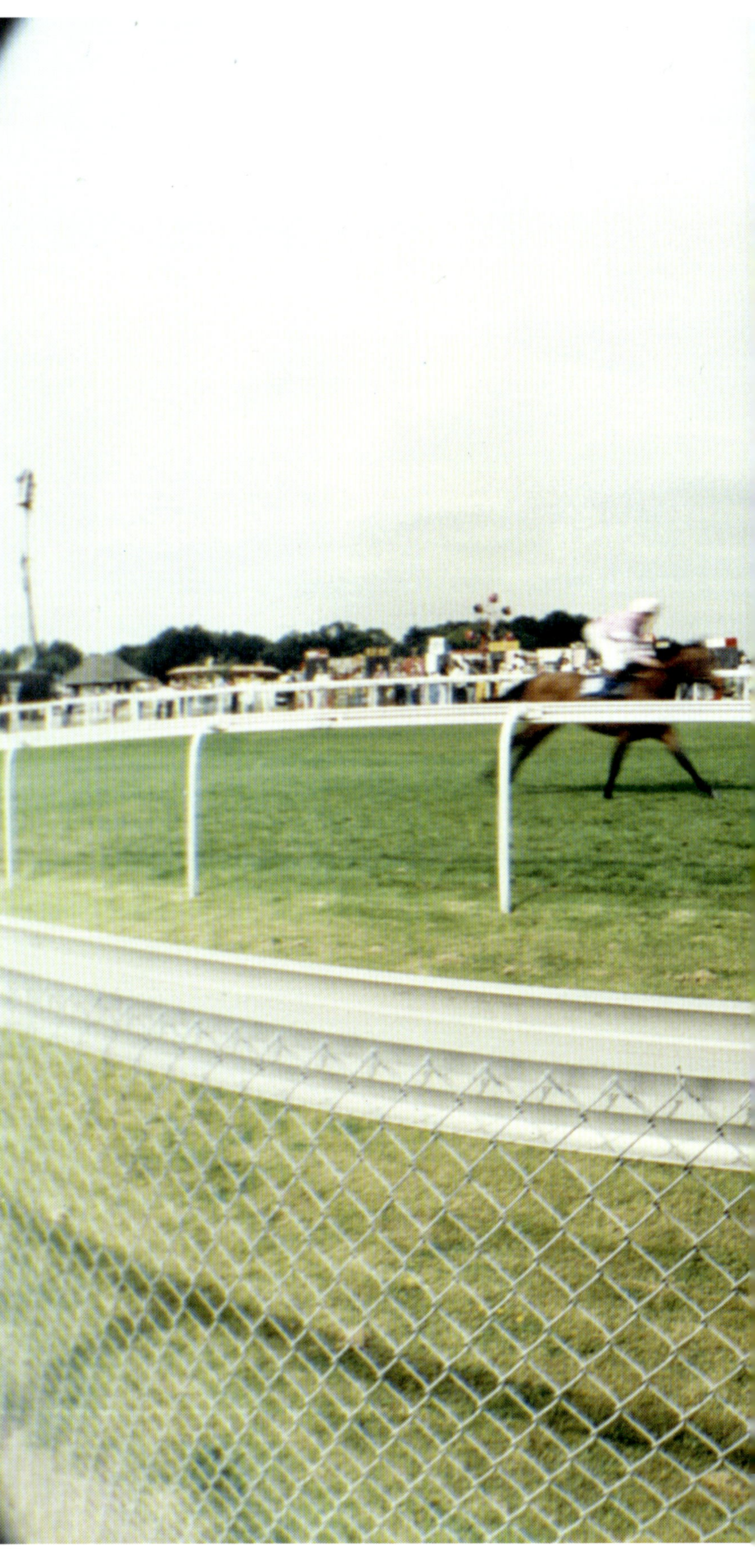

118

Mark Wallinger
Self Portrait as Emily Davison   1993

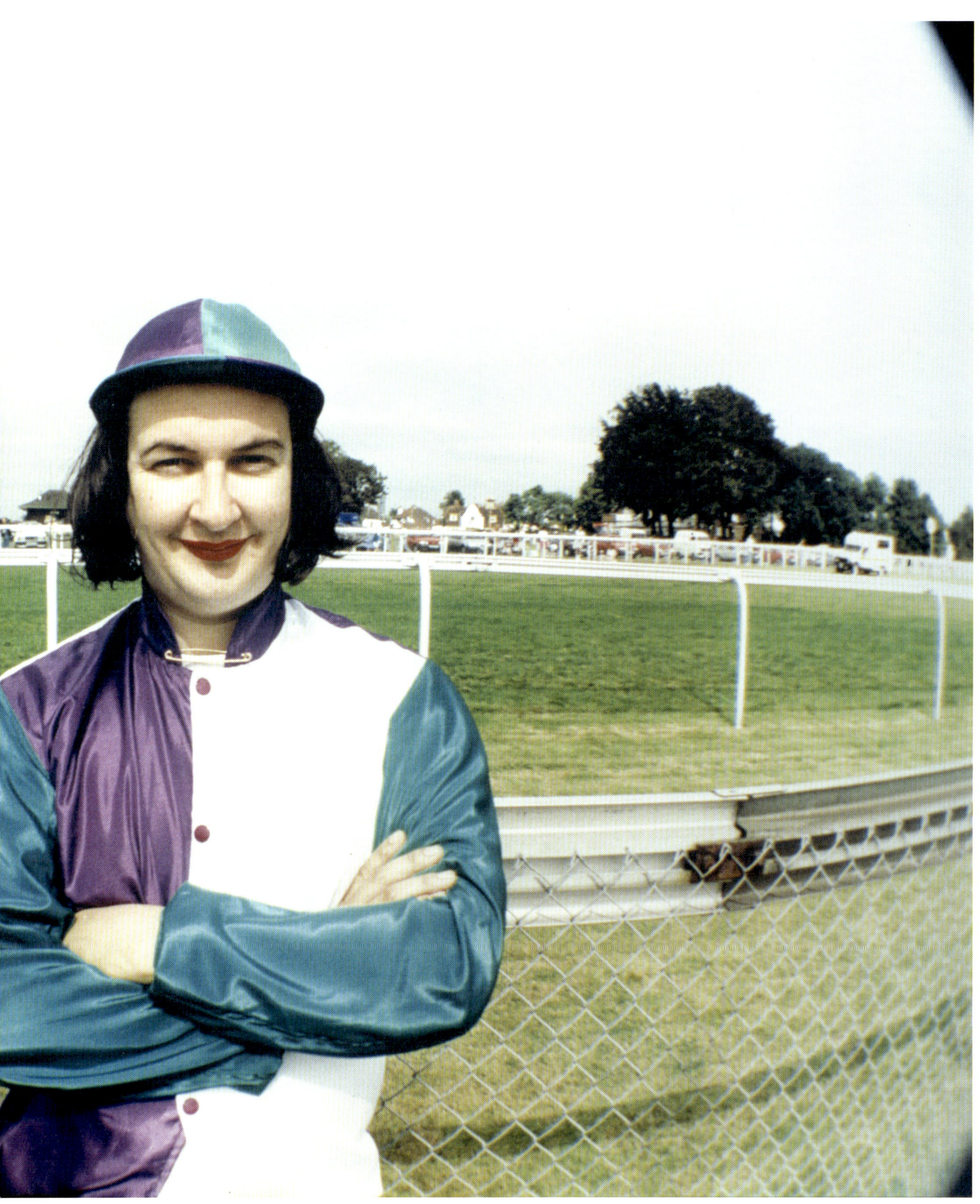

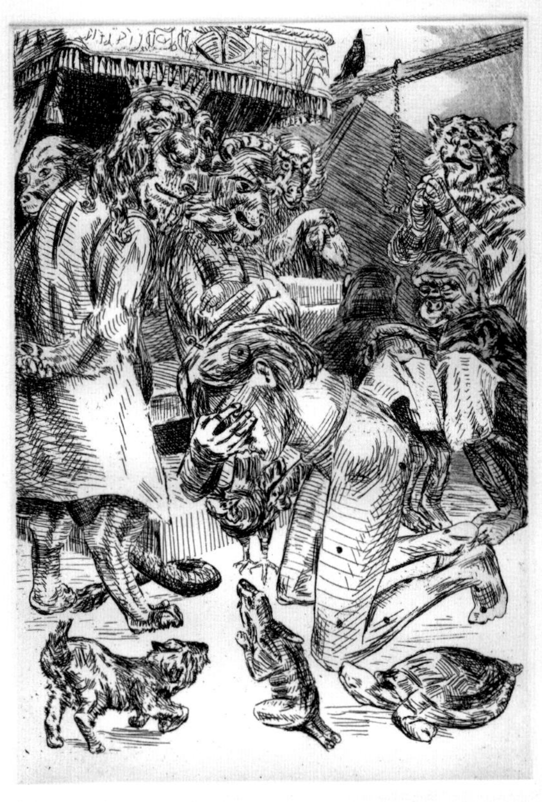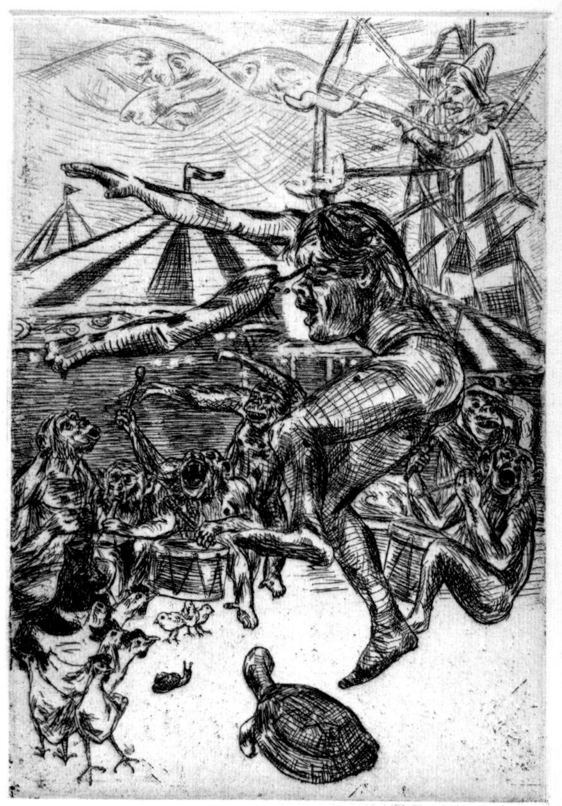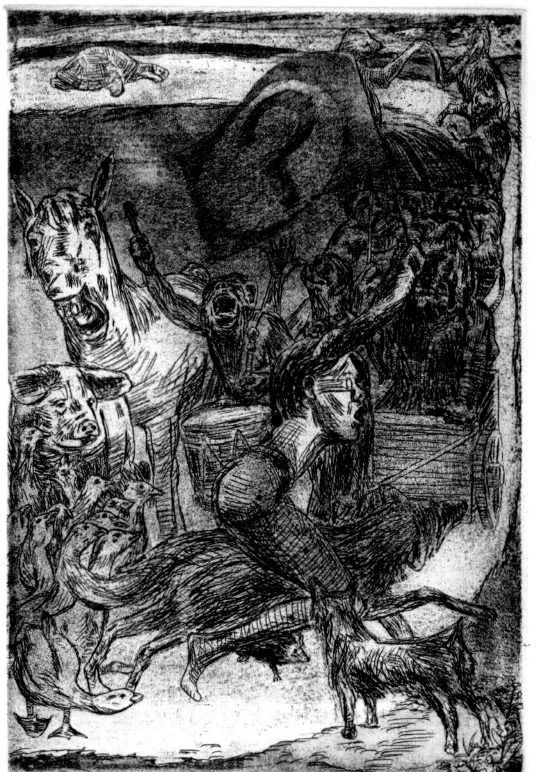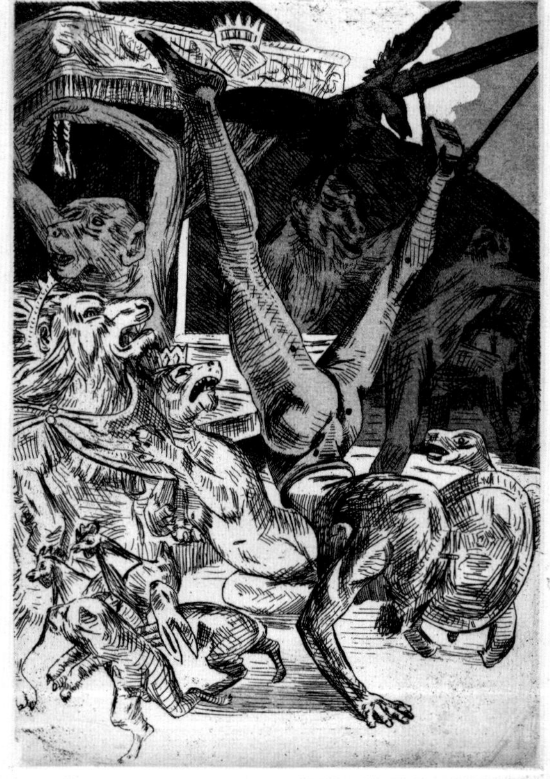

120

John Yeadon
The Travails of Blind Bifford Jelly   1989–91

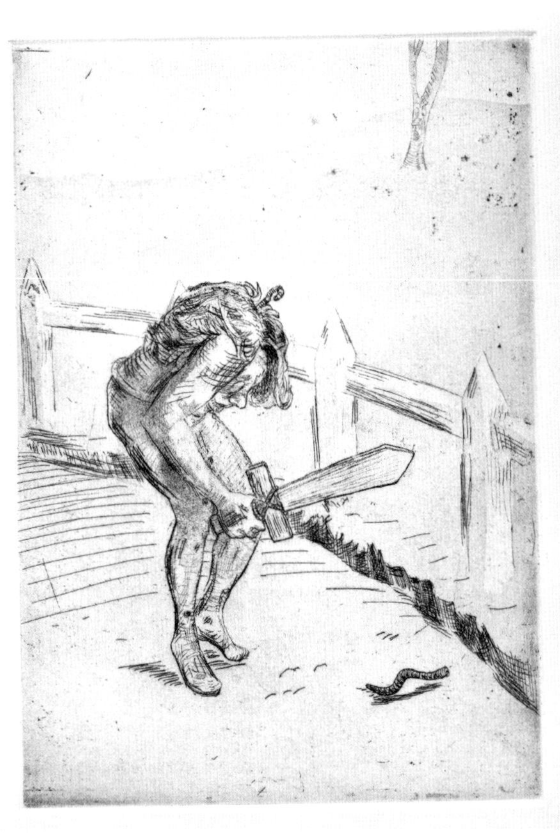

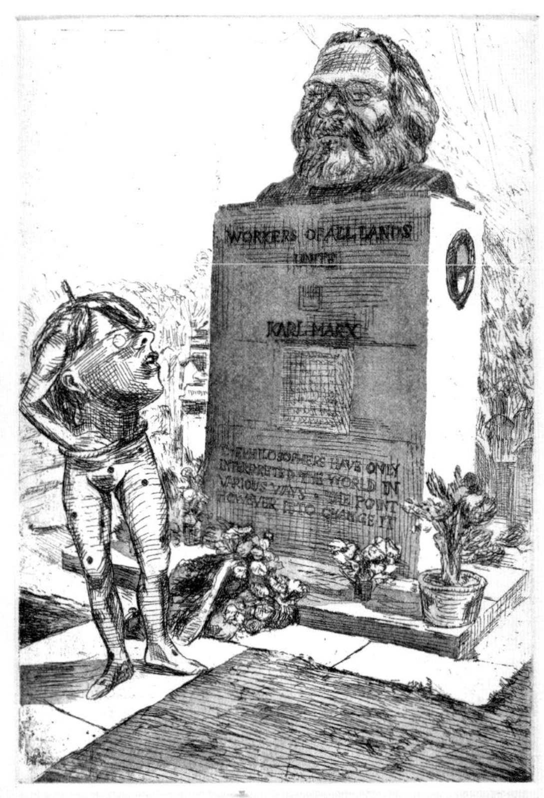
WORKERS OF ALL LANDS
UNITE
KARL MARX
THE PHILOSOPHERS HAVE ONLY
INTERPRETED THE WORLD IN
VARIOUS WAYS. THE POINT
HOWEVER IS TO CHANGE IT.

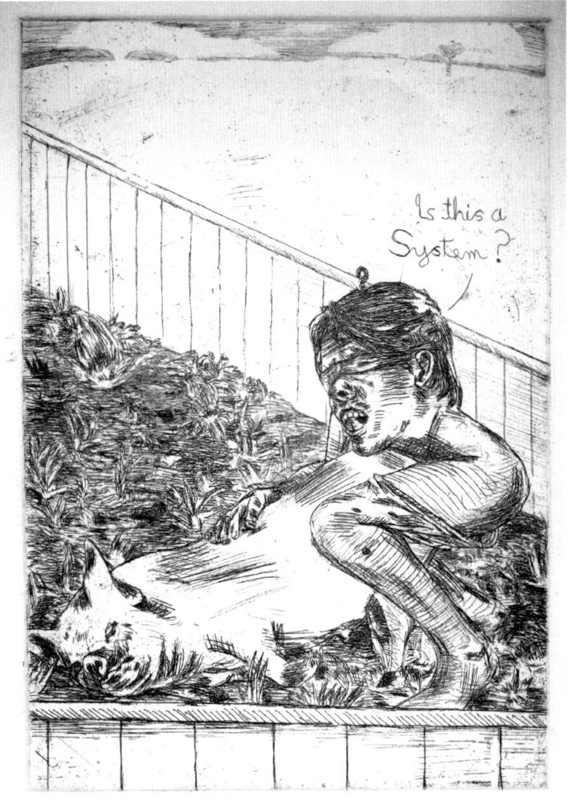
Is this a
System?

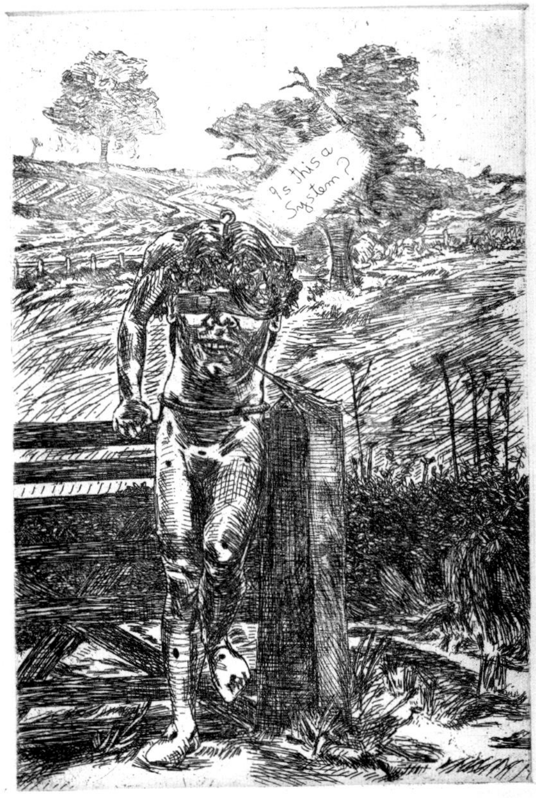
Is this a
System?

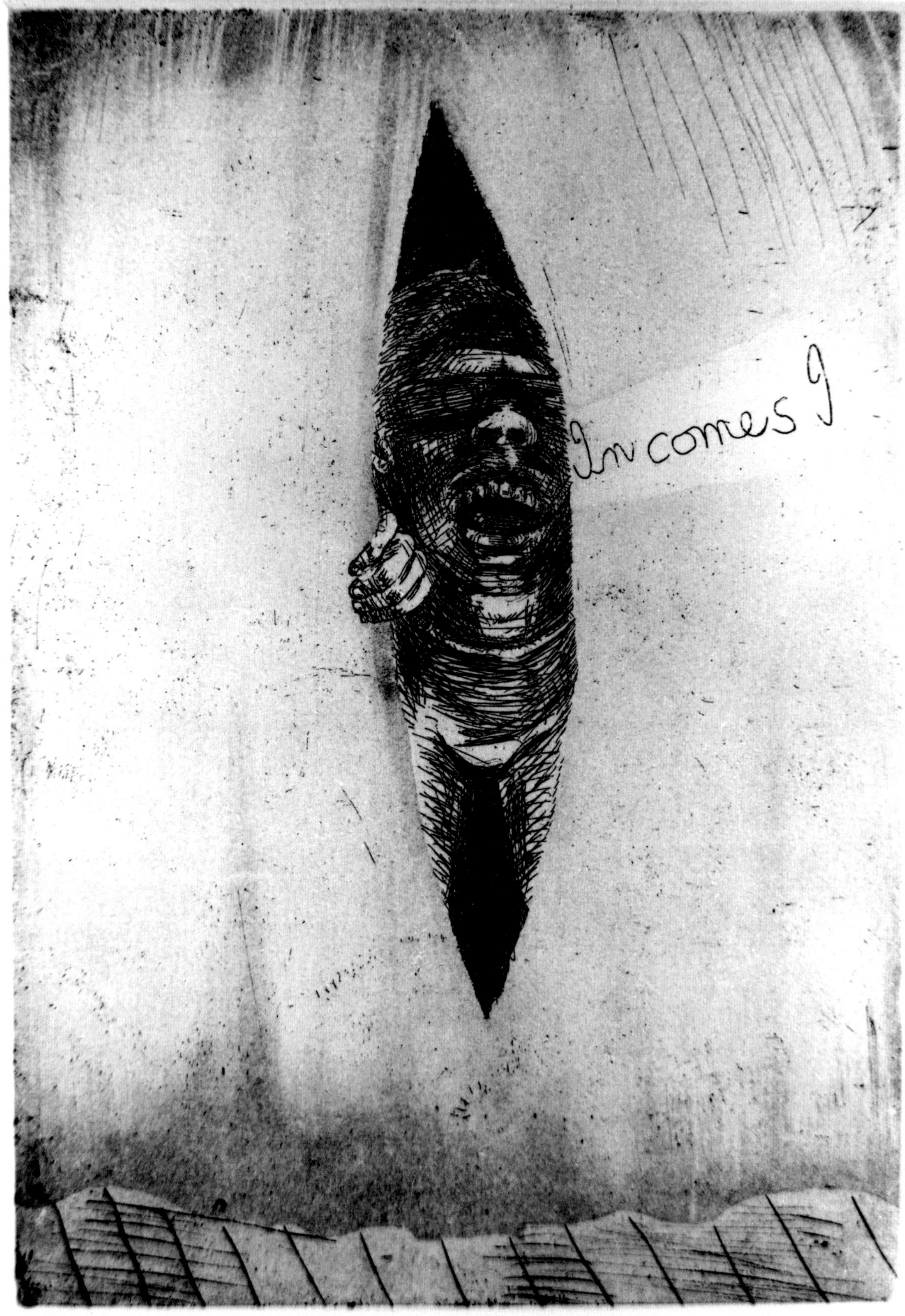
In comes 9

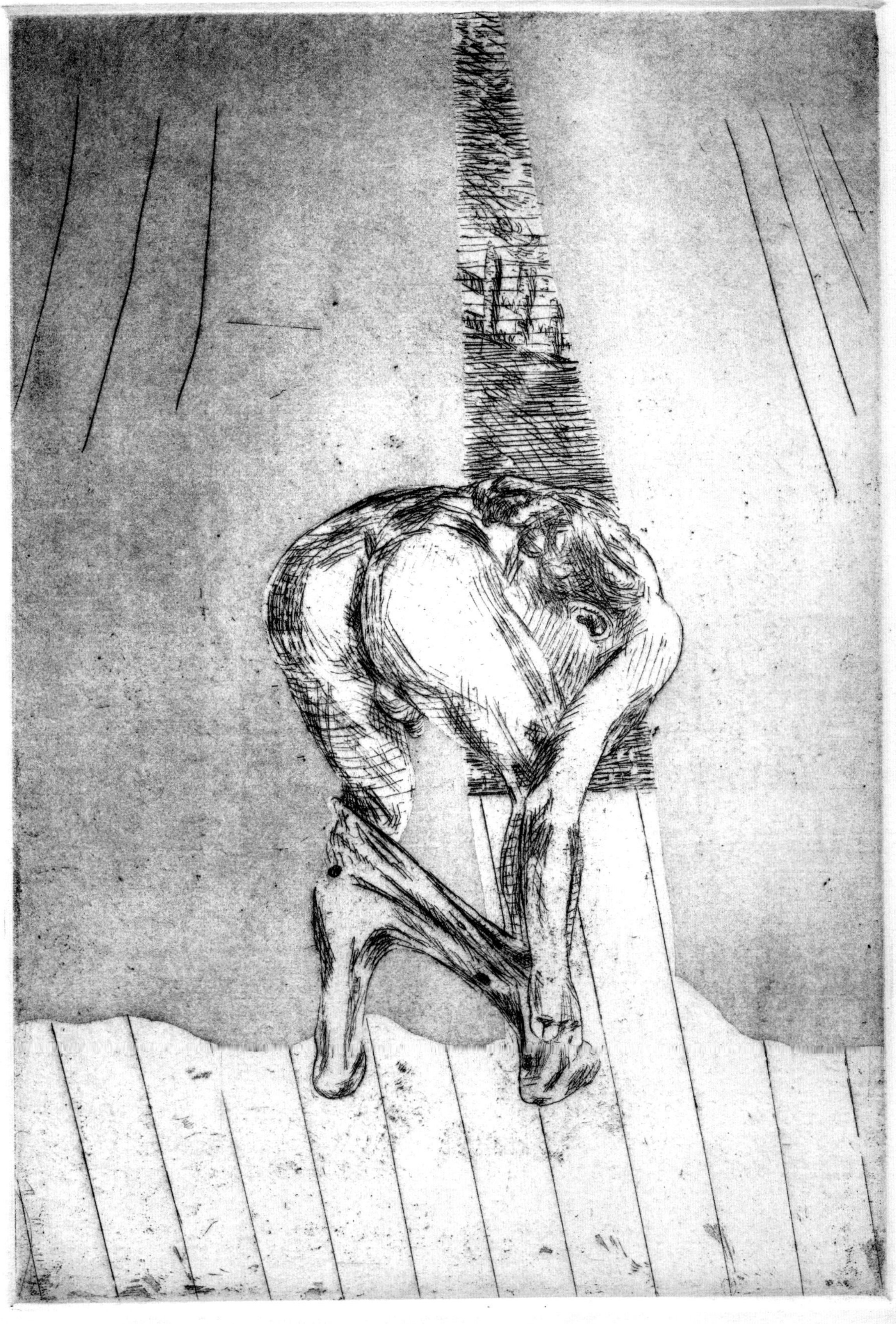

List of Works

Felicity Allen
Baby II 1989*
Photograph
200 × 140 cm
Courtesy the artist

Edward Allington
Unfinished Instruments 1989
Ink, emulsion and paper on canvas
152.4 × 213.2 cm
Arts Council Collection,
Southbank Centre, London

Edward Allington
Decorative Forms Over the World 1996
Emulsion and ink on MDF
Various dimensions
Courtesy the Estate of Edward Allington

Edward Allington
Curved Pediment 1990
MDF and zinc sheet
90 × 186 × 38.5 cm
Courtesy the Estate of Edward Allington

Siah Armajani
*Gazebo for Two Anarchists: Emilio Coda
and Richard Henry Dana* 1991
Wood and steel
30.5 × 59.7 × 24 cm
Richard Saltoun Gallery

Basil Beattie
Imagine If 1993*
Oil and wax on canvas
259.5 × 304.7 cm
Arts Council Collection, Southbank Centre,
London

Gordon Bennett
Suprematist Painting II (Purity) 1993
Acrylic on canvas
50 × 50 cm
Private Collection, London

Zarina Bhimji
Untitled 1992*
Photograph
96 × 72 × 2 cm (framed)
Courtesy the artist

Zarina Bhimji
Untitled 1992*
Photograph
96 × 72 × 2 cm (framed)
Courtesy the artist

Zarina Bhimji
Untitled 1992*
Photograph
96 × 72 × 2 cm (framed)
Courtesy the artist

Ansuya Blom
… this human being … 1993–95
Gouache and ink on photograph on paper
Support: 25 × 20 cm,
frame: 38.8 × 31.2 × 2.5 cm
Tate: Purchased 2010

Adam Chodzko
Nightvision 1998*
2-channel video projection, colour, sound
13 minutes 20 seconds
Presented by Tate Members 2010

Juan Davila
Love 1988
Oil paint on canvas
200 × 200 cm
Tate and Museum of Contemporary Art
Australia, presented through the Australian
Government's Cultural Gifts Program by the
artist, and with the support of the Qantas
Foundation 2018

Mark Dion and Jason Simon
Artful History, a Restoration Comedy
1988*
Single-channel video, colour, sound
28 minutes 20 seconds
Video courtesy the artists; Callicoon Fine Arts,
New York; and Tanya Bonakdar, New York

Eugenio Dittborn
To Return (RTM) Airmail Painting No.103
1993
Oil paint, charcoal and screenprint
on 6 fabrics
Each image: 201 × 140 cm
Tate: Presented by the Latin American
Acquisitions Committee, with funds provided
by the American Fund for the Tate Gallery
2004

Rose Finn-Kelcey
God Kennel – A Tabernacle – (Model)
1992
Black and white photograph of artist's model
for Documenta IX, Kassel, Germany
18 × 21.5 cm (image), 44 × 49 cm (framed)
Courtesy The Estate of Rose Finn-Kelcey

**Rose Finn-Kelcey and
Donald Rodney**
Truth Dare, Double-Dare 1994*
Sound
1 hour 30 minutes 15 seconds
Courtesy The Estate of Rose-Finn Kelcey
and The Estate of Donald Rodney

Ellen Gallagher
Untitled 1998*
Oil paint and enamel on paper on canvas
Support: 305.3 × 244.4 × 3.8 cm
Tate: ARTIST ROOMS. Acquired jointly with
the National Galleries
of Scotland through The d'Offay Donation
with assistance from the National Heritage
Memorial Fund and the Art Fund 2008

Antony Gormley
Maquette for 'Iron Man' 1991
Plaster, paint, wooden plinth
96 × 61.3 × 61.3 cm
Lent by Birmingham Museums Trust
on behalf of Birmingham City Council

Víctor Grippo
Tables of Work and Reflection 1978–94
7 wooden desks with chalk and marker pen,
clay, handkerchief, beans, stones, mirror,
lights and fishing line
Overall display dimensions variable
Tate: Presented by the Latin American
Acquisitions Committee 2005

Graham Gussin
Surrendering 1 1994–95*
Archival digital print
42.5 × 28 cm
Courtesy the artist

Graham Gussin
Surrendering 2 1994–95
Archival digital print
42.5 × 28 cm
Courtesy the artist

Graham Gussin
Surrendering 3 1994–95
Archival digital print
42.5 × 28 cm
Courtesy the artist

Callum Innes
*Exposed Painting Paynes Grey/Yellow
Oxide/Red Oxide on White* 1999
Oil paint on canvas
228.9 × 223.5 × 3.5 cm
Tate: Purchased 1999

Permindar Kaur
Falling 1995*
Polar fleece and arctic fur, 120 figures
Display dimensions variable
Courtesy the artist

Permindar Kaur
Loss 1995*
Copper and ash
38 × 57 × 28 cm
Courtesy the artist

Tania Kovats
Peninsula 1998
Acrylic composite and MDF
68.5 × 176 × 59 cm
British Council Collection

Tania Kovats
Little Vera 1998
Plaster and flocking
32 × 7.5 × 6.5 cm
British Council Collection

Tania Kovats
Plinth 1998*
Welsh Brathay Slate
38.30 × 26.58 × 1.86 m
Commissioned by Ikon Gallery

Cildo Meireles
Jogo de Velha AX/OP 8B 1993–94
Wooden tape measure, paint,
mounted on board
62 × 65 × 5 cm
The Tiqui Atencio Collection

Lisa Milroy
Kyoto House 1994*
Oil on canvas
71.5 × 99.2 cm
Arts Council Collection, Southbank Centre,
London

Lisa Milroy
Kyoto House 1994*
Oil paint on canvas
71.5 × 99.2 cm
Arts Council Collection, Southbank Centre,
London

Lisa Milroy
Finsbury Square 1995*
Oil paint on canvas
Support: 175.5 × 229.1 cm
Tate: Presented by the Patrons of New Art
(Special Purchase Fund) through the Tate
Gallery Foundation 1996

Antoni Miralda
*The Miralda Honeymoon Project.
Birmingham: The Eternity Ring* 1991*
Single-channel video
3:4 aspect ratio, colour, sound
14 minutes 44 seconds
Courtesy the artist and Ikon

Avis Newman
Compass 1992–93
2 tables, paint on canvas, 2 portfolios and
lithographs on paper
Overall display dimensions variable
Tate: Presented in memory of Adrian
Ward-Jackson by Weltkunst Foundation 2013

Lucia Nogueira
Two into One Won't Go 1993
MDF, watercolour on paper and felt
86.4 × 218.4 × 53.3 cm
Arts Council Collection, Southbank Centre,
London

Lucia Nogueira
Untitled 1990
Watercolour, graphite and ink on paper
50.1 × 40 × 3 cm (framed)
Tate: Presented by Tate Members 2009

Lucia Nogueira
Untitled c.1991–92
Watercolour, ink and graphite on paper
40.7 × 50.2 × 2.9 cm (framed)
Tate: Presented by Tate Members 2009

Lucia Nogueira
Untitled 1993
Watercolour and ink on paper
40.7 × 50.2 × 2.9 cm (framed)
Tate: Presented by Tate Members 2009

Vong Phaophanit
Fragments 1990
Slide projection with electric fans
Projected image: 200 cm (diameter)
Arts Council Collection, Southbank Centre,
London

Adrian Piper
Please God 1990
Video
61 minutes (looped)
Collection Adrian Piper Research Archive
Foundation Berlin

Keith Piper
Four Corners, a Contest of Opposites
1995
Computer montage prints on
transparency film in lightboxes
4 parts, each 182.9 × 50.8 × 53.3 cm
Arts Council Collection, Southbank Centre,
London

Donald Rodney
In the House of my Father 1997
Photographic print on aluminium
Photograph: Andra Nelki
122 × 153 cm
Arts Council Collection, Southbank Centre,
London

Martha Rosler
Housing is a Human Right 1989*
Short animation produced by
The Public Art Fund, Messages
to the Public
1 minute 17 seconds
© Martha Rosler; Courtesy the artist and
Mitchell-Innes & Nash, New York

Yinka Shonibare
Diary of a Victorian Dandy 9.00hrs.
1998*
C-Type print
122 × 183 cm (image)
130.5 × 192 × 3.5 cm (framed)
Collection of The New Art Gallery Walsall,
purchased through the Contemporary Arts
Society Special Collection Scheme, with lottery
funding from Arts Council England, 1999

Nancy Spero
Carnival 2000
Hand printing and printed collage on paper
260.7 × 60 cm
Cathy Wills Collection, London

Georgina Starr
The Nine Collection of the 7th Museum
1994
Silkscreen on paper
175 × 118 cm
Courtesy the artist

Amikam Toren
Of the Times Monday March 19th 1990
Pulped newspaper and PVA on canvas,
newspaper on cardboard
235 × 220 cm
Courtesy the artist and Anthony Reynolds
Gallery, London

Amikam Toren
Armchair Painting Untitled (these diverse individual embodiments of the national spirit)   1991
Oil on canvas
91.5 × 70.5 cm (unframed)
112.5 × 92 cm (framed)
Courtesy the artist and Anthony Reynolds Gallery, London

Suzanne Treister
Picassoids Video Game   1989*
Oil on canvas
213 × 153 cm
Courtesy the artist, Annely Juda Fine Art, London; and P.P.O.W. Gallery, New York

Alison Turnbull
The Echoing Green   1990*
Oil on canvas
162 × 216 cm
Courtesy the artist and Matt's Gallery, London

Shelagh Wakely
Rug for CBSO Centre, date unknown
Hand-tufted rug, pure wool
6.5 × 3.5 m (approx.)
On permanent display at CBSO Centre
Berkley Street, Birmingham B1 2LF

Maxine Walker: UNTITLED
Exhibition, Midlands Arts Centre
4 April – 21 June 2021
Cannon Hill Park,
Birmingham B12 9QH

Mark Wallinger
Royal Ascot   1994*
Video installation on 4 monitors,
with flight cases
Overall display dimensions variable
British Council Collection

Mark Wallinger
Self Portrait as Emily Davison   1993*
Colour photograph on aluminium
89 × 137 cm (framed)
British Council Collection

Mark Wallinger
A Real Work of Art   1993*
Painted die-cast metal, wood and
metal plaque
12 × 13 × 7.5 cm
British Council Collection

John Yeadon
The Travails of Blind Bifford Jelly
1989–91*
39 etchings
each 59 × 40 cm (framed)
Courtesy the artist

*Previously exhibited at Ikon Gallery

Breaking Down the Barriers

Elizabeth Macgregor
interviewed by Jonathan Watkins

How was it for you, starting at Ikon?

When I moved to Ikon I had had very little management experience. To be honest it was a big jump for me professionally. What got me the job was my passion for bringing artists and audiences together. I remember having a lovely conversation with the then Chair (Jeannette Koch) about this gallery that had done so many wonderful exhibitions, how it began in Birmingham's Bull Ring with a very strong public ethos, developing over time, but certainly it needed more funding and a higher profile … That was the challenge that drew me to the job.

I had to take a deep breath and jump in with both feet but it was very exciting. My predecessor, Antonia Payne, had done an amazing job; I had big shoes to fill. It was a lot of fun for me in those early days, getting to grips with a lot of things I had never done before, such as fundraising and managing staff. I very much learnt on the job.

And Birmingham?

I had been living in London for a few years previously and it was tricky to move away, especially with everything there having been at my fingertips. After leaving I had to make much more of an effort to see things that were happening in London. I went back quite regularly … I was famous for catching the last train out of Euston Station!

On the other hand, Birmingham was changing. The local authority was determined to dispel popular perceptions of the city as being depressed and behind-the-times, recognising the regenerative role that culture could play. They wanted to change its appearance, literally, to make it look less down-trodden. They made a huge investment in the new Symphony Hall, acknowledging that Simon Rattle – then Chief Conductor of the City of Birmingham Symphony Orchestra – was a great ambassador for the city.

There was a great sense of everyone working together. We worked with the other arts organisations and it was very collaborative. We always felt we were working against the grain, that we were "up against it". And, with London, people didn't come the other way very often – we had to work very hard to get people out of London. I look back on my time in Birmingham with enormous fondness; I really enjoyed living in this vibrant city with its great music scene, great fun and great clubs ...

When she left, Antonia Payne was in the process of (re-) making Ikon more international. Hence the Transcontinental exhibition which you brought to fruition. And then you went on to preside over an exhibition programme that ranged from the Americas to Australia. How did you square that internationalism with what you were encountering locally?

Transcontinental was a project that curator Guy Brett had been trying to present for many years and it really framed the way we decided to take Ikon's programme forward. It's hard to think back to a time when South America wasn't being looked at seriously in an art world still fixated on Europe and North America. The planning for *Transcontinental*, which was a highly ambitious project for a regional gallery, coincided with the ground breaking but controversial *Magiciens de la terre* exhibition in Paris. We decided that looking outside of the so-called mainstream should be our focus. What was important was that this not only helped us select our international artists, but also drove our thinking on artists from the UK. In a city where a very large percentage of the population was not Anglo/white, profiling artists from different cultural backgrounds had an added potency as we strove to make Ikon relevant to a broader audience.

However, we also wanted to offer our audience a range of exhibitions, not all of one "type". Having different curatorial standpoints was also important. In the end, I believe that the best programmes are driven by curators being passionate about the artists they want to work with so we didn't have a rigid policy.

Did you have a position on the YBAs (Young British Artists) at the time? They were more or less absent from Ikon's programme in the 1990s.
It depends who you define as YBAs! We did do a major exhibition of Mark Wallinger and later Yinka Shonibare, both of whom were included in shows of the so-called young British artists. It is certainly interesting to look back at that period which was defined by the media frenzy attacking the work. I wrote at the time that I didn't believe in deliberately courting controversy and that presenting sensational work was not an effective way of building long term audiences, as audiences would always be looking for the next thrill. My ambition was to engage people in debate about art and the issues raised by artists. There is no doubt that this generation fundamentally changed the relationship between art and audience in the UK, making a small number of artists household names. I was frustrated by the constant media attacks on contemporary art which misrepresented the way in which audiences respond. Our focus on artists who were not part of the mainstream also turned our gaze in a different direction.

That tabloid reaction to contemporary art – in Birmingham, epitomised by the *Evening Mail* – was rife in the 1990s. A number of artists presented by Ikon were targeted, including Victor Grippo and Avis Newman. Did you discern a pattern in the criticism or the reasons for it? On the whole, how did you deal with it?
Sadly, it wasn't just the tabloids. The so-called quality press could be just as bad – the announcement of the Turner Prize shortlist always brought out the anti-contemporary art critics in full force. The Grippo coverage was exceptionally vicious because the *Daily Mail* erroneously linked the exhibition to our lottery grant for the new building! It was distressing for staff to get hate calls from the public who believed the claim that the money had gone to a pile of potatoes rather than a children's hospital. Minimal and conceptual work is an easy target.

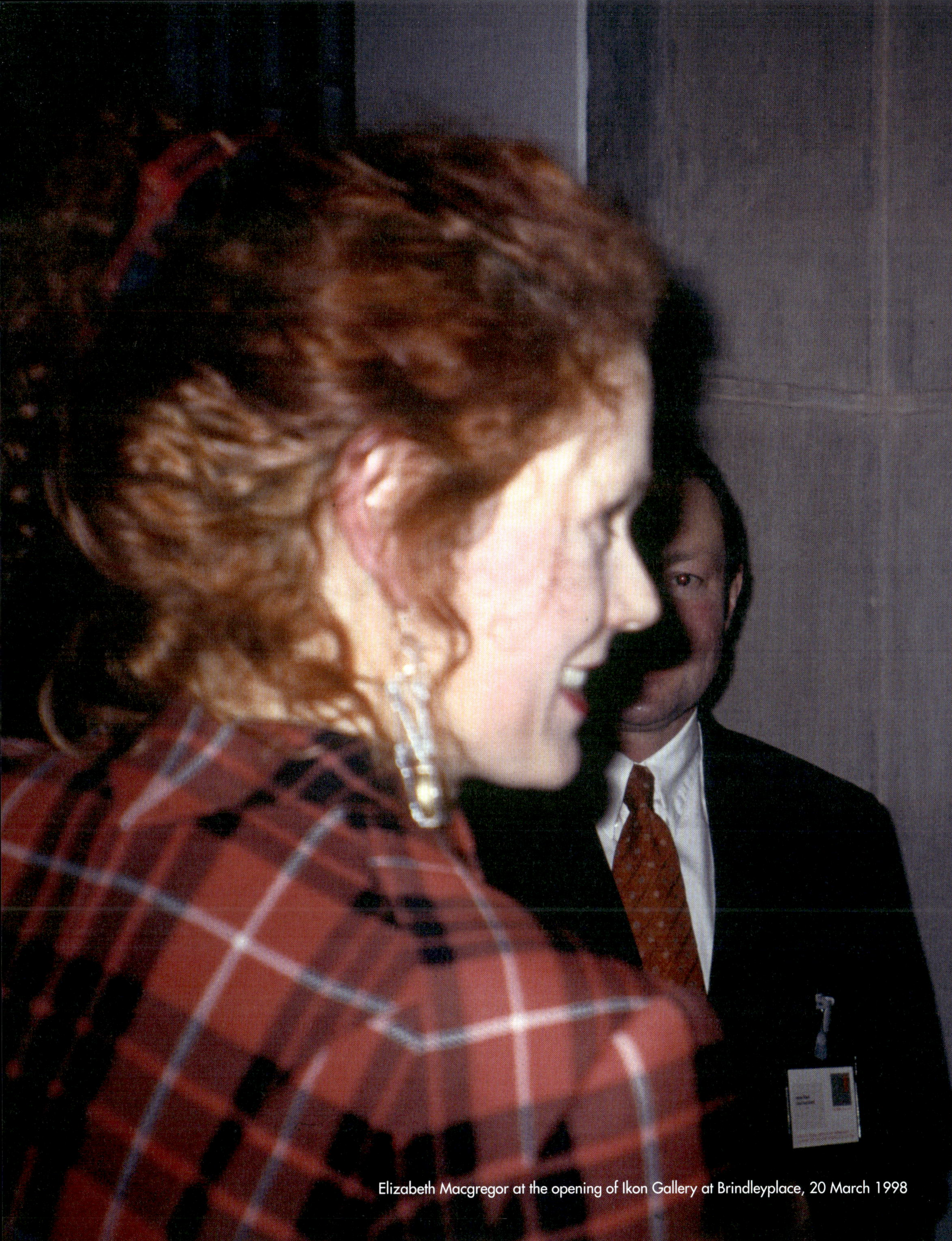

Elizabeth Macgregor at the opening of Ikon Gallery at Brindleyplace, 20 March 1998

We spent a lot of time trying to counter this kind of misinformation. I do think though that galleries then often didn't bother to explain why such work was important. This focus on talking about why we were exhibiting these artists became an important aspect of our audience building strategy. Many people who came to see Victor's exhibition commented on how different it was from the tabloid description.

The tide did begin to turn though – in 1995 I was asked to write an article for *The Sunday Times* in response to the derision heaped on contemporary art. I had always argued that the public was much more open minded and responsive than the media.

How did the tide turn? Was it a question of bringing the media around with convincing arguments, or (in keeping with the maritime metaphor) was there some kind of sea change occurring then that transformed perceptions of contemporary art in the UK?

There were a number of factors. The late 80s and 90s saw the introduction of a range of education and outreach programmes that engaged younger audiences who were more receptive. I also think higher profile exhibitions of various kinds demonstrated the capacity of the audience to engage with new ideas. The championing of contemporary art by high profile public figures also helped to change perceptions – Princess Diana becoming Patron of the Serpentine catapulted one contemporary art gallery into the public consciousness! Exhibition programmes became more diverse – not just culturally but in the kind of work that was shown. Postmodernism opened the door to a less rigid definition of contemporary art. By the time Tate Modern opened in 2002, even *The Sun* was positive in is coverage.

Postmodernism was supposed to counteract an imbalance between cultural centres and peripheries. Did artistic communities in British regional cities such as Birmingham feel a beneficial effect?

The short answer is no! London very much considered itself the centre of the art world. I can remember certain high-profile curators questioning why they would even bother to visit major centres like Glasgow, assuming that all good things came to London in the end! We didn't see many London-based curators at Ikon openings. But ironically (or perhaps inevitably) it was precisely because of this "peripheral" position that Ikon could take a lead in looking outside the mainstream. We could take risks and experiment and above all think seriously about how to engage our audience.

What did you find were the most effective ways of developing new audiences, in a city that was not inclined traditionally to give visual arts the benefit of the doubt?

More like contemporary art! Birmingham has always lauded its Pre-Raphaelites! I think the key was to overcome people's prejudices, which were fed by the negative press coverage. To make artists more accessible as well as art. I think it is interesting that Ikon began in a shopping centre – those artists really did want to engage with an audience – it wasn't one of those spaces that was just for artists. Ikon Touring, the small-scale exhibitions that went to schools and community venues, was a great way to help break down barriers and our education programmes were also critical. We were particularly keen to overcome the perception that contemporary art is only for the elite and a big part of that was making people feel comfortable coming to the gallery.

All too often contemporary galleries in those days reinforced people's feelings that this kind of art wasn't for them – I remember it all too well as an art history student myself! One of the first things I did when I arrived at Ikon was to change the front desk, to lower it so that visitors didn't feel intimidated. We also challenged the artworld orthodoxy that "art speaks for itself". Simple things, like sharing with our visitors why we were putting on the shows. When curators go to artists' studios, they ask questions, they have access to a lot of information that helps them make up their minds about the work. Sharing that information in an accessible manner was critical. Art jargon reinforces a sense of alienation and puts people off. We wanted to encourage our visitors to approach often complex work with an open mind, and to do that they have to feel comfortable in the gallery. You don't change the art but you do change the context.

Location too was important for attracting a wider audience and when we had to think about the end of the lease [of John Bright Street], it became a key consideration.

For a while you entertained the idea of Ikon staying in John Bright Street, but by 1991 it seems that you were set on moving Ikon to the old Oozells Street school building ...
When it became clear that we were likely to face a substantial rent increase on the John Bright Street premises, we began the search for a new building. We wanted something in the city centre in the belief that contemporary galleries should be accessible and contribute to city life. We were approached about Oozells Street school by the developers of Brindleyplace who were obliged to find a public use for it. It was derelict but after some initial investigations with architect Axel Burroughs of Levitt Bernstein we felt it could provide a wonderful new home. It required significant renovation and we were fortunate to attract one of the first lottery grants.
We felt it was a big advantage to have a building that was so well loved by the local community – one of the few buildings of its kind to survive. Its location on the canal behind the new International Convention Centre brought the gallery closer to other facilities. Our choice was not without controversy. The architecture committee advising the Arts Council on the lottery funding initially advised against support on the grounds that we should be seeking support for a new building on a greenfield site which in their view would be more appropriate. This ran counter to our desire to be where people could drop in rather than make a specific trip. We were also backed by research

undertaken by Tate in relation to the proposed conversion of Bankside power station into Tate Modern that revealed artists preference for renovated old buildings over new architecture. In the end the Arts Council decided to fund the project as we had a clear vision and purpose that the school suited. In 1999 Ikon was the winner of the Royal Society of British Architects Awards and received the Building of the Year Award from the Royal Fine Art Commission Trust.

How was it for you on the day of the opening at Oozells Street?
I will never forget the moment I looked out the window and saw the wonderful group of African Caribbean women who had been working with Yinka Shonibare while we were closed queuing up waiting for the doors to open. They were dressed up for the occasion and determined to be the first over the doorstep – their first visit to a contemporary art gallery. It was a clear demonstration that Ikon could connect with new audiences and that the location in a much-loved building on the edge of one of the poorest areas of the city would help break down the barriers that prevent people from engaging with contemporary art. Claire Short, the popular local MP who officially opened the new building reiterated this in her speech. (We had considered having a celebrity but the decision to invite Claire was so right for our ambitions to connect art with audiences.)

I loved the fact that there were people from all different walks of life at that opening. Even artworld colleagues from London had made the trip! We celebrated into the night with a much-deserved party for staff and supporters in the adjacent empty office building – another feat of organisation! After the mega-stress of the renovation, which was extremely challenging, it was a much-needed opportunity to celebrate. I knew that we had made the right decision.

Now, more than twenty years later, what occurs to you as the greatest challenges and most significant achievements for Ikon during the 1990s.
One of my greatest challenges throughout my time at Ikon was persuading local government to get involved with contemporary art. Despite certain initiatives, it still had the perception within the city that contemporary art was only for a few people, artists and those who knew about the subject. We were determined to change that perception; by encouraging councillors to visit the gallery and look at what we were doing, and by getting the community involved.

Looking back on it, what I am most proud of was how Ikon reflected the changes that occurred in the art world during that decade – the recognition that we needed to be more inclusive in an art world which had been too exclusive, only paying attention to certain kinds of work. Antonia Payne had done a lot with respect to feminism, showing wonderful artists like Mona Hatoum. We were very interested in looking at the cultural diversity of Birmingham as a city and reflecting that in our programmes, both British and international. I brought to Birmingham the first European survey of Adrian Piper, the American conceptual artist, and Zarina Bhimji also had her first solo show under my directorship at Ikon.

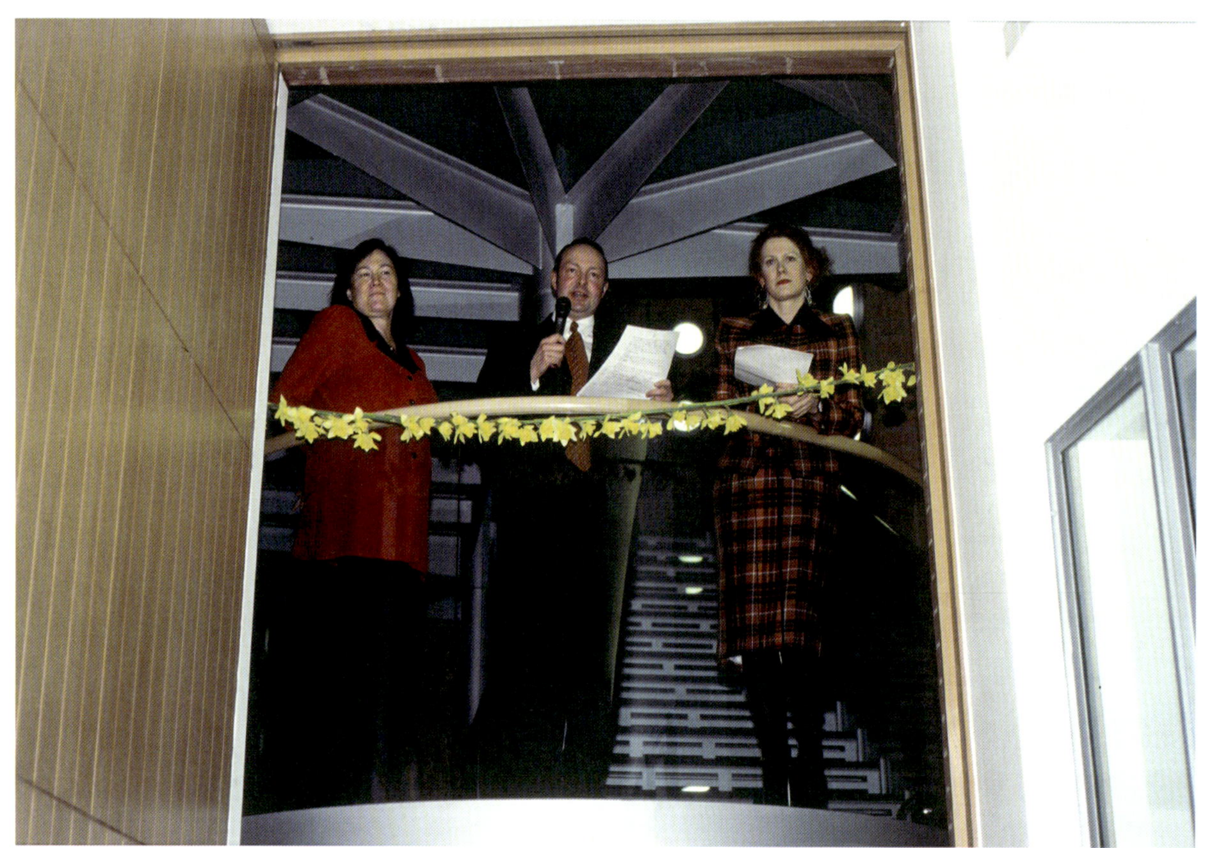

Opening of Ikon Gallery at Brindleyplace, 20 March 1998

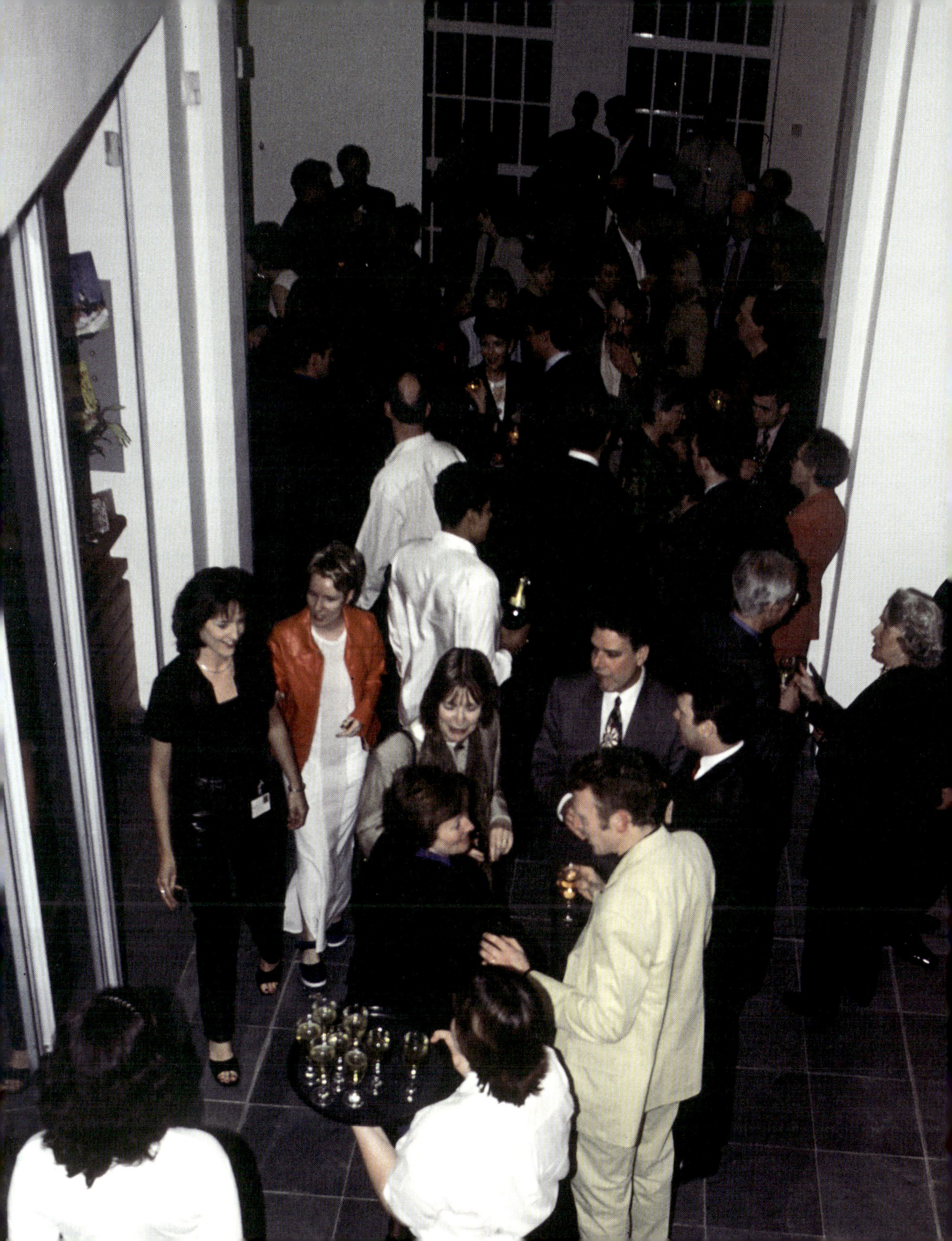

From Oozells Street School to Ikon Gallery

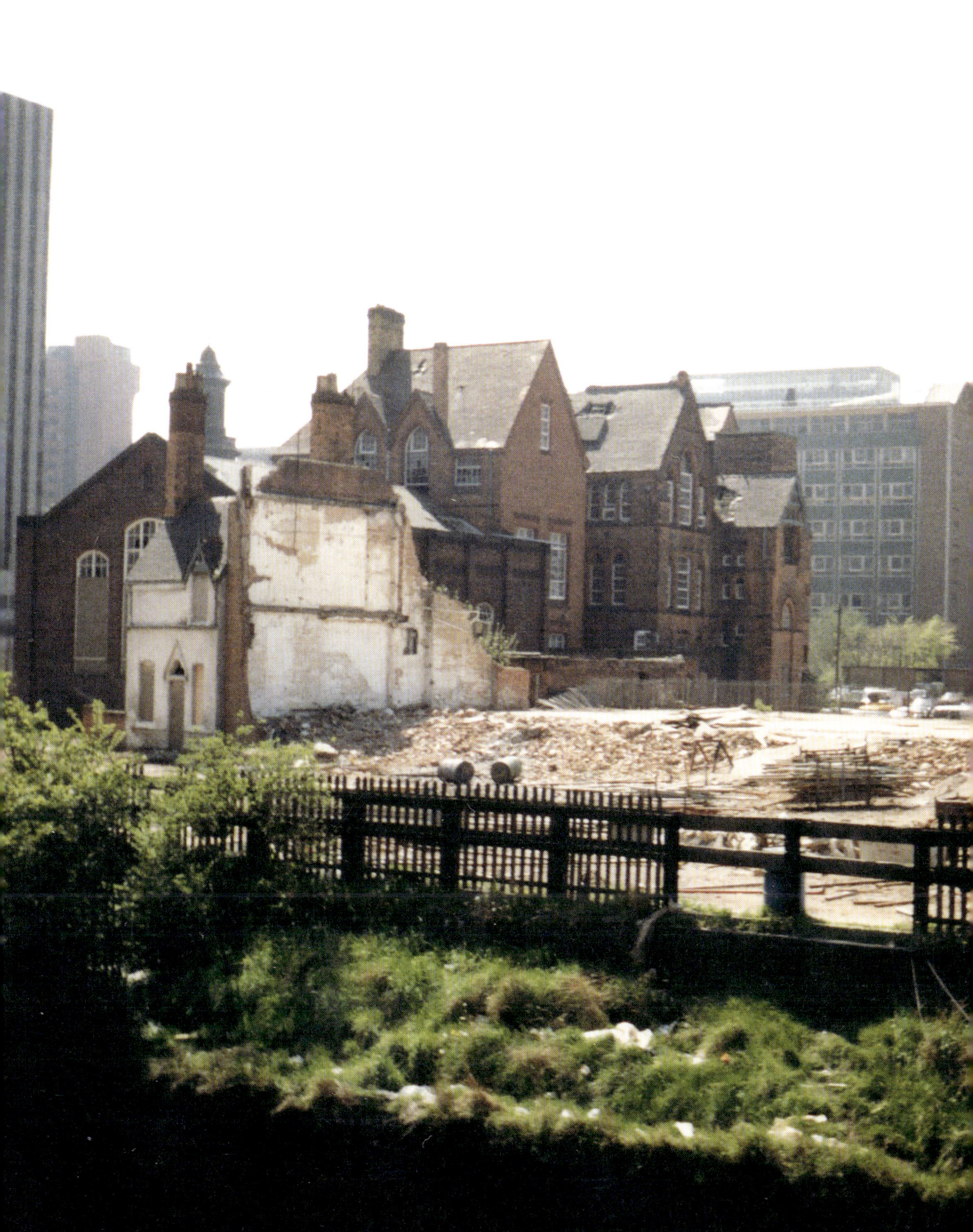

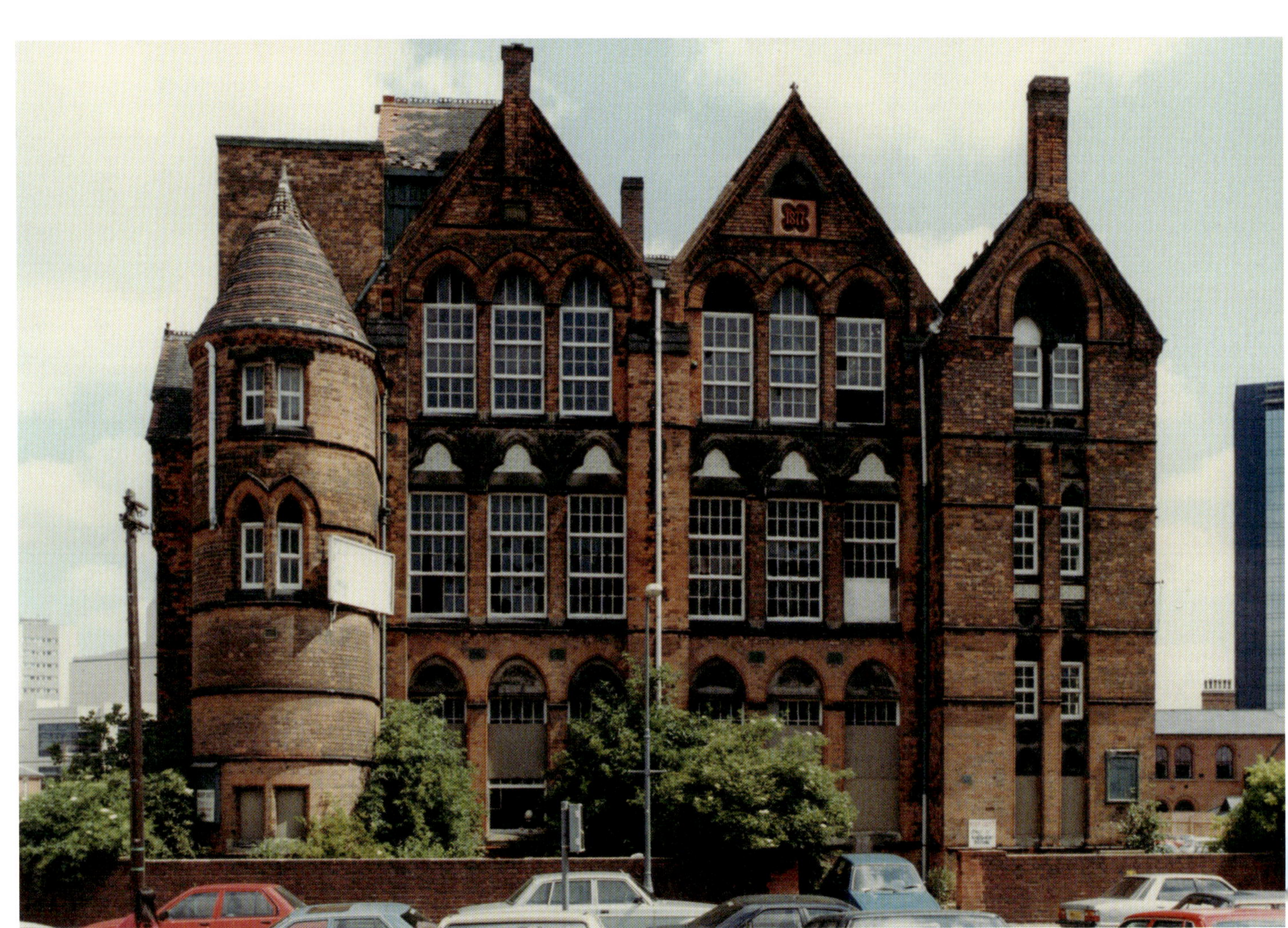

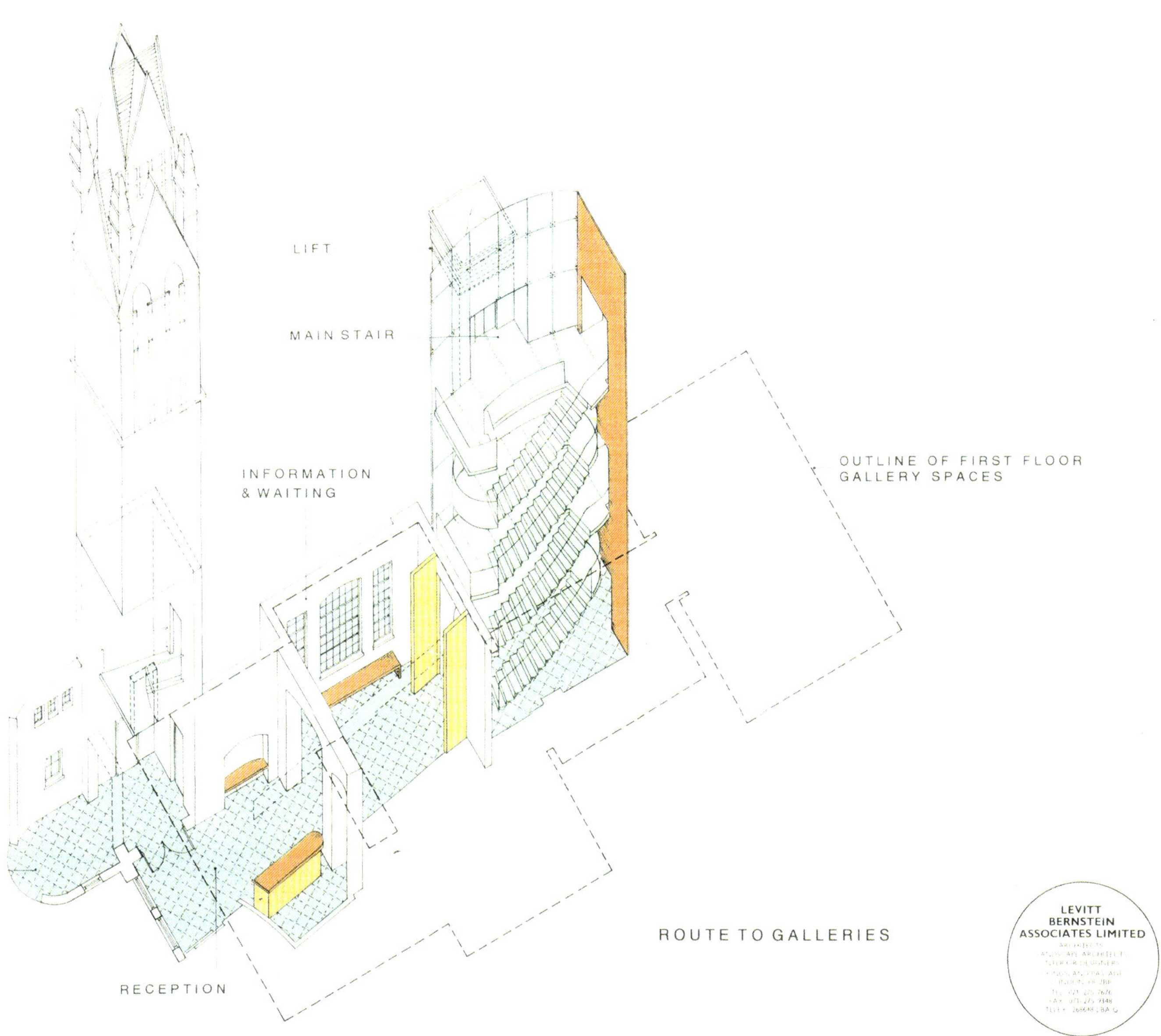

LIFT
MAIN STAIR
INFORMATION
& WAITING
OUTLINE OF FIRST FLOOR
GALLERY SPACES
ANCE
ROUTE TO GALLERIES
RECEPTION
LEVITT
BERNSTEIN
ASSOCIATES LIMITED

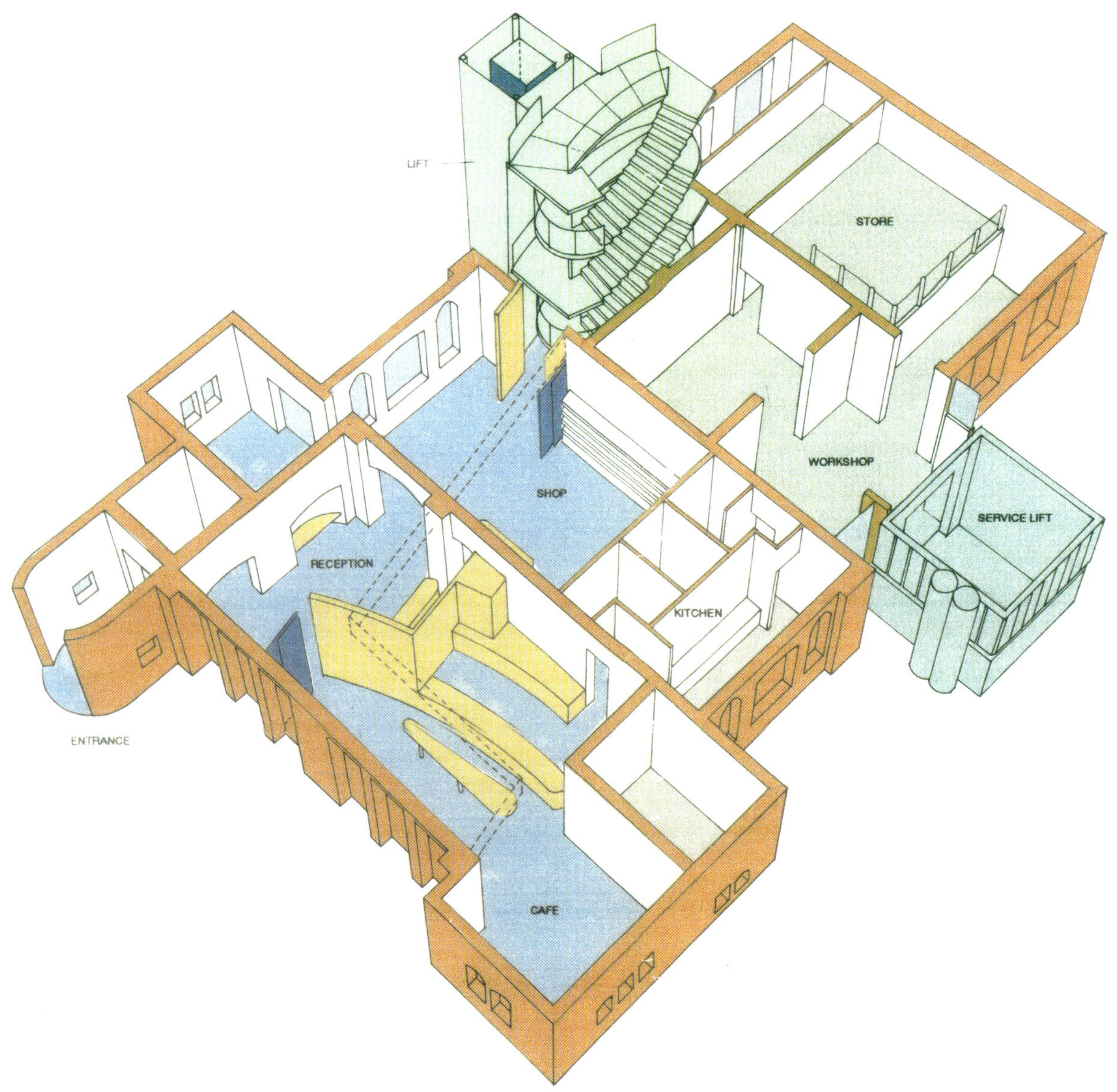

GROUND FLOOR

142

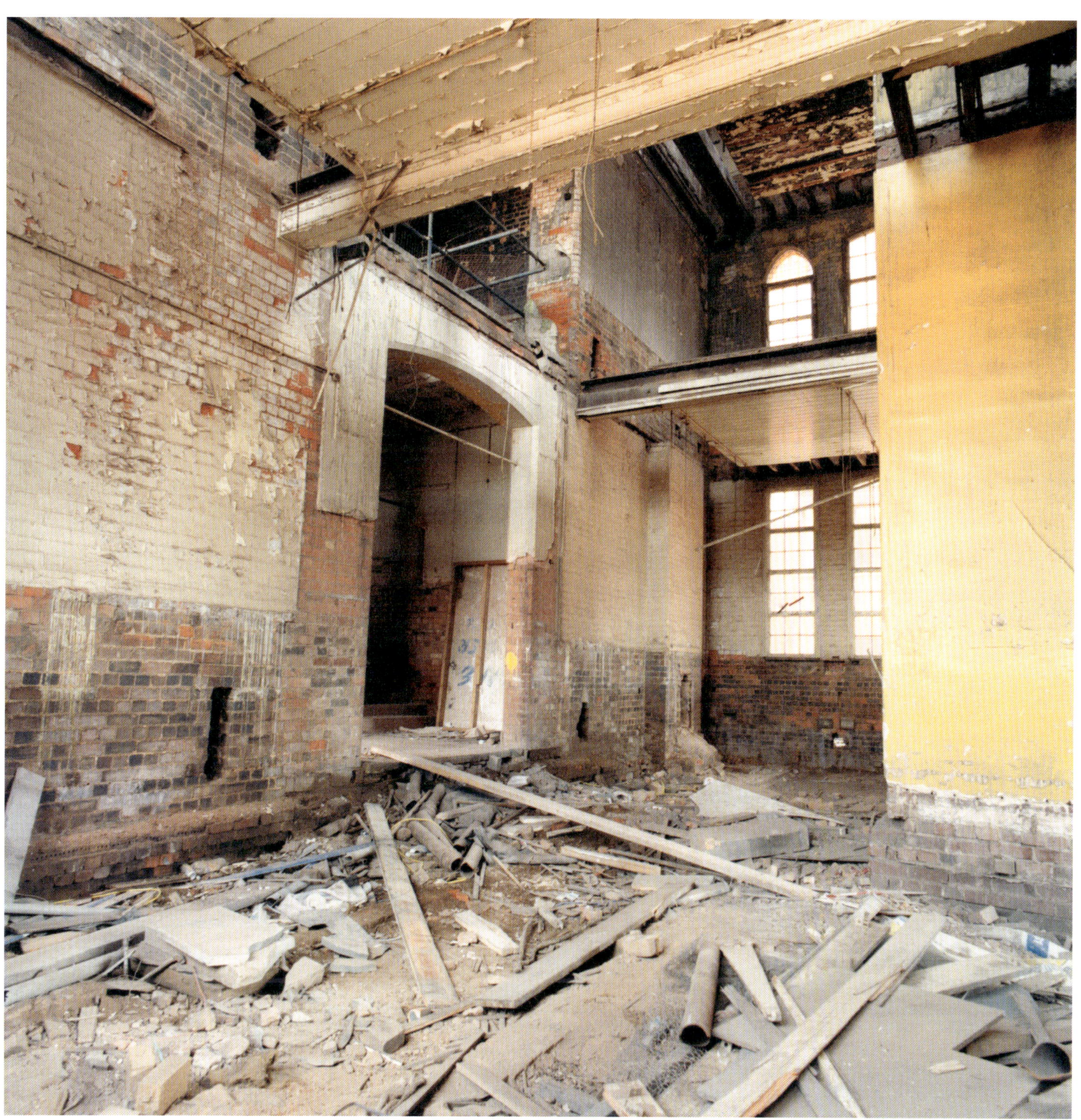

144

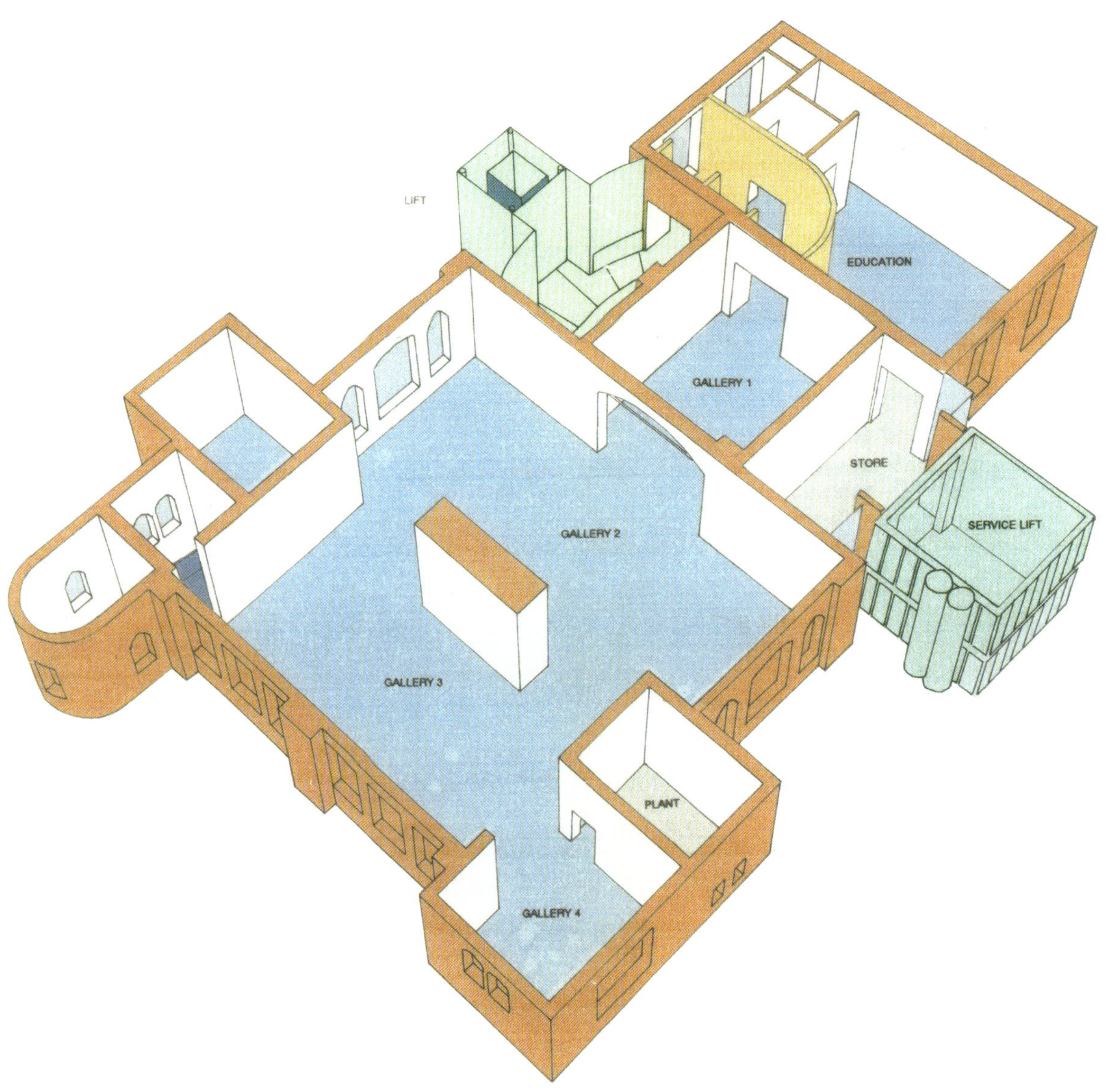

FIRST FLOOR

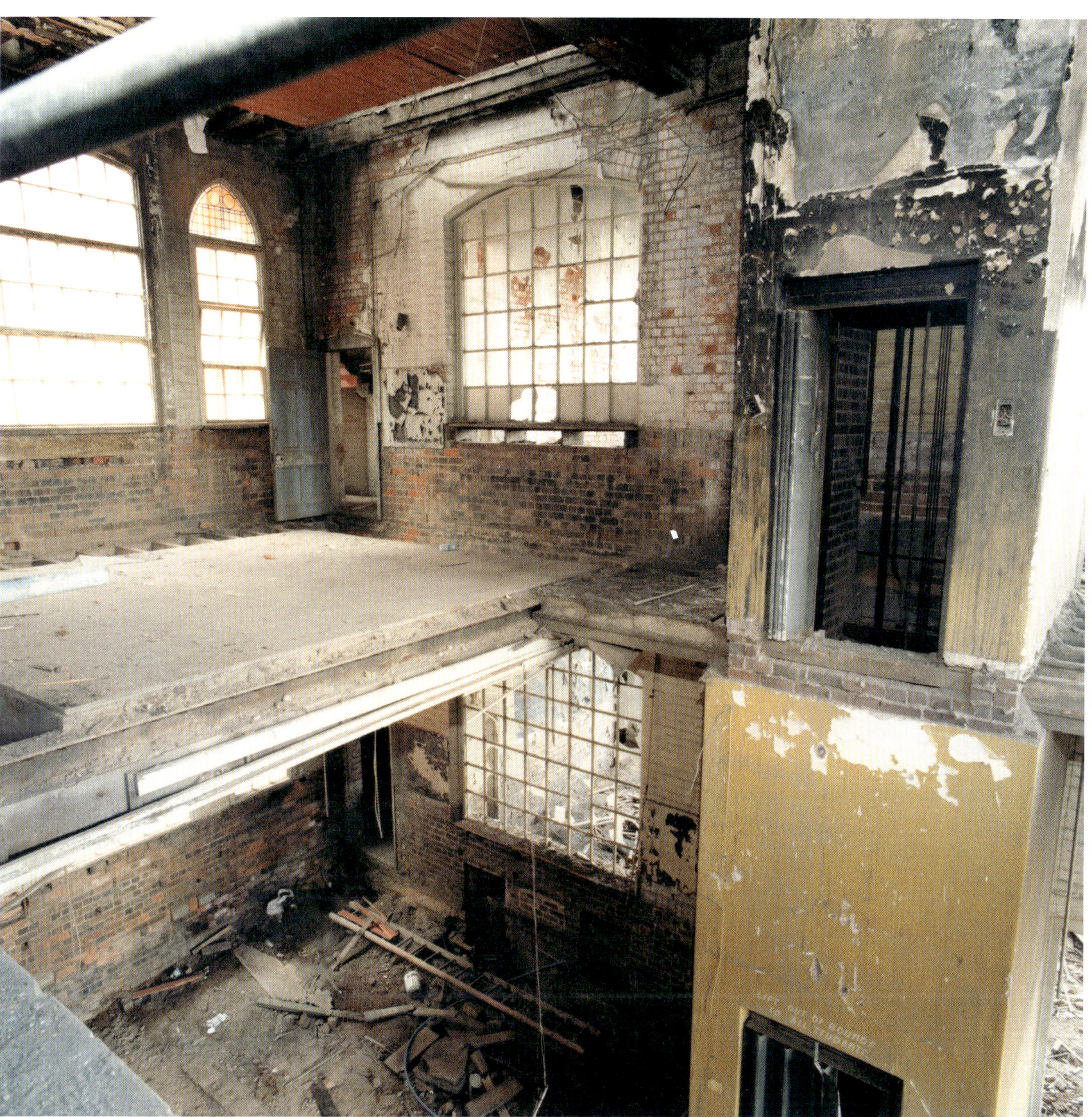

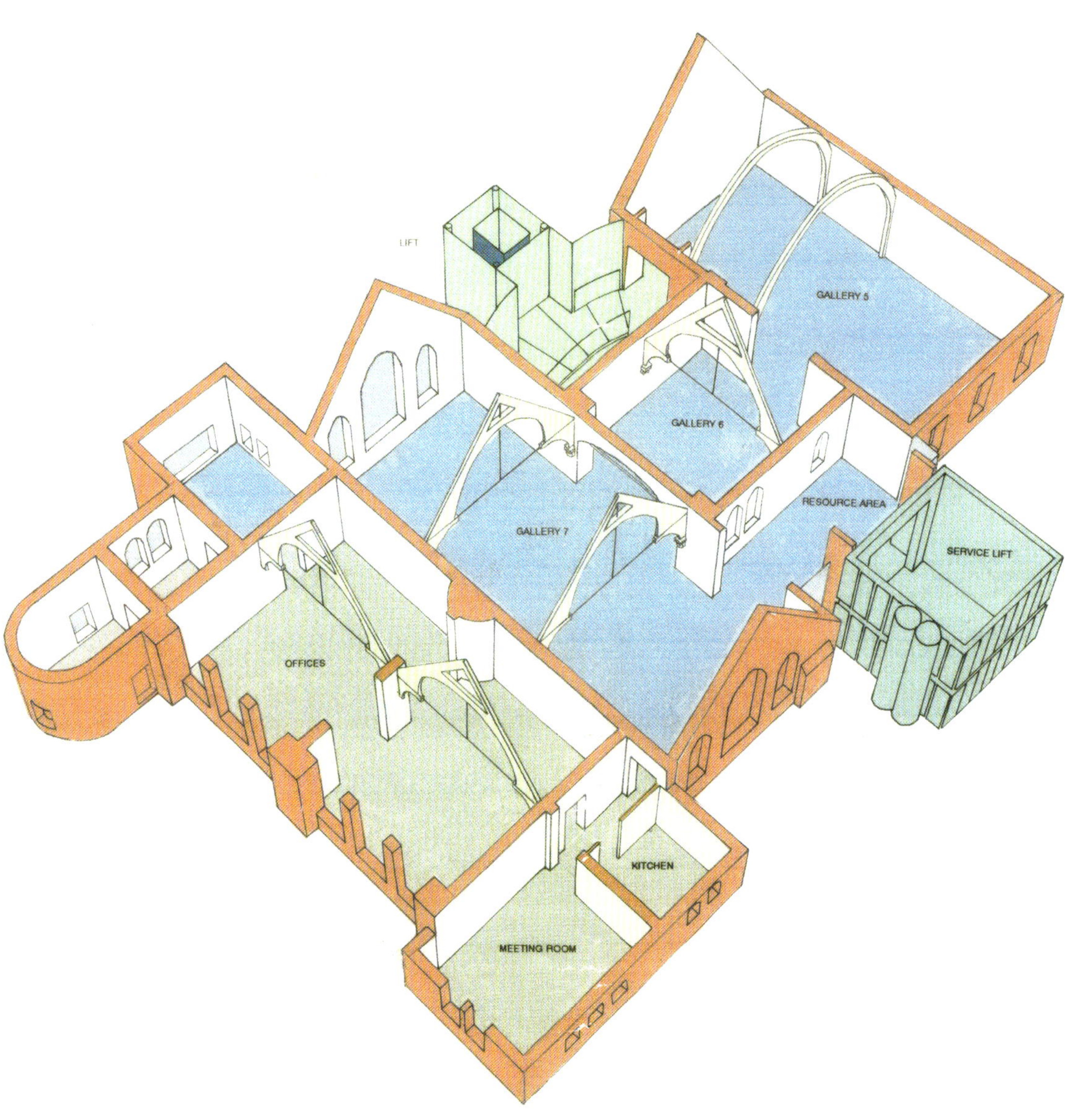

SECOND FLOOR

146

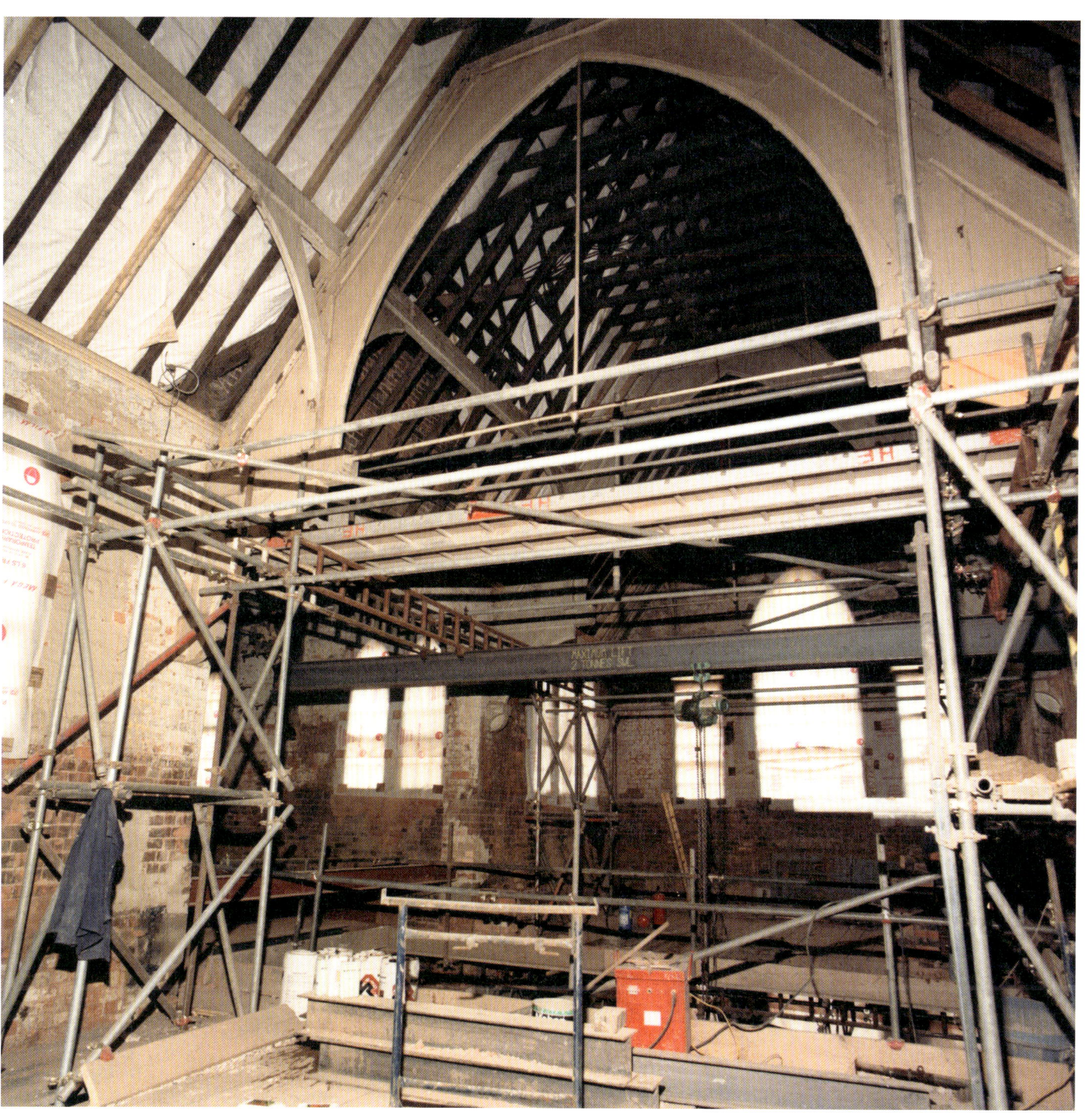

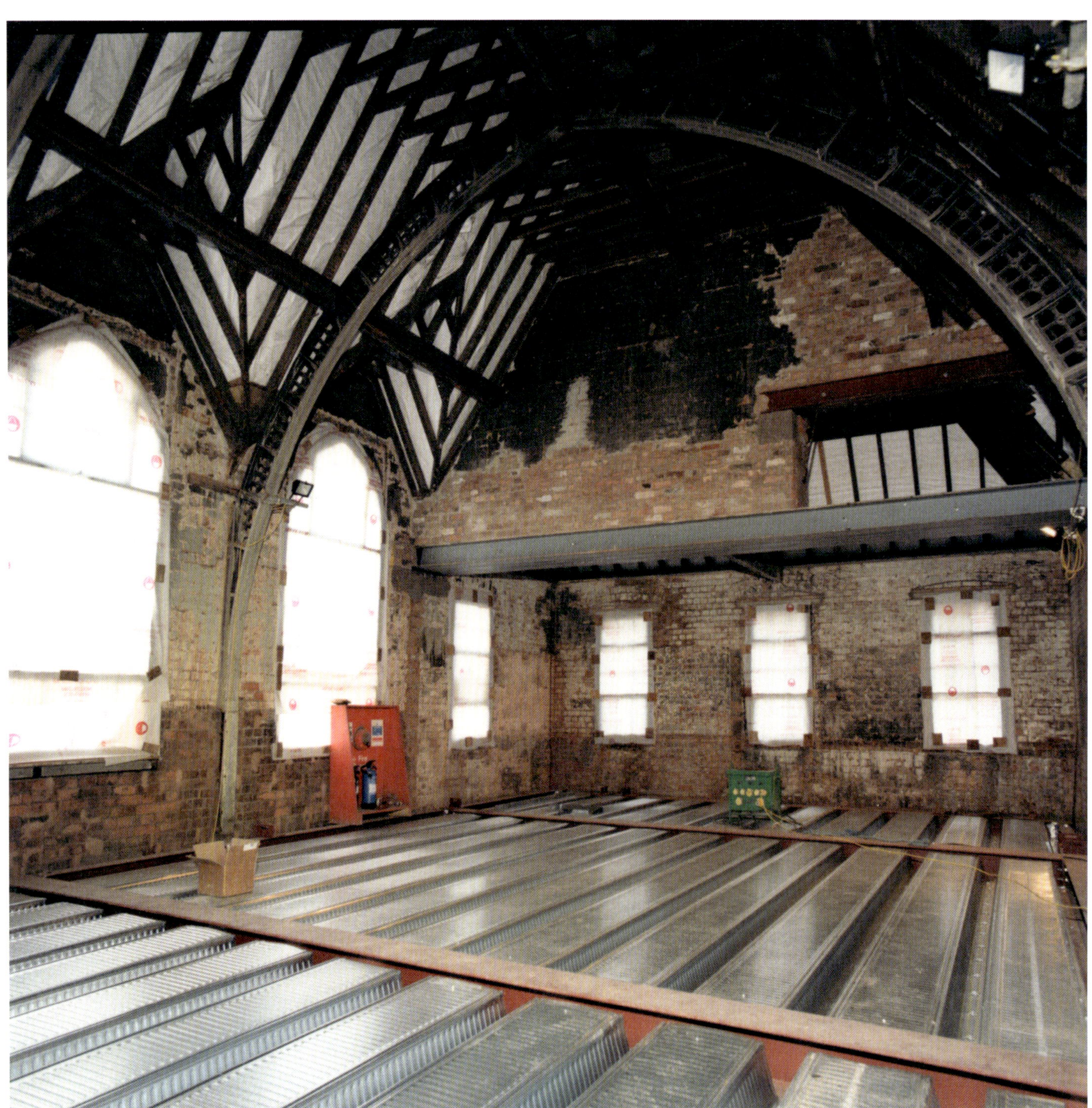

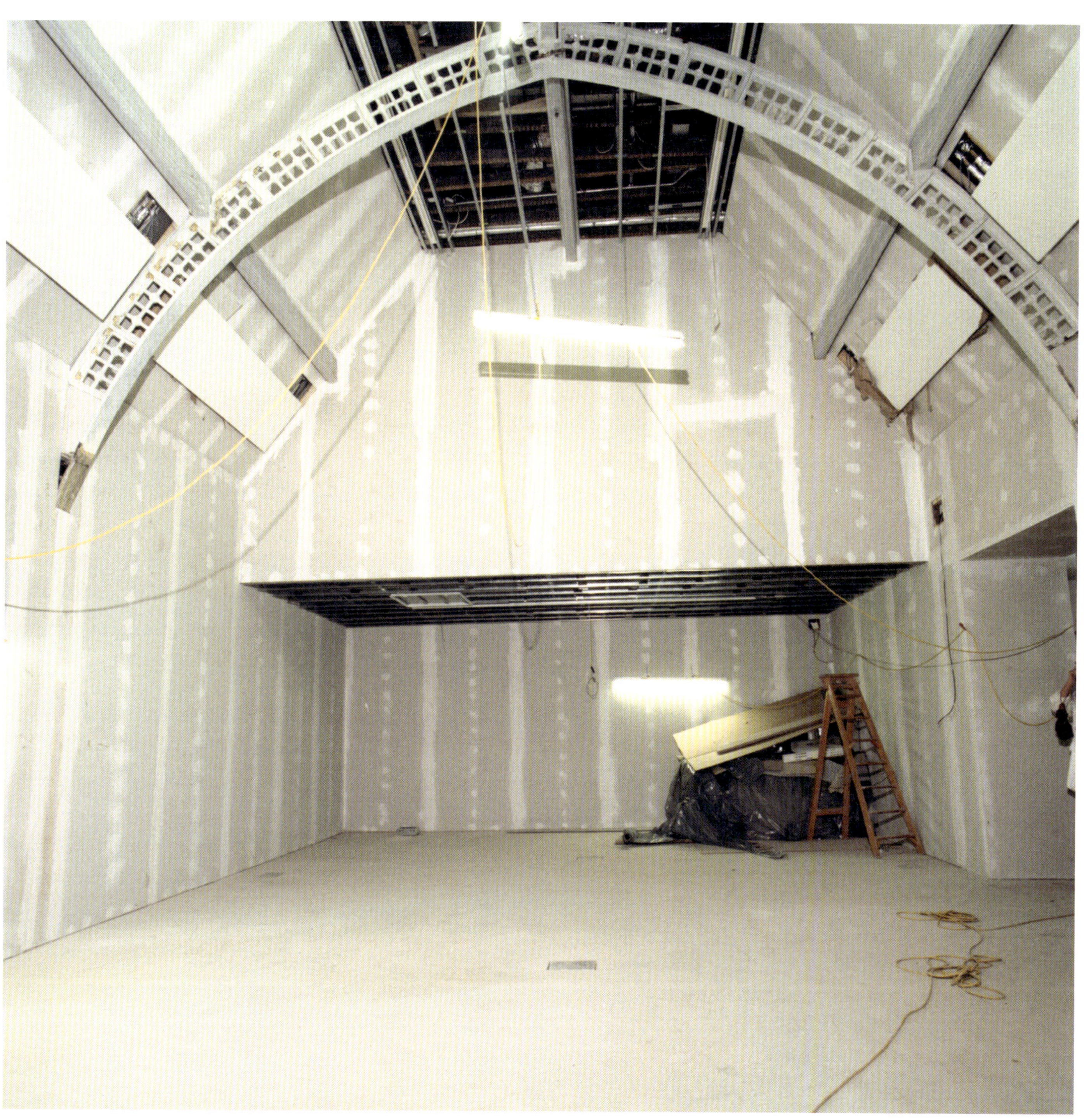

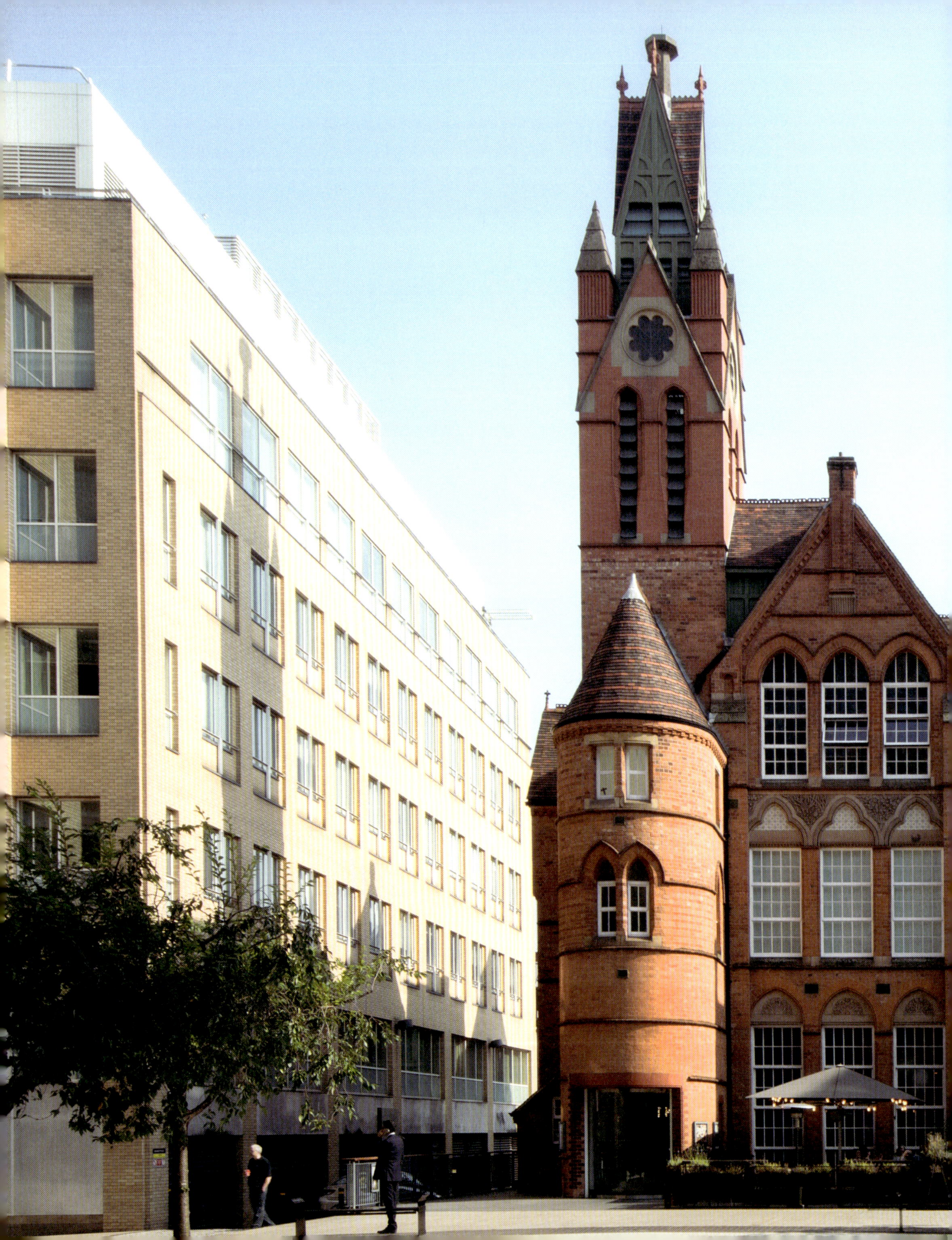

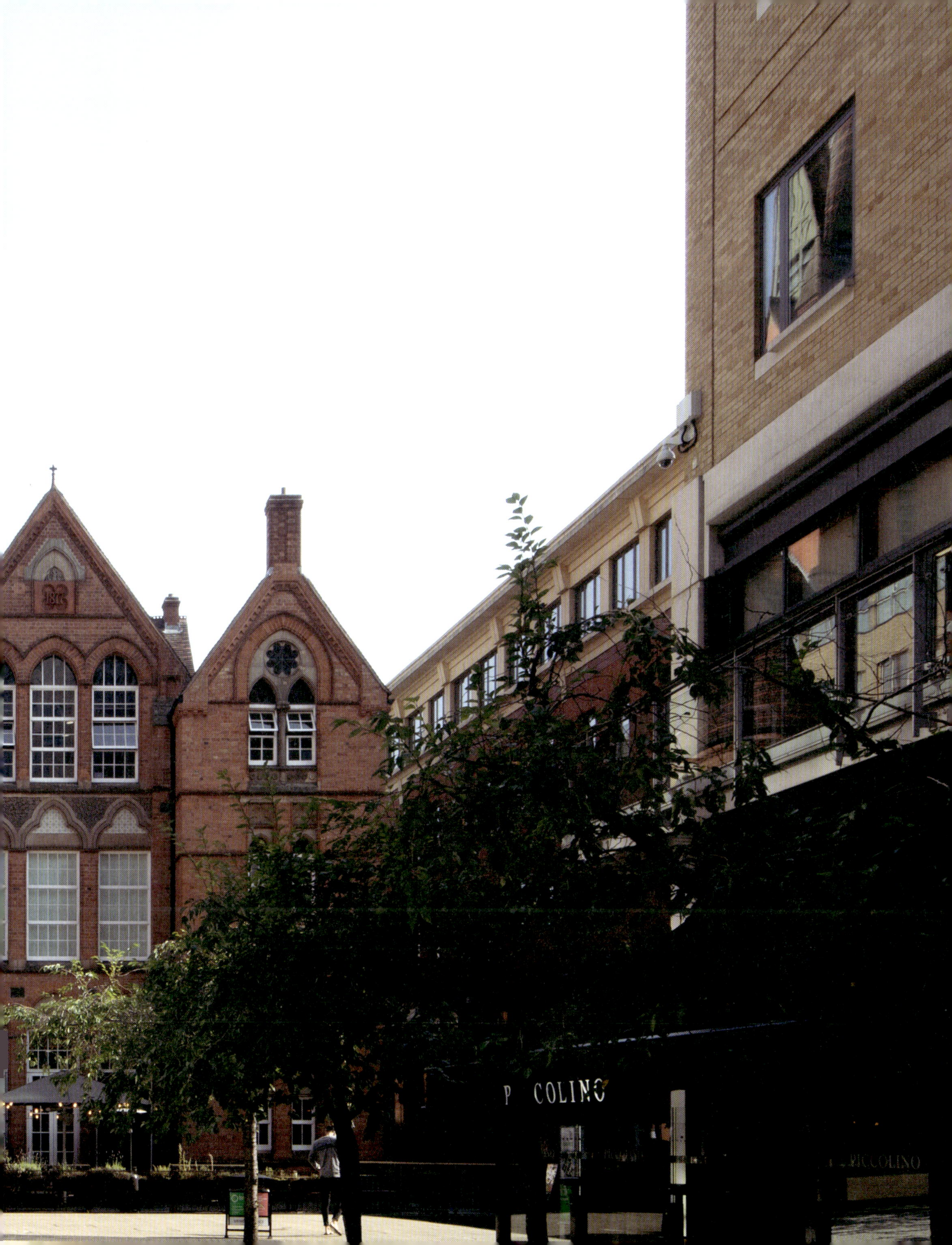
P COLINO
PICCOLINO

Ikon Exhibitions
1990–1999

John Bright Street

1990

January – February
Joan Miró, *Sculpture*

March – May
Transcontinental. Nine Latin American Artists

May – June
Futureland: Photographs by John Kippin and Chris Wainwright
Fabled Territories: New Asian Photography in Britain

June – July
Suzanne Treister

July – August
Shafique Uddin
The Subjective City
The Lie of the Land: Painting and Photography by West Midlands Artists

September – October
Ecstatic Antibodies: Resisting the AIDS Mythology
Television Intervention

October – November
Mothers

November – January
Amikam Toren

1991

January – February
Keith Piper, *A Ship Called Jesus*
Re-Writing History

March
Sharon Kivland, *The Fire of Tongues*
Tom Gilhespy, *Leniniana*

April – May
British Telecom New Contemporaries

May – June
With This Ring ...
Antoni Miralda, *Honeymoon Project*

July – August
Stephen Chambers, *Felonies and Errors*
Tony Phillips, *Jazz and the 20th Century*
John Yeadon, *Chronicles & Continuing Tales, The Travails of Blind Bifford Jelly*

August – September
Shocks to the System

September – November
Adrian Piper

November – December
Maud Sulter, *Hysteria*
The Secret Life of Objects

1992

January – February
Site Work: Architecture in Photography Since Early Modernism
Human Properties

February – March
Vong Phaophanit, *Tok Tem Dean Kep Kin Bo Dai (What Falls to the Ground but Can't be Eaten)*
Shelagh Wakely, *Gold Dust*

April – May
Zarina Bhimji, *I Will Always Be Here*
French Window

May – June
Turning the Map
Photovideo: The Camera Never Lies

June – August
Bruise: Painting for the Nineties

August – September
Alan Davie, *Works on Paper*
White Noise

October – November
Lee Jaffe, *The Harder They Come the Harder They Fall*

November – January
Rosa Sanchez and Motionhouse, *Déjà Vu*
Refusing to Surface

1993

January – February
According to Sensation, Bridget Riley 1982 – 1992

February – April
In Fusion: New European Art

April – June
Alison Wilding, *BARE*
Ilya Kabakov and Ülo Sooster, *Illustration as a Way to Survive*

June – July
WILD: Landscapes by Six Painters

July – September
Barbara Steinman, *Oracle*
Paul Graham, *New Europe*

September – October
Beyond Destination
Tony Oursler, *Dummies, Dolls, and Poison Candy ...*

November – December
Edward Allington
Lucia Nogueira

1994

January – February
Eric Bainbridge, Una Rosie Smith, Craig Wood, *Clean*
Brian Jenkins, Locky Morris, Nicola Petrie, Alistair Raphael, *Dirty*

February – March
Roger Hilton

April – May
Disrupted Borders

May –July
Basil Beattie

June – July
Rose Finn-Kelcey and Donald Rodney, *Truth, Dare, Double-Dare ...*

July – August
Boyd Webb
Ron Haseldon, *Maid of the Mist*

September – October
Ansuya Blom
Close Encounters

October – December
Siah Armajani

1995

January – February
Juan Davila, *Juanito Laguna*
New British Architecture

February – April
Mark Wallinger

April – May
Victor Grippo

May – July
Antony Gormley

July – August
V-topia: Visions of a Virtual World
August – September
Self Evident

September – November
Avis Newman

November – January
Distant Relations

1996
January – March
Diller + Scofidio, *The Desiring Eye:
reViewing the Slow House*
Lisa Milroy, *Travel Paintings*

March – May
Into the Void
Dalziel + Scullion

May – June
Permindar Kaur, *Cold Comfort*
Dorothy Cross, *Even*

June – August
Desert
Pervaiz Kahn and Felix de Rooy,
The Garden of A...

August – October
Eve Arnold, *In Retrospect*

November – January
Loaded

1997
January – March
Mark Dion

Brindleyplace

1998
March – May
Georgina Starr, *Tuberama*
Nancy Spero

June – August
Claustrophobia

August – September
Keith Piper, *Relocating the Remains*
Sorted

October – November
Callum Innes
Ellen Gallagher

December – January
Martha Rosler, *Positions in the Life World*

1999
February – April
Yinka Shonibare, *Dressing Down*
*Secret Victorians: Contemporary Artists
and a 19th Century Vision*

April – June
*E.S.P. Contemporary Artists Investigate
the Paranormal*

June – August
Adam Chodzko
Clement Cooper, *PRIMARY*

September – November
*Babel: Contemporary Art and
the Journeys of Communication*

November – January
*History and Memory in the Art
of Gordon Bennett*

Cildo Meireles *Jogo de Velha AX/OP 8B* (detail) 1993–94

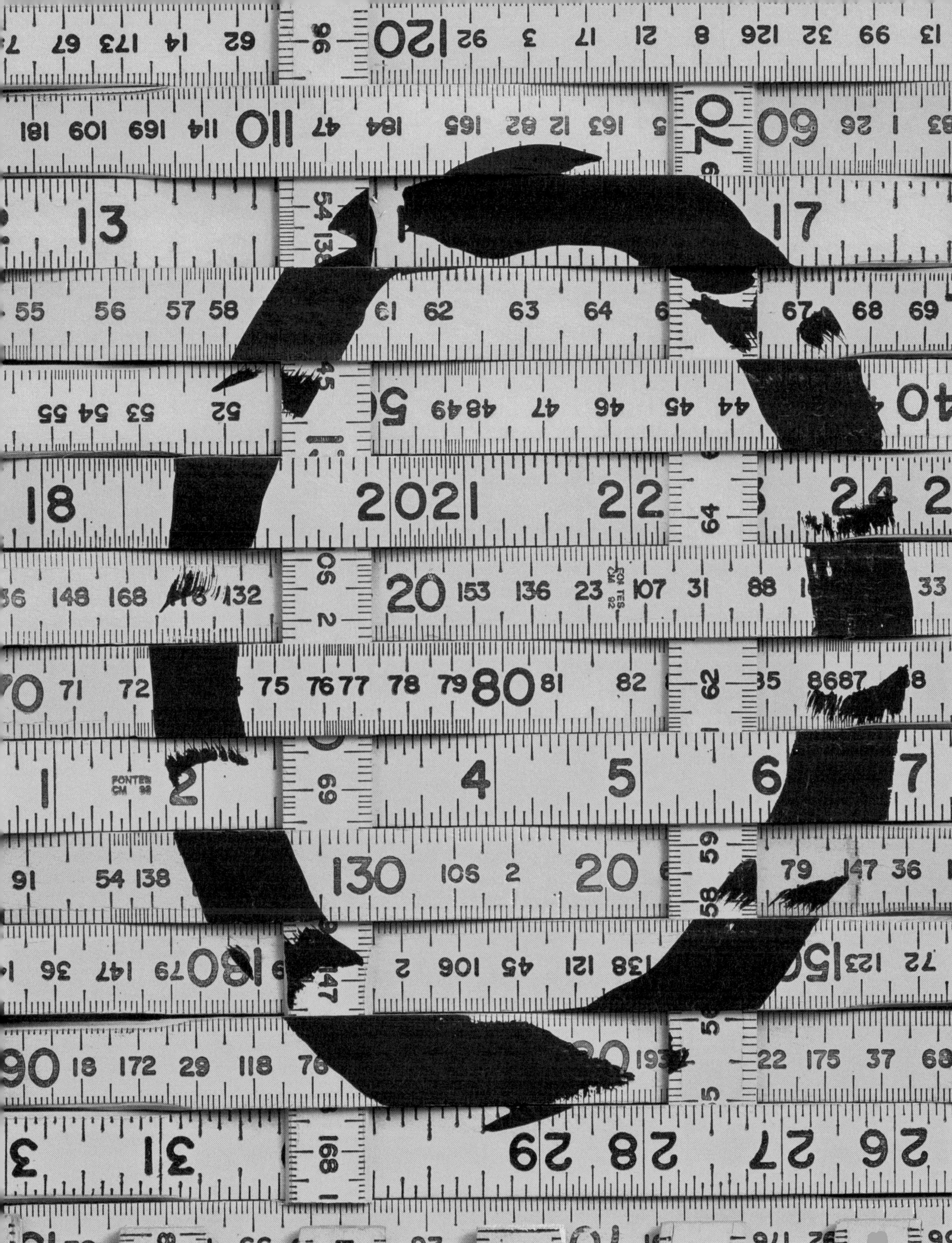

Artists' Biographies

Felicity Allen
Born in Wirral, 1952. Lives in London and Ramsgate

Selected Solo Exhibitions
1984–85
Cafe Royal, ICA, London

1986
Shape, Albert Dane Centre; Bentley Day Centre; John Wilson House; Mereway Day Centre; Randall Close Day Centre; St Pancras Hospital; Sunberry Day Centre, London
The Naked City: Durham Effigy, Air Gallery, London

1987
Durham Cathedral, Dartington Gallery, Totnes

1989
1 Finsbury Avenue, Broadgate, London
Mario Flecha Gallery, London

1991
Elements and Senses, St Vincent VI Form College, Gosport; Upton Park Heritage Centre, Dorset; Winchester Gallery; South Hill Park Arts Centre, Bracknell

1993
Towner Art Gallery, Eastbourne

1997
Priory School Gallery, Lewes

1998
Brief Encounters, Photo 98, St George's Square, Huddersfield

2015
Dialogic Portraits: As If They Existed, Turner Contemporary, Margate
As If They Existed, Electro Studios Project Space, St Leonards-on-Sea

2018
The Disoeuvre, Ex Libris Gallery, Newcastle upon Tyne
(with Althea Greenan) *Slidewalking Towards a Disoeuvre*, LIMBO, Margate

Selected Group Exhibitions
1985
Variations, with Judy Chicago's 'The Dinner Party', The Warehouse, London
Rooms, The Spitalfields Practice, London

1986
Love: Sacred and Profane, Plymouth Arts Centre; Stoke-on-Trent City Museum & Art Gallery
Critics' Space, Air Gallery, London
Four Painters, Guildhall, London

1987
European Invitational, George Ciscle Gallery, Baltimore
8 x 8, Curwen Gallery, London
Ikons, Mario Flecha Gallery, London

1988
Graven Images, Harris Museum and Art Gallery, Preston
Print Show, Pomeroy Purdy Gallery, London

1989
Critics Space, Air Gallery, London
A Spiritual Dimension, Peterborough Museum & Art Gallery; Herbert Art Gallery & Museum, Coventry; Worcester City Art Gallery & Museum; Winchester Gallery; Christchurch Mansion; Shipley Art Gallery, Gateshead
Painters at Winchester, Winchester Gallery

1990
Mothers, Ikon Gallery, Birmingham; Cleveland Gallery, Middlesbrough; Tullie House Museum and Art Gallery, Carlisle
Secret Spaces: Still Life & Interiors, Pride Gallery, London

1996
CAS Art Market, Contemporary Art Society, London
Durham Cathedral Artists in Residence 1983–1996, Durham Art Gallery

1997
What's for Dinner?, Towner Gallery, Eastbourne

2012
Off the S{H}Elf: The Self and Subjectivity in the Artist's Book, Stockwell Studios, London

2016
Meaning Making Meaning: Art and Pedagogy, A–venue, Gothenburg

2017
Strange Love, International Time Based Arts Festival, Folkestone

2018
Complicit, part of POW! Festival of Arts, Heimat 29, Ramsgate

2019
Dark Energy. Feminist Organizing, Working Collectively, Xhibit, Academy of Fine Arts Vienna
POW! Painters, part of POW! Thanet Festival, LIMBO, Margate

Edward Allington
Born in Westmorland, 1951. Died 2017

Selected Solo Exhibitions
1983
Sculpture, Lisson Gallery, London
Drawing Towards Sculpture, ICA, London

1984
New British Sculpture, Gallery Schmela, Dusseldorf

1991
Pictured Bronzes and Drawings, Kohji Ogura Gallery, Nagoya

1993
Ikon Gallery, Birmingham
Cell-Cella-Celda, Henry Moore Institute, Leeds

1996
From Figure to Object, Karsten Schubert & Frith Street Gallery, London

1997
Pictured Bronzes, Yorkshire Sculpture Park, Wakefield

2003
Titled Vase and Other Projects, Bury Art Gallery & Museum

2012
Trees, Small Fires, and Japanese Joints, Daiwa Anglo Japanese Foundation, London

2016
The Hidden Sculptures, Megan Piper, London

2019
Things Unsaid, Henry Moore Institute, Leeds
In Pursuit of Sculpture, UCL Gallery, London

2020
Edward Allington and Pablo Bronstein, Tate Britain, London

Selected Group Exhibitions
1981
Objects and Sculpture, Arnolfini, Bristol

1982
British Drawing, Hayward Annual 82,
Hayward Gallery, London

1983
The Sculpture Show, Hayward Gallery,
London

1988
Sculpture/Drawings, Fuji Television Gallery,
Tokyo

1989
British Sculpture 1960–1988, MuKHA,
Antwerp

1991
*Objects for the Ideal Home: The Legacy
of Pop Art*, Serpentine Gallery, London

1994
*Sculptors' Drawings Presented by the
Weltkunst Foundation,* Tate Gallery, London

1998
*A Changed World: Contemporary British
Sculpture 1963–1996*, Johannesburg Art
Gallery

2002
*Blast to Freeze, British Art in the 20th
Century,* Kunstmuseum, Wolfsburg

2004
MULTIPLICATION, Museum of Modern Art,
Skopje

2008
British Sculptors' Drawings, British Museum,
London

2012
Then and Now, The Piper Gallery, London

2014
A Thousand Doors, NEON, Athens
Ruin Lust, Tate Britain, London

2015
Classicicity, Breese Little, London
Making it: Sculpture in Britain 1977–1986,
Yorkshire Sculpture Park, Wakefield

2019
*Pushing Paper: Contemporary Drawing
from 1970 to Now*, British Museum, London

Siah Armajani
Born in Tehran, 1939. Died 2020

Selected Solo Exhibitions
1992
Streets: Sculptures and Notations, Arts
Club of Chicago; The Poetry Garden, Lannan
Foundation, Los Angeles

1994
Anarchistic Contributions 1962–1994,
Villa Arson, Nice
Ikon Gallery, Birmingham

1995
MAMCO, Geneva

1996
Anarchistic Contributions 1962–1994,
Neue Galerie am Landesmuseum Johanneum,
Graz
Reading Spaces, MACBA, Barcelona
*The Staten Island Ferry Pedestrian Bridge
and Other Works*, Newhouse Center for
Contemporary Art, Staten Island, New York
The Customs House, Newcastle upon Tyne

1999
Museo Nacional Centro de Arte Reina Sofia,
Madrid

2007
Fallujah, Artium, Vitoria-Gasteiz, Spain;
Centro de Arte y Naturaleza/Fundación
Beulas, Huesca, Spain; Fundación Cesar
Manrique, Lanzarote; Santa Fe Art Institute
*L'art n'est pas le salon de beauté de la
civilisation*, MAMCO, Geneva

2013
'An Ingenious World', Parasol unit, London
Bridges for Paris Transit System, MAMCO,
Geneva

2016
Bridge Builder, Kemper Museum of
Contemporary Art, Kansas City

2017
Rossi & Rossi, Hong Kong

2018
Follow This Line, Walker Art Center,
Minneapolis

2019
The Met Breuer, New York

Selected Group Exhibitions
1987
Avant-Garde in the Eighties, Los Angeles
County Museum of Art
documenta 8, Kassel

1988
Carnegie International, Pittsburgh
Sculpture Inside Outside, Walker Art
Center, Minneapolis
*View Points: Post-War Painting and
Sculpture*, Solomon R. Guggenheim
Museum, New York

1992
Century of Sculpture, Stedelijk Museum
and Nieuwe Kerk Foundation, Amsterdam
Like Nothing Else in Tennessee, Serpentine
Gallery, London

1998
Projects/Installations, PS1, New York

2004
*Gardens of Iran: Ancient Wisdom, New
Visions*, Tehran Museum of Contemporary Art

2006
*The Contemporary Persian Scene:
The American and European Experience*,
LTMH Gallery, New York
*Word into Art: Artists of the Modern
Middle East*, British Museum, London

2007
*Arte y derechos civiles en el nuevo(des)
orden global*, Fundación César Manrique,
Lanzarote

2008
Artists and War, North Dakota Museum
of Art, Grand Forks

2009
Event Horizon, Walker Art Center,
Minneapolis

2011
9/11, MoMA PS1, New York
The Spectacular of Vernacular, Walker Art
Center, Minneapolis

2015
*Cycle des histoires sans fin, séquence
automne-hiver 2015–2016*, MAMCO,
Geneva

2016
*(INFRA) STRUCTURE: complex, below and
further on*, Lannan Foundation Gallery,
Santa Fe

Passages in Modern Art: 1946–1996,
Dallas Museum of Art

Basil Beattie

Born in West Hartlepool, 1935. Lives in
London

Selected Solo Exhibitions
1994
Ikon Gallery, Birmingham
New Town Gallery, Johannesburg

1995
New Paintings, Angel Row Gallery,
Nottingham; Todd Gallery, London

2000
The Storey Gallery, Lancaster

2007
Tate Britain, London

2008
The Janus Series, Two Rooms Gallery,
Auckland

2010
*Basil Beattie: Paintings from the Janus
Series II*, Abbot Hall Art Gallery, Kendal

2013
Promises, promises, Jerwood Gallery,
Hastings
Hilton Fine Art, Bath

2016
When Now Becomes Then: Three Decades,
Middlesbrough Institute of Modern Art

2018
A Passage of Time, Royal Academy of Arts,
London

Selected Group Exhibitions
1994
Paintmarks, Kettle's Yard, Cambridge; City
Art Gallery, Southampton; Mead Gallery,
Coventry

1967
Survey '67, Camden Art Centre, London

1971
Big Paintings for Public Places, Whitworth
Art Gallery, Manchester

1974
British Painting, Hayward Gallery, London

1984
British Art Show 2, Ikon Gallery, Birmingham;
Birmingham Museum and Art Gallery; Royal
Scottish Academy, Edinburgh; Mappin Art
Gallery, Sheffield; Southampton City Art Gallery

1996
Ace! New Purchases, Hatton Gallery,
Newcastle upon Tyne; Harris Museum and
Art Gallery, Preston, Oldham Art Gallery;
Hayward Gallery, London; Walsall Museum
& Art Gallery; Weston Park Museum,
Sheffield; Sheffield City Art Galleries; Angel
Row Gallery, Nottingham; Arnolfini, Bristol

1999
Thinking Aloud, Camden Art Centre, London

2001
*A Master Class – British Painting: Basil
Beattie, John Hoyland, John Walker,
John Edwards*
Stephen Lacey Gallery, London

2009
Invisible Cities, Jerwood Space, London

2016
Towards the Night, Towner Art Gallery,
Eastbourne

2019
Fully Awake 5.6, Freelands Foundation
Gallery, London

Gordon Bennett

Born in Monto, Australia, 1955. Died 2014

Selected Solo Exhibitions
1990
Psycho(d)rama, Institute of Modern Art,
Brisbane

1991
Dialogues with Self, Art Gallery of Western
Australia, Perth

1993
Mirrorama, Ian Potter Gallery, University of
Melbourne
Painting History, Contemporary Art Centre
of South Australia, Adelaide

1995
BLACK: Fear of Shadows, Bellas Gallery,
Brisbane

1996
*Mirror Mirror: The Narcissism of
Coloniality*, Canberra School of Art Gallery

1999–2000
*History and Memory in the Art of Gordon
Bennett*, Brisbane City Gallery; Ikon Gallery,
Birmingham; Arnolfini, Bristol; Henie Onstad
Kunstsenter, Oslo

2002
Notes to Basquiat: 9 11, Greenaway Art
Gallery, Adelaide

2007
The Expiation of Guilt, Museum of
Archaeology and Anthropology, University
of Cambridge

2007–09
Gordon Bennett Survey, National Gallery
of Victoria, Melbourne; Queensland Art
Gallery | Gallery of Modern Art, Brisbane;
Art Gallery of Western Australia, Perth

2012
*Outsider/Insider: The Art of Gordon
Bennett*, AAMU Museum of Contemporary
Aboriginal Art, Utrecht

2014
*In Memoriam Gordon Bennett 1955–
2014*, Milani Gallery, Brisbane

2015–18
Be Polite, Institute of Modern Art, Brisbane;
Perth Institute of Contemporary Arts;
Contemporary Art Gallery, Vancouver; Mc-
Master Museum of Art, Hamilton, Canada

2020–21
*Unfinished Business: The Art of Gordon
Bennett*, Gallery of Modern Art, Brisbane

Selected Group Exhibitions
1988
Australian Art of the Last Twenty Years,
Museum of Contemporary Art, Brisbane

1990
Adelaide Biennial, Art Gallery of South
Australia
Paraculture, Artists' Space, New York

1992
9th Biennale of Sydney

1993
Aratjara: Art of the First Australians,
Kunstsammlung Nordrhein-Westfalen,
Dusseldorf, Germany; Hayward Gallery,
London; Louisiana Museum of Contemporary
Art, Humlebaek, Denmark

1994
5th Havana Biennial
*Localities of Desire: Contemporary Art
in an International World*, MCA, Sydney

1994–95
Antipodean Currents, John F Kennedy
Centre, Washington DC; Guggenheim
Museum SoHo, New York

1995
Seven Histories of Australia, ACCA,
Melbourne

1997
*In Place (Out of Time): Contemporary Art
in Australia*, Museum of Modern Art Oxford

1999
Perspecta 99, MCA, Sydney

1999–2001
*Global Conceptualism: Points of Origin
1950s–1980s*, Queens Museum of Art, New
York; Walker Art Center, Minneapolis; Miami
Art Museum; MIT List Visual Arts Center,
Cambridge, USA, Vancouver Art Gallery

1999–2000
*New Republics, Contemporary Art from
Australia, Canada & South Africa*, Canada
House Gallery, London; Edmonton Art
Gallery, Canada; ACCA, Melbourne;
Johannesburg Art Gallery

2000
3rd Shanghai Biennale
Mirror With a Memory, National Portrait
Gallery, Canberra
On the Brink; Abstraction of the 90s,
Heide Museum of Modern Art, Melbourne

2003
*War Without Boundaries – Australia and
the War Against Terrorism*, Australian War
Memorial, Canberra

2005
2nd Prague Biennale

2008
16th Biennale of Sydney

2009
*Avoiding Myth and Message: Australian
Artists and the Literary World*, MCA,
Sydney

2012
dOCUMENTA (13), Kassel

2013
Australia, Royal Academy of Arts, London
*My Country, I Still Call Australia Home:
Contemporary Art From Black Australia,*
Gallery of Modern Art, Brisbane
*Vivid Memories: An Aboriginal Art
History*, Musee d'Aquitaine, Bordeaux

2014
8th Berlin Biennale
An Appetite for Painting, National Museum,
Oslo

2016
Shut Up and Paint, NGV International,
Melbourne
Today Tomorrow Yesterday, MCA, Sydney
1st *Yinchuan Biennale*

2017
*Every Brilliant Eye: Australian Art of the
1990s*, National Gallery of Victoria,
Melbourne

2018
Colony: Frontier Wars, National Gallery
of Victoria, Melbourne
National Picture, National Gallery of
Australia, Canberra

2019
Micro Histories, Museum of Brisbane
IN-Formalism, Casula Powerhouse Arts
Centre, Sydney

Zarina Bhimji
Born in Mbarara, Uganda, 1963. Lives in
London

Selected Solo Exhibitions
1989
Tom Allen Community Art Centre, London

1992
I Will Always Be Here, Ikon Gallery,
Birmingham

1995
Kettle's Yard, Cambridge

1998
Cleaning the Garden, Harewood House,
Terrace Gallery, Leeds

2001
Cleaning the Garden, Talwar Gallery,
New York

2003
Zarina Bhimji / Matrix 150, Wadsworth
Athenium Museum of Art, Hartford
Art Now, Tate Britain, London

2004
Archive Season, Iniva, London

2006
Haunch of Venison, London

2007
Haunch of Venison, Zürich

2009
Art Institute of Chicago

2012
Whitechapel Gallery, London; Kunstmuseum
Bern
Yellow Patch, New Art Gallery Walsall
de Appel, Amsterdam

2015
Jangbar, New Art Exchange, Nottingham

2018
Lead White, Tate Britain, London

2020–21
Black Pocket, Sharjah Art Foundation

2021
Fruitmarket Gallery, Edinburgh

Selected Group Exhibitions
1985
Artists Against Apartheid, South Bank,
London

1986
From Two Worlds, Whitechapel Gallery,
London

1987
Dislocation, Kettle's Yard, Cambridge
Black Women Photographers, Camden Art
Centre, London
*The Image Employed: The Use of
Narrative in Black Art*, Cornerhouse,
Manchester

1988
The Essential BLACK ART, Chisenhale
Gallery, London

1989
Towards a Bigger Picture, Victoria and
Albert Museum, London; Tate Liverpool

1990
Intimate Distance, The Photographers'
Gallery, London

1992
Critical Decade, Museum of Modern Art
Oxford

1993
Antwerp '93, MuKHA, Antwerp

1994
Inauguration exhibition, Iniva, London
Revir/Territory, Kulturhuset, Stockholm

1995
The Impossible Science of Being,
The Photographers' Gallery, London

1996
In/Sight, Solomon R. Guggenheim Museum,
New York

1997
No Place (Like Home), Walker Art Center,
Minneapolis
2nd Johannesburg Biennale
Out of India, Queens Museum of Art,
New York
Strange Day, Gian Ferrari Arte
Contemporanea, Milan

2001
The Short Century, Museum Villa Stuck,
Munich; Haus der Kulturen der Welt, Berlin;
Museum of Contemporary Art Chicago; PS1,
New York

2002
documenta 11, Kassel

2003
8th Istanbul Biennale
50th Venice Biennale

2004
Experiments With Truth, The Fabric
Workshop and Museum, Philadelphia
*In Our Time, Works from the Moderna
Museet Collection*, Moderna Museet,
Stockholm

2005
*50 Jahre / Years documenta: 1955
– 2005*, Kassel, Kunsthalle Fridericianum
British Art Show 6, BALTIC, Gateshead,
and touring UK

2006
*How to Improve the World: 60 Years
of British Art*, Hayward Gallery, London
15th Biennale of Sydney
*Snap Judgments: New Positions in
Contemporary African Photography*,
International Center of Photography,
New York

2007
Turner Prize 2007, Tate Liverpool

2008
3rd Guangzhou Triennial

2009
Capturing Time, Kadist Art Foundation,
Paris
Out of Blue, The Art Institute of Chicago

2010
29th Bienal de São Paulo
Who Knows Tomorrow, Nationalgalerie
im Hamburger Bahnhof, Berlin

2011
*HE DISAPPEARED INTO COMPLETE
SILENCE*, De Hallen Museum, Haarlem
*Pandemonium: Art in a Time of Creativity
Fever*, Göteburg International Biennial

2014
Prospect.3: Notes for Now, New Orleans
Paradise Lost, NTU Centre for Contemporary
Art, Singapore

2015
Poetics of Relations, Perez Art Museum,
Miami

2017
The Place is Here, Nottingham Contempo-
rary; Middlesbrough Institute of Modern Art;
South London Gallery, London

2018
The Fabric of Felicity, Garage Museum
of Contemporary Art, Moscow

2019
Here We Are Today, Bucerius Kunst Forum,
Hamburg

2020
Lahore Biennale 02

Ansuya Blom
Born in Groningen, Netherlands, 1956.
Lives in Amsterdam

Selected Solo Exhibitions
1991
Scanning, Deweer Art Gallery, Otegem,
Belgium

1992
Galerie van Gelder, Amsterdam

1993
Associated Publishers, Amsterdam

1994
Ikon Gallery, Birmingham

1998
Galerie van Gelder, Amsterdam

2001
Stedelijk Museum Schiedam

2002
House of Invertebrates, AP, Amsterdam

2004
Tintinnabulation, Galerie van Gelder,
Amsterdam

2005
The Paradise Project, The Douglas Hyde
Gallery, Dublin

2008
The Fall, Galerie van Gelder, Amsterdam

2009
The Fall, Fred Gallery, London

2014
Through Shutters, Galerie van Gelder,
Amsterdam

Selected Group Exhibitions
1989
*Amsterdam Art-Regards: designs
contemporains*, Institut Néerlandais, Paris
30 Anni de Disegni, Instituto Universitario
Olandese di Storia dell'Arte, Florence

1992
The Last Rose of Summer, Gallery Wanda
Reiff, Amsterdam
Art for ASAP, Beurs van Berlage, Amsterdam

1993
Avant-garde Films From The Netherlands,
Cinematheek, Brussels
The Return of the Cadavre Exquis,
The Drawing Center, New York

1994
I Find Your Work Very Interesting,
Wetering Galerie, Amsterdam

1996
The Eye as a Welding Machine, Stedelijk
Museum Schiedam, Netherlands

1997
The Wedding Report, Centraal Museum,
Utrecht
One Line Drawings, Ubu Gallery, New York

1998
27th International Filmfestival, Rotterdam
Lines of Desire, Bluecoat, Liverpool

1999
Lie of the Land: Earth Body and Material,
John Hansard Gallery, Southampton;
Arnolfini, Bristol

2000
Flash, Contemporary Art Centre, Vilnius

2001
Grinding differently!, Smart Projects,
Amsterdam

2002
Line = Shape = Content. Works on Paper,
Stadsgalerij Heerlen, Netherlands
Transformer, Porin Taidemuseo, Pori, Finland

2003
Nightwood, Rhodes and Mann, London
Until Now, Stedelijk Museum, Amsterdam
The Seven Year Itch, Stedelijk Museum
Schiedam
The Portable Museum, Centre for
Contemporary Art, Dordrecht, Netherlands
Flash, Listasafn, Reykjavíkur Hafnarhús,
Reykjavik

2005
Green Film Festival, Seoul
Cross Art, Kunsthalle Bonn, Germany

2006
Kosmopolis 06, Centre de Cultura
Contemporània de Barcelona
The Projection Project, MuKHA, Antwerp

2007
Lucassen's Choice, Ramakers Gallery,
The Hague
*Art From House III, Armando Collects
and Draws*, Stedelijk Museum Schiedam

2008
*Prospects and Interiors: Sculptors'
Drawings of Inner Space*, Henry Moore
Institute, Leeds

2009
Rencontres Internationales, Haus der
Kulturen der Welt, Berlin

2010
*Remember Me – About Death and
Memory*, Museum Arnhem, Netherlands

2011
All About Drawing. 100 Dutch Artists,
Stedelijk Museum Schiedam, Netherlands
Contemporary Classic, Allard Pierson
Museum, Amsterdam

2012
To Make a Show It Takes a Thought …,
Galerie van Gelder, Amsterdam
30 Days of Peace, Love and Painting,
Ellen de Bruijne Projects, Amsterdam

2013
International Film Festival Rotterdam,
Netherlands
AAA Festival, Stedelijk Museum, Amsterdam
This and That and That, Galerie van Gelder,
Amsterdam

2014
De Keuze van Lucassen, Nouvelles Images,
The Hague
AD XL, New Dakota, Amsterdam
Dark Rooms, Museum Dr Ghislain, Ghent

Adam Chodzko
Born in London, 1965. Lives in Whitstable

Selected Solo Exhibitions
1996
Lotta Hammer, London

1998
Galleria Franco Noero, Turin
Northern Gallery of Contemporary Art,
Sunderland

1999
Ikon Gallery, Birmingham

2002
Arizona State University Art Museum, Tempe
Plains Art Museum, Fargo
Cubitt, London

2007
Signal, Malmö
Then, Dublin City Gallery The Hugh Lane
MAMbo, Bologna

2008
Proxigean Tide, Tate St Ives

2013
You'll See; This Time it'll be Different,
Benaki Museum, Athens
We are Ready for your Arrival, Raven
Row, London

2015
Channel, Rupture, Beppu Triennial, Japan
Great Expectations, Guildhall Museum,
Rochester

Selected Group Exhibitions
1991
City Racing, London

1993
Making People Disappear, Cubitt, London

1995
Zombie Golf, Bank, London
General Release, Scoula San Pasquale,
Venice Biennale
Brilliant, Walker Arts Center, Minneapolis

1997
Sensation, Royal Academy of Arts, London;
Museum für Gegenwart, Berlin; Brooklyn
Museum, New York

1998
Wrapped, Vestjælands Kunstmuseum, Sorø,
Denmark

2000
Artifice, Deste Foundation, Athens

2001
1st Auckland Triennial

2003
Electric Earth, The State Russian Museum,
St Petersburg
Micro/Macro: British Art 1996–2002,
Mucsarnok Kunsthalle, Budapest
Independence, South London Gallery,
London

2004
Romantic Detachment, PS1, New York

2005
Documentary Creations, Kunstmuseum
Luzern
Monuments for the USA, CCA Wattis
Institute for Contemporary Arts, San
Francisco; White Columns, New York
British Art Show 6, BALTIC, Gateshead,
and touring UK

2006
Belief and Doubt, Aspen Art Museum,
Colorado

2007
Breaking Step, Museum of Contemporary
Art, Belgrade

2008
Martian Museum of Terrestrial Art, Barbican
Centre, London
Tales of Time and Space, Folkestone
Sculpture Triennial

2009
Dark Monarch, Tate St Ives; Towner Gallery,
Eastbourne
Journeys with No Return, Akbank Art
Centre, Istanbul
Plot 09: This World & Nearer Ones,
Governors Island, New York
Athens Biennale

2012
In the Belly of the Whale Part III,
Montehermoso, Vitoria-Gasteiz, Spain

2013
*Assembly: A Survey of Recent Artists'
Film and Video in Britain 2008–2013*,
Tate Britain, London
How is it towards the East?, Calvert 22,
London
Schwitters in Britain, Tate Britain, London

2014
Somewhat Abstract, Nottingham
Contemporary
*Private Utopia: Contemporary Art from
the British Council Collection*, Tokyo Station
Gallery; Itami City Museum of Art; Kochi
Museum of Art; Okayama Museum of Art,
Japan

2015
Postcard Views, 1 Shantiroad, Bangalore
Sculpture in the City, Leadenhall Market,
London

2016
Estuary 2016, Essex

2019
*24/7: A Wake-Up Call for our Non-Stop
World*, Somerset House, London
Being Human (permanent exhibition),
Wellcome Collection, London

2020
Towner International, Eastbourne
Die Sonne Does Not Shine Like Słońce,
Trafostacja Sztuki, Szczecin, Poland
The Botanical Mind, Camden Art Centre,
London
Essex Road VI, TINTYPE, London

Juan Davila
Born in Santiago de Chile, 1946. Lives
in Melbourne

Selected Solo Exhibitions
1991
Centre for Contemporary Art of South
Australia, Adelaide

1994–95
Juanito Laguna, Chisenhale Gallery,
London; Ikon Gallery, Birmingham; Tolarno
Galleries, Melbourne

1998
Verdeja, Project Room, ARCO 98,
Greenaway Art Gallery, Madrid

2000
Greenaway Art Gallery, Adelaide

2001
The Ruins of Adelaide, Greenaway Art
Gallery, Adelaide

2002
Works 1988–2002, Australian National
University Drill Hall Gallery, Canberra

2006
Retrospective, MCA, Sydney; National
Gallery of Victoria, Melbourne

2009
A Panorama of Melbourne, Cowen
Gallery, State Library of Victoria, Melbourne

2011
The Moral Meaning of Wilderness, Griffith
University Art Gallery, Brisbane; Monash
University Museum of Art, Melbourne
Paintings at BLOC, BLOC, Santiago de Chile

2013
*A Man Renounces Love, Wagner Ring
Cycle*, Arts Centre Melbourne

2018
pintura y ambigüedad, Museo de Arte
Contemporáneo de Castilla y León, Spain

Selected Group Exhibitions
1984
5th Biennale of Sydney

1990
Transcontinental, Ikon Gallery, Birmingham;
Cornerhouse, Manchester
Add Magic, a Billboard Project, Australian
Centre for Photography, Sydney

1991
Blue Chip, The Instant Decorator, Tolarno
Galleries, Melbourne
4th Havana Biennial

1992
America, Bride of the Sun, Royal Fine Arts
Museum, Antwerp
My Head is a Map, Australian National
Gallery, Canberra
You Are Here, Institute of Modern Art,
Brisbane

1993
You Are Here, ACCA, Melbourne
Currents '93 Dress Codes, ICA, Boston
Dislocations, National Gallery of Victoria,
Melbourne
*Art from Latin America, La Cita
Transcultural*, MCA, Sydney
States of Loss, Jersey City Museum,
New Jersey

1994
Unbound: Possibilities in Painting, Hayward
Gallery, London
Cocido y Crudo, Museo Nacional Centro de
Arte Reina Sofia, Madrid
*Don't Leave Me This Way: Art in the Age
of AIDS*, Australian National Gallery,
Canberra

1997
Power, Corruption and Lies, Institute of
Modern Art, Brisbane
1st Bienal de Artes Visuales del Mercosur,
Porto Alegre, Brazil

1999
On the Road, the Car in Australian Art,
Heide Museum of Modern Art, Melbourne

163

2002
Icon Interior, Howard Arkley and Juan Davila, Drill Hall Gallery, Australian National University, Canberra

2006
Arte Contemporaneo Chile: Desde el Otro Sitio/Lugar, National Museum of Contemporary Art, Seoul; Museo de Arte Contemporaneo, Santiago de Chile
Pie de Pagina, Fundacion Cultural Gil de Castro, Plaza Mulato, Santiago de Chile

2007
documenta 12, Kassel
Andy and Oz: Parallel Visions, The Andy Warhol Museum, Pittsburgh

2013
Mix Tape, National Gallery of Victoria, Melbourne
Melbourne Now, National Gallery of Victoria, Melbourne

2015
Hysterical Tears, Institute of Modern Art, Brisbane

2015–16
Asia Pacific Triennial of Contemporary Art – APT8, Queensland Art Gallery | Gallery of Modern Art, Brisbane, Australia

2016
Painting More Painting, ACCA, Melbourne

2017
Every Brilliant Eye, Australian Art of the 1990s, National Gallery of Victoria, Melbourne

2018
The Shape of Things to Come, Buxton Contemporary, Melbourne
38th EVA International
Intimacy, Activism and AIDS, Tate Modern, London

Mark Dion
Born in New Bedford, USA, 1961. Lives in Copake

Selected Solo Exhibitions
1994
When Dinosaurs Ruled the Earth (Toys 'R' U.S.), American Fine Arts, Co., New York

1995
American Fine Arts, Co., New York

1997
Natural History and Other Fictions, Ikon Gallery, Birmingham; Kunstverein Hamburg

1998
Tate Thames Dig (*Two Banks*), Tate Gallery, London

2004
Projects 82, Rescue Archaeology, A Project for The Museum of Modern Art, MoMA, New York

2006
Microcosmographia and the Secret Garden Biological Field Unit, South London Gallery, London

2007
Systema Metropolis, Natural History Museum, London

2014
The Lost Museum: A Project of the Jenks Society, Department of Social Humanities, Brown University, Providence, USA

2017
ExtraNaturel: Voyage initiatique dans la collection des Beaux-Arts de Paris, Palais des Beaux-Arts, Paris
Scandinavian Pavilion, 57th Venice Biennale

2018
Theatre of the Natural World, Whitechapel Gallery, London

Selected Group Exhibitions
1987
Fake, New Museum, New York
The Castle, Fridericianum, Kassel

1989
Here and There: Travels, Part II: Sad Travels, PS1, New York
The Desire of the Museum, Whitney Museum of American Art, New York
Le Magasin L'École L'Exposition, Le Magasin, Grenoble

1990
The (Un)Making of Nature, Whitney Museum of American Art, New York

1992
True Stories: Part II, ICA, London

1994
Crudo, Museo Nacional Centro de Arte Reina Sofia, Madrid

1996
Multiple Pleasure, Tanya Bonakdar Gallery, New York
100 Photographs, American Fine Arts, Co., New York
Hybrids, De Appel, Amsterdam
The Crude and the Rare, 41 Cooper Gallery, The Cooper Union, New York

1997
The Spiral Village, Bonnefanten Museum, Maastricht
Nordic Pavilion, 47th Venice Biennale

1998
The Sound of One Hand: The Collection of Collier Schorr, Apex Art C.P., New York

1999
The Museum as Muse, MoMA, New York

2000
The Greenhouse Effect, Serpentine Gallery, London
Crossing the Line, The Queens Museum of Art, New York

2002
Play's the Thing: Critical and Transgressive Practices in Contemporary Art, Whitney Museum of American Art, New York

2008
In Stock—uit stock, Galerie Tanya Rumpff, Haarlem
16th Biennale of Sydney
Underkammer: A Century of Curiosities, MoMA, New York

2009
Radical Nature: Art and Architecture for a Changing Planet 1969–2009, Barbican Centre, London; Dick Institute, Kilmarnock, Scotland
Classified, Tate Modern, London

2010
The Traveling Show, Museo Jumex, Mexico City

2011
The Luminous Interval: An Exhibition of the D.Daskalopoulos Collection, Guggenheim Museum Bilbao, Spain

2012
La Triennale: Intense Proximité, Palais de Tokyo, Paris

2013
Le Surréalisme et l'objet – La sculpture au défi, Centre Pompidou, Paris
The Way of the Shovel: Art as Archaeology, Museum of Contemporary Art Chicago
EXPO 1: New York, MoMA PS1, New York

2016
Don't Look Back: The 1990's at MOCA, The Geffen Contemporary at MOCA, Los Angeles

2017
15ᵗʰ Istanbul Biennial
Dioramas, Palais de Tokyo, Paris

Eugenio Dittborn
Born in Santiago de Chile, 1943.
Lives in Santiago de Chile

Selected Solo Exhibitions
1993
La Casa de Erasmo de Rotterdam, Witte de With Center for Contemporary Art, Rotterdam

1993–94
Mapa, John Hansard Gallery, Southampton; City Gallery Wellington, New Zealand

1994–95
Transmission Gallery, Glasgow

1997
Remota, New Museum, New York

1998
Taciturna (recent and non-recent airmail paintings), Alexander and Bonin, New York

2010
Museo De Artes Visuales, Santiago de Chile

2013
Your Letters. Pinturas Aeropostales 1986–2012, Museum Het Domein, Sittard, Netherlands

2014
Pinturas Aeropostales, KOW, Berlin

2015
Las Dos, Galeria Macchina, Pontificia Universidad Catolica de Chile, Santiago de Chile

2020
Airmail Paintings, Goldsmiths Centre for Contemporary Art, London

Selected Group Exhibitions
1990
Transcontinental, Ikon Gallery, Birmingham; Cornerhouse, Manchester

1992
documenta IX, Kassel
The Absent Body, ICA, Boston

1992–93
Latin American Artists of the 20th Century, MoMA, New York; Estacion Plaza de Armas, Seville; Hotel des Arts, Paris; Museum Ludwig, Cologne

1997
2nd Johannesburg Biennale

2000
Around 1984: A Look at Art in the Eighties, PS1, New York
Más Allá del Documento, Museo Nacional Centro de Arte Reina Sofia, Madrid
3rd Gwanju Biennale

2001
Going Places, SMART Project Space, Amsterdam
Total Object Complete with Missing Parts, Tramway, Glasgow
Lugares de la Memoria, Espai d'Art Contemporani de Castelló, Spain

2003
Traces of Friday. Art, Tourism, Displacement, ICA, Philadelphia

2004
26th Bienal de São Paulo
Faces in the Crowd: The Modern Figure and Avant-Garde Realism, Whitechapel Gallery, London; Castello di Rivoli Museo d'Arte Contemporanea, Turin

2005
Classified Materials: Accumulations, Archives, Artists, Vancouver Art Gallery

2006
The 80s: A Topology, Museu Serralves, Porto
If It Didn't Exist You'd Have to Invent It: A Partial Showroom History, The Showroom, London

2008
BAGHDAD/ SPACE COG/ ANALYST, Frith Street Gallery, London

2009
Ordinary Revolutions: Contemporary Latin American Art, Museum Morsbroich, Leverkusen, Germany
9th Sharjah Biennial

2010
The Traveling Show, Museo Jumex, Mexico City

2010–11
América Latina: arte y confrontación, 1910–2010, Museo del Palacio de Bellas Artes, Mexico City

2011
8ᵗʰ Mercosul Biennial

2012
7th Liverpool Biennial
Printin', MoMA, New York
This Will Have Been: Art, Love, & Politics in the 1980s, Museum of Contemporary Art Chicago; Walker Art Center, Minneapolis; ICA, Boston

2013
Xerography, Firstsite, Colchester

2014
Unbound: Contemporary Art After Frida Kahlo, Museum of Contemporary Art Chicago

2014–16
Art from Elsewhere, Gallery of Modern Art, Glasgow; Bristol Museum & Art Gallery

2017
As If Sand Were Stone: Latin American Contemporary Art, Art Gallery of Ontario, Toronto

2018
The Matter of Photography in the AmerICA, Cantor Arts Center, Stanford University

2019–20
Crossing Lines, Constructing Home: Displacement and Belonging in Contemporary Art, Harvard Art Museums, Cambridge, USA

Rose Finn-Kelcey
Born Northampton, 1945. Died 2014

Selected Solo Exhibitions
1976
One for Sorrow Two for Joy, London Calling, Acme Gallery, London

1977
(with H Walton) *Her Mistress's Voice*,
The Eisteddfod, Wrexham, Wales

1978
(with Tina Keane) *Book and Pillow,* Galleria
del Cavallino, Venice

1980
Mind the Gap, About Time, ICA, London;
Franklin Furnace, New York

1982
Cut-Out, 4th Symposium of Performance Art,
Lyon, Gallerie L'Ollave, Lyon

1983
Glory, Serpentine Gallery, London

1984
*Black and Blue – The Button Pusher's
View of Paradise*, Matt's Gallery, London

1985
Bull's Eye,The British Show, Gallery of
New South Wales, Sydney; EAF Foundation,
Adelaide; Performance Space, Melbourne,
Australia
(with H Walton and Nirrup) *Ascending
Order*, The British Art Show, Royal Scottish
Academy, Edinburgh

1988
Bureau de Change, Matt's Gallery, London

1992
Steam Installation, Chisenhale Gallery,
London

1993
Galerie l'Ollave, Lyon

1994
Just Minus, The British School at Rome
(with Donald Rodney) *Truth, Dare,
Double-Dare …* Ikon Gallery, Birmingham

1997
Camden Art Centre, London

2004
Angel, St Paul's Church, Bow, London

2006
Milton Keynes Gallery

2017
Life, Belief and Beyond, Modern Art
Oxford

2018
Power for the People, Firstsite, Colchester

2019
*Truth, Dare, Double-Dare … by Rose
Finn-Kelcey and Donald G Rodney, 1994.*
Part of *On Allyship*, ICA, London.

2020
Works 1971–2001, Kate MacGarry, London

Selected Group Exhibitions
1977
*International Exhibition of Women Artists:
100 Years of Women's Art*, Charlottenburg
Palace, Berlin

1986
The Window Box, AIR Gallery, London

1988
Rhetorical Image, New Museum, New York

1989
The Suitcase Show, Harris Museum and Art
Gallery, Preston; Aberdeen City Art Gallery;
Wolverhampton Art Gallery

1990
Signs of the Times, Museum of Modern Art
Oxford

1991
Shocks to the System, Royal Festival Hall,
London; Northern Centre for Contemporary
Art, Sunderland; Ikon Gallery, Birmingham;
Chapter Arts Centre, Cardiff; Royal Albert
Memorial Museum, Exeter; Plymouth City
Museum and Art Gallery; Maclaurin Art
Gallery, Ayr, Scotland

1992
documenta IX, Kassel

1993
Young British Artists Part 2, The Saatchi
Gallery, London

1998
*Out of Actions: Between Performance and
the Object 1949–1979*, MOCA, Los Angeles

1997
Through the Viewfinder, Stichting de Appel,
Amsterdam

2000
*Live in Your Head: Concept and
Experiment in Britain 1965–75*,
Whitechapel Gallery, London; Museo de
Chiado, Lisbon

2001
House Rules, The Multiple Store, numerous
venues including Tate Gallery, Liverpool, Ikon
Gallery, Birmingham and Brooke Alexander
Gallery, New York

2005
Size Matters, Longside Gallery, Yorkshire
Sculpture Park, Wakefield; Millais Gallery,
Southampton

2006
*How to Improve the World: 60 Years of
British Art*, Hayward Gallery, London

2011
Modern British Sculpture, Royal Academy
of Arts, London
Re.act Feminism #2, Centro Cultural
Montehermoso, Victoria-Gasteiz, Spain

2014
Interchange Junctions, Howick Place,
London
*Keywords: Art, Culture & Society in 1980s
Britain*, Tate Liverpool

2017
IT IS JUST A BEGINNING, National Gallery
of Modern and Contemporary Art, Rome

2021
*Breaking the Mould, Sculpture by Women
since 1945*, Ferens Art Gallery, Hull;
Djanogly Art Gallery, Nottingham; Lakeside
Arts, Nottingham

Ellen Gallagher
Born in Providence, USA, 1965. Lives in
Rotterdam and New York

Selected Solo Exhibitions
1998
Ikon Gallery, Birmingham

2001–02
Watery Ecstatic, ICA, Boston; MCA, Sydney
Preserve, Des Moines Art Center; Yerba
Buena Center for the Arts, San Francisco;
Drawing Center, New York

2003
POMP-BANG, Saint Louis Art Museum

2004–05
Orbus, Fruitmarket Gallery, Edinburgh

2005
DeLuxe, Whitney Museum of American Art,
New York
Ichthyosaurus, Freud Museum, London
Murmur and DeLuxe, Museum of
Contemporary Art, Miami

2007
Coral Cities, Tate Liverpool; Dublin City
Gallery The Hugh Lane

2009
An Experiment of Unusual Opportunity,
South London Gallery, London
Moby Dick, CCA Wattis Institute for
Contemporary Arts, San Francisco

2013
Don't Axe Me, New Museum, New York

2013–14
AxME, Tate Modern, London; Sara Hildén Art
Museum, Tampere, Finland; Haus der Kunst,
Munich

2014
Haus de Kunst, Munich

2018
Are We Obsidian?, Art Institute of Chicago
Nu-Nile, The Power Plant, Toronto

2019
(with Edgar Cleijne) *Liquid Intelligence*,
WIELS, Contemporary Art Centre, Brussels

Selected Group Exhibitions
1992
Word and Image, Boston Public Library

1993
Traveling Scholars' Exhibit, Museum of Fine
Arts, Boston

1994
In Context, ICA, Boston

1995
Whitney Biennial, New York

1996
Inside the Visible, ICA, Boston; Whitechapel
Gallery, London; Art Gallery of Western
Australia, Perth; National Museum of Women
in the Arts, Washington, DC

1997
Projects, Irish Museum of Modern Art, Dublin

1998
Postcards from Black America, De Beyerd
Center for Contemporary Art, Breda,
Netherlands

1999
(Corps) Social, École Nationale Supérieure
des Beaux-Arts, Paris

2000
*Strength and Diversity: A Celebration of
African American Artists*, Carpenter Center
for the Visual Arts, Harvard University,
Cambridge, USA

2003
50th Venice Biennale

2005–06
Drawing From the Modern, 1975–2005,
MoMA, New York

2006
Heart of Darkness, Walker Art Center,
Minneapolis

2007
Passages from History, Tate Modern, London

2008
Eclipse. Art in a Dark Age, Moderna
Museet, Stockholm

2009
Medals of Dishonour, British Museum,
London

2010
*Afro Modern: Journeys through the Black
Atlantic*, Tate Liverpool

2012
La Triennale: Intense Proximité, Palais de
Tokyo, Paris

2013
The Shadows Took Shape, The Studio
Museum in Harlem, New York

2015
56th Venice Biennale
FOUND, New Art Gallery Walsall
How to Construct a Time Machine, MK
Gallery, Milton Keynes
14th Istanbul Biennial

2016
*The Color Line: African-American Artists
and Civil Rights*, Musée du Quai Branly,
Paris

2017
Elements of Vogue, Centro de Arte Dos de
Mayo, Madrid
A Global Table, Frans Hals Museum, Haarlem

2018
*Posing Modernity: The Black Model from
Manet to Matisse and Beyond*, Wallach
Art Gallery, Columbia University, New York;
Musée d'Orsay, Paris

2021
*sonsbeek20→24: Force Times Distance
– On Labour and its Sonic Ecologies*,
Arnhem, Netherlands

Antony Gormley
Born in London, 1950. Lives in London

Selected Solo Exhibitions
1981
Whitechapel Gallery, London
Serpentine Gallery, London

1986
Salvatore Ala Gallery, New York
Drawings, Victoria Miro Gallery, London

1987
Five Works, Serpentine Gallery, London

1988
Contemporary Sculpture Centre, Tokyo
The Holbeck Sculpture, Leeds Art Gallery

1989
Louisiana Museum of Modern Art,
Copenhagen; Scottish National Gallery of
Modern Art, Edinburgh

1991
American Field and Other Figures,
Modern Art Museum, Fort Worth, USA

1992
American Field, Centro Cultural Arte
Contemporáneo, Mexico City; San Diego
Museum of Contemporary Art; Corcoran
Gallery of Art, Washington DC; Montreal
Museum of Fine Arts, Canada
Learning to Think, The British School at Rome

1993
Malmö Konsthall, Sweden; Tate Liverpool;
Irish Museum of Modern Art, Dublin

1994
Lost Subject, White Cube, London

1995
Kohji Ogura Gallery, Nagoya, Japan
Critical Mass, Remise, Vienna

1996
Inside the Inside, Galerie Xavier Hufkens,
Brussels
Field for the British Isles, Hayward Gallery,
London; Ikon Gallery, Birmingham

1998
Angel of the North, The Gallery, Central
Library, Gateshead
Critical Mass, Royal Academy of Arts,
London

1999
Intimate Relations, MacClaren Art Centre,
Barrie, Canada
European Field, Malmö Konsthall

2001
Contemporary Sculpture Centre, Tokyo
Some of the Facts, Tate St. Ives

2002
Drawing, British Museum, London

2003
Domain Field, BALTIC, Gateshead

2004
Asian Field, Guangdong Museum,
Guangzhou
Unform, Yale Centre for British Art, New Haven
Tate Britain, London

2005
Field for the British Isles, Longside Gallery,
Yorkshire Sculpture Park, Wakefield
Asian Field, ICA Singapore

2006
Parco and Museo di Scolacium, Catanzaro,
Italy
Critical Mass, Museo d'Arte Contemporanea
Donna Regina, Naples

2007
Blind Light, Hayward Gallery, London

2008
Between You and Me, Kunsthal Rotterdam;
Musée d'Art Moderne de Saint-Etienne
Metropole, France

2009
Garage Museum of Contemporary Art,
Moscow
One and Other, Fourth Plinth, Trafalgar
Square, London

2010
Critical Mass II, De La Warr Pavilion,
Bexhill-on-Sea
Event Horizon, Madison Square Park,
New York

2012
Horizon Field, Deichtorhallen, Hamburg

2014
Expansion Field, Zentrum Paul Klee, Bern

2015
Space Stations, Hatton Gallery, Newcastle
upon Tyne

2016
Object, National Portrait Gallery, London

2017
Another Time, Bordeaux

2018
Subject, Kettle's Yard, Cambridge

2019
Royal Academy of Arts, London

Selected Group Exhibitions
1981
British Sculpture in the 20th Century,
Whitechapel Gallery, London
Objects and Sculpture, ICA, London;
Arnolfini, Bristol

1982
Figures and Objects, John Hansard Gallery,
Southampton; Fruitmarket Gallery, Edinburgh
Contemporary Choices, Serpentine Gallery,
London

1983
New Art, Tate Gallery, London
Tongue and Groove, Coracle Press, London;
St. Paul's Gallery, Leeds; Ferens Art Gallery,
Hull
Portland Clifftop Sculpture, Camden Art
Centre, London

1985
Walking and Falling, Plymouth Arts Centre;
Kettle's Yard, Cambridge; Interim Art, London

1984
Camden Art Centre, London
From the Figure, Ikon Gallery, Birmingham

1986
42nd Venice Biennale

1987
documenta 8, Kassel

1988
Made to Measure, Kettle's Yard, Cambridge
*Starlit Waters: British Sculpture 1968–
1988*, Tate Liverpool

1991
Inheritance and Transformation, Irish
Museum of Modern Art, Dublin

1993
The Raw and the Cooked, Barbican Centre,
London; Museum of Modern Art Oxford;
Glynn Vivian Art Gallery, Swansea; The
Shigaraki Ceramic Cultural Park, Japan

1994
Turner Prize, Tate Gallery, London

1995
Gwangju Biennale

1998
L'Empreinte, Centre Pompidou, Paris

2000
3rd Gwangju Biennale
Enclosed and Enchanted, Museum of
Modern Art Oxford; Mappin Art Gallery,
Sheffield
Conversation, Milton Keynes Gallery

2002
Blast to Freeze, Kunstmuseum Wolfsburg,
Germany
*Self-Evident: Making the Self the Subject
of Art from 1970 to the Present Day*, Tate
Britain, London

2003
Independence, South London Gallery

2004
*A Secret History of Clay: From Gauguin
to Gormley*, Tate Liverpool

2006
*Sixty Years of Sculpture in the Arts
Council Collection*, Longside Gallery,
Yorkshire Sculpture Park, Wakefield

2008
*Fourth Plinth Commission: The New
Proposals*, National Gallery, London
Space to Draw, Jerwood Space, London

2012
Fourth Plinth: Contemporary Monument,
ICA, London

2015
Self, Turner Contemporary, Margate

2017
Folkestone Triennial
Rodin: L'Exposition du Centenaire, Grand Palais, Paris

2019
Pompei e Santorini: l'eternità in un giorno, Scuderie del Quirinale, Rome

Victor Grippo
Born in Junín, Argentina, 1936. Died 2002

Selected Solo Exhibitions
1966
Lirolay Gallery, Buenos Aires

1972
Analogy IV, MoMA, New York

1976
Algunos oficios, Galería Artemúltiple, Buenos Aires

1977
14th Bienal de São Paulo

1990
Cornerhouse, Manchester

1991
Fawbush Projects, New York

1994
Energía 1971–1994, Museo de Arte Carrillo Gil, Mexico City

1995
Ikon Gallery, Birmingham; Palais des Beaux-Arts, Brussels

2006
Works 1971–2001, Miami Art Central
Table of Work and Reflection, Camden Art Centre, London
Selected Works 1978–2001, Alexander and Bonin, New York

2013–14
Transformation, Centro Gallego de Arte Contemporánea, Santiago de Chile

2019
Sculpture and Drawings 1955–2001, Alexander and Bonin, New York

Selected Group Exhibitions
1960
Exposición de la colección Alperte, Peña de Arte, Buenos Aires

1962
11 expresiones de la plástica actual, Galería Arte Nuevo, Buenos Aires

1969
6th Biennale des Jeunes, Musée d'Art Moderne de Paris

1973
Art and Ideology in Latin America, Galerie Paramedia, Berlin

1977
VII Encuentro Internacional de Video y Coloquio de la Comunicación, Fundació Joan Miró, Barcelona
14th Bienal de São Paulo

1985
Brainwork, Artificial Intelligence in the Arts, Steirischer Herbst, Graz; Municipal Art Gallery, Los Angeles

1986
42nd Venice Biennale

1992
Artistas latinoamericanos del siglo XX, Sevilla Plaza de Armas, Spain
Latin American Artists of the Twentieth Century, MoMA, New York

1993
CAYC Group, Striped House Museum of Art, Tokyo

1994
Arte argentino contemporáneo, Museo Nacional de Bellas Artes, Fundación Arte y Technología, Madrid
Art from Argentina: 1920–1994, Museum of Modern Art Oxford; Sudwestdeutsche Landesbank, Stuttgart; Royal College of Art Galleries, London; Fundação das Descobertas, Centro Cultural de Belém, Lisbon; Fundación para las Artes-Centro Borges, Buenos Aires

1996
Inklusion – Exklusion. Kunst im Zeitalter von Postkolonialismus und Global Migration, Reininghaus, Graz

1997
A Quality of Light, Tate St. Ives

1998
Wounds: Between Democracy and Redemption in Contemporary Art, Moderna Museet, Stockholm

1999
Cantos Paralelos. Visual Parody in Contemporary Argentinean Art, Jack S. Blanton Museum of Art, Austin; Phoenix Art Museum; Biblioteca Centro Cultural Luis Ángel Arango, Bogotá

1999–2001
Global Conceptualism: Points of Origin 1950s–1980s, Queens Museum of Art, New York; Walker Art Center, Minneapolis; Miami Art Museum; MIT List Visual Arts Center, Cambridge, USA, Vancouver Art Gallery

2000
Beyond Preconceptions: The Sixties Experiment, Collection of Modern and Contemporary Art of the National Gallery, Prague; Zacheta National Gallery of Contemporary Art, Warsaw; Museo de Arte Moderno de Buenos Aires; Fundação Armando Alvarez Penteado, São Paulo; Berkeley Art Museum

2001
Antagonismos, MACBA, Barcelona
Da adversidade vivemos, Musée d'Art Moderne de la Ville de Paris

2002
documenta 11, Kassel

2007
New Perspectives on Latin American Art 1930–2006, MoMA, New York

2008
Arte ≠ Vida: Actions by Artists of the AmerICA, 1960–2000, El Museo del Barrio, New York

2008–09
Here Is Every. Four Decades of Contemporary Art, MoMA, New York

2009
Horizonte Expandido, Santander Cultural, Porto Alegre, Brazil

2010–12
Animism: Modernity through the Looking Glass, Extra City Kunsthal Antwerpen; the Museum van Hedendaagse Kunst Antwerpen; Kunsthalle Bern; Generali Foundation, Vienna; Haus der Kulturen der Welt, Berlin

2013
*Open Work in Latin America, New York
& Beyond: Conceptualism Reconsidered,
1967–1978*, Hunter College, New York

2015
Museum of Fine Arts, Houston
*Geometries On and Off the Grid: Art
from 1950 to the Present*, The Warehouse,
Dallas
*Dark Mirror. Art from Latin America Since
1968*, Kunstmuseum Wolfsburg

2017
Museum of Contemporary Art, San Diego

Graham Gussin
Born in London, 1960. Lives in London

Selected Solo Exhibitions
1993
Chisenhale Gallery, London

1997
Camden Art Centre, London

1998
Art Now, Tate Britain, London

2001
States of Mind, New Museum, New York

2002
Ikon Gallery, Birmingham

2004
Centre d'Art Santa Monica, Barcelona

2006
Spill, Ikon Eastside, Birmingham

2008
Solar, Galeria de Arte Cinematica, Vila do
Conde, Portugal

2012
In and Out, Back and Forth, New Art
Centre, Salisbury
Animated Environments, Siobhan Davies
Studios, London

2013
CLEARBLUESKYDEEPDARKWATER, Centro
Galego de Arte Contemporánea, Santiago
de Compostela, Spain

2014
FORSAKENFOCUSVERTIGOPREDICTION,
Marlborough Contemporary, London

Selected Group Exhibitions
2000
Intelligence: New British Art 2000, Tate
Britain, London

2000–01
The British Art Show 5, Inverleith House,
Royal Botanical Gardens, Edinburgh;
Southampton City Art Gallery, Southampton;
National Museum of Wales, Cardiff; Ikon
Gallery, Birmingham; Birmingham Museum
and Art Gallery

2003
The Distance Between Me and You, Lisson
Gallery, London

2006
One Year, One Second, Palais de Tokyo,
Paris

2007
8th Sharjah Biennial

2009
*Sequelism Part 3: Possible, Probable
or Preferable Futures*, Arnolfini, Bristol
À la surface de l'infini, La Galerie, Centre
d'art Contemporain, Noisy-le-sec, Paris

2010
*Never The Same River (Possible Futures,
Probable Pasts)*, Camden Art Centre,
London
Cage Mix, BALTIC, Gateshead

2011
As If, Art House Foundation, London
Illumination Rig, Turner Contemporary,
Margate

2012
4th Guangzhou Triennial
The Space Between, Tate Britain, London

2017
BIENALSUR, 1st International Biennial of
Contemporary Art of South America
Neo-Geometry, New Art Centre, Salisbury

2018
Criminal Ornamentation, Attenborough
Arts Centre, Leicester; Royal Albert Memorial
Museum, Exeter; Longside Gallery, Yorkshire
Sculpture Park, Wakefield; Southampton City
Art Gallery

Callum Innes
Born in Edinburgh, 1962. Lives in Edinburgh
and Oslo

Selected Solo Exhibitions
1992
ICA, London
Scottish National Gallery of Modern Art,
Edinburgh

1995
Mackintosh Gallery, Glasgow School of Art

1996
Callum Innes (1990–1996), Inverleith
House, Royal Botanic Garden, Edinburgh

1997
Kunsthaus, Zürich

1998
Ikon Gallery, Birmingham

1999
Irish Museum of Modern Art, Dublin
Kunsthalle, Bern

2005
Resonance, Tate St Ives

2006
From Memory, Fruitmarket Gallery,
Edinburgh; Modern Art Oxford; MCA,
Sydney

2013
Malerei als Prozess, Neues Museum
Staatliches Museum für Kunst, Nuremberg

2016
I'll Close my Eyes, De Pont Museum, Tilburg

Selected Group Exhibitions
1990
The British Art Show 3, McLellan Galleries,
Glasgow; Leeds Art Gallery; Hayward
Gallery, London

1992
New Voices, Centre de Conférences Albert
Borschette, Brussels; Musée Nationale
d'Histoire et d'Art, Luxembourg; Taksim Art
Gallery, Istanbul; State Fine Arts Gallery,
Ankara; State Painting and Sculpture
Museum, Izmir, Turkey; Centre d'Art Santa
Mònica, Barcelona; Museo de Bellas Artes,
Bilbao, Spain
Moving into View: Recent British Painting,
Royal Festival Hall, London; Darlington Arts
Centre; Chapter, Cardiff; Oriel Gallery, Mold;
Newlyn Orion Gallery, Penzance; University

of Northumbria, Newcastle upon Tyne;
Drumcroon Arts Centre, Wigan; Harrogate
Museum & Art Gallery; Victoria Art Gallery
Coalition, CCA, Glasgow

1994
Paintmarks, Kettle's Yard, Cambridge; City
Art Gallery, Southampton; Mead Gallery,
Coventry

1997
*Abstraction / Abstractions: géométries
provisoires*, Musée d'Art Moderne de
Saint-Étienne

1998
Abstract Painting, Once Removed,
Contemporary Arts Museum, Houston;
Kemper Museum of Contemporary Art,
Kansas City

1999
*New Work: Painting Today, Recent
Acquisitions*, San Francisco Museum of
Modern Art

2004
*Singular Forms (Sometimes Repeated):
Art from 1951 to the Present*, Solomon
R. Guggenheim Museum, New York

2005
*Miradas Y Conceptos En La Colección
Helga de Alvear*, Museo Extremeño e
Iberoamericano de Arte Contemporáneo,
Badajoz, Spain

2006
*Helga de Alvear – Concepts for a
Collection*, Exhibition Centre of Centro
Cultural de Belém, Brazil

2011
Watercolour, Tate Britain, London

2013
HAUPTSACHE GRAU #03 Farbiges Grau,
Mies van der Rohe Haus, Berlin

2014
*GENERATION: 25 Years of Contemporary
Art in Scotland*, Scottish National Gallery
of Modern Art, Edinburgh; Dovecot Studios,
Edinburgh; Gallery of Modern Art, Glasgow;
Glasgow School of Art; Inverness Museum
and Art Gallery, Scotland

2015
Chromophobia, Gagosian Gallery, Geneva
Absent Presence, Manchester Art Gallery

2017
Ages of Wonder, Royal Scottish Academy,
Edinburgh
Abstract Painting Now!, Kunsthalle Krems,
Austria

Permindar Kaur
Born in Nottingham, 1965. Lives in St. Albans

Solo Exhibitions
1996
Cold Comfort, Ikon Gallery, Birmingham;
Mead Gallery, Coventry
Backspace, Galeria Alejandro Sales,
Barcelona

1997
Secrets Must Circulate, Galeria Carles Poy,
Barcelona
Fetish, Art Gallery of Windsor, Canada

1998
Independent Thoughts, Nottingham Castle
Museum & Art Gallery

1998–99
Comfort of Little Places, Aspex Gallery,
Portsmouth; Fabrica, Brighton

1999
Out of Breath, East London Gallery, London
Untitled, Berwick Gymnasium Art Gallery

2001
Photos of Simran, Galeria 44, Barcelona

2014
Hiding Out, Djanogly Gallery, Lakeside Arts,
Nottingham

2016
Interlopers, UH Art & Design Gallery,
Hatfield

2017
Black and Blue, New Art Projects, London

2020
Home, 5 Howick Place, London

Selected Group Exhibitions
1995
The British Art Show 4, Manchester;
Edinburgh; Cardiff

1997
Pictura Britannica, Art from Britain, MCA,
Sydney
Out of India, Queens Museum, New York

Crosscurrents, University Museum of
Ethnography, Oslo
Flexible Co-existence, Art Tower Mito,
Japan
Krishna, The Divine Lover, Hayward
National Touring Exhibitions; Whitechapel
Gallery, London
Las Ninas de Mis Ojos, Galerai Trajecto,
Vitoria, Spain

1998
Claustrophobia, Ikon Gallery, Birmingham

1999
Hot Air, Granship, Shizuoka Arts Centre,
Japan

2000
Through the Looking Glass, University of
Essex, Colchester
See for Yourself, Peterborough Museum and
Art Gallery

2004
Changing Rooms, Wakefield Art Gallery

2005
Spoilt rotten: Young Curators 2005,
Oriel Davies Gallery, Newtown, Wales

2006
*Revelation: Reflecting British Art in
the Arts Council Collection*, The Lowry,
Manchester

2013
What's Going On? Usher Gallery, Lincoln

2014
Bad Copy: Cardiff by Parris, Cardiff Story
Museum

2016
Now for Tomorrow II, Nottingham Castle
Museum & Art Gallery

2017
Tread Softly, Yorkshire Sculpture Park,
Wakefield

2018
Crossing Lines , F.E. McWilliam Gallery
& Studio, Banbridge, Ireland
Animals & Us, Turner Contemporary,
Margate

2019
NAE Open, New Art Exchange, Nottingham

2020
MK Calling, MK Gallery, Milton Keynes

2021
Breaking the Mould: Sculpture by Women since 1945, Longside Gallery, Yorkshire Sculpture Park, Wakefield; Djanogly Gallery, Nottingham; Ferens Art Gallery, Hull; New Art Gallery Walsall

Tania Kovats
Born in London, 1966. Lives in Devon

Selected Solo Exhibitions

1991
Riverside Studios, London

1992
Lokaal 01, Breda, Netherlands

1993
Laure Genillard Gallery, London

1994
Galerie Philip Rizzo, Paris
Galerie Staten, Den Haag

1995
Laure Genillard Gallery, London

1997
Erosion (with Carlo Guiata), British School at Rome
Laure Genillard Gallery, London

1998
Asprey Jacques Gallery, London
Galleria Marina Marabini, Bologna

1999
New Art Centre, Salisbury

2001
Schist, Asprey Jacques Gallery, London

2002
Slip, Yorkshire Sculpture Park, Wakefield

2004
Offshore, Newlyn Art Gallery; Oriel Mostyn Gallery, Llandudno

2007
Small Finds, Peer Arts, London

2008
Catch This, Yorkshire Sculpture Park, Wakefield

2010
Small Finds, Salisbury Museum

2011
LOG, Bath Spa College of Art and Design, Bath

2014
Oceans, Fruitmarket Gallery, Edinburgh; Hestercombe Gallery, Taunton

2015
Evaporation, Museum of Science and Industry, Manchester
Watermark, Pippy Houldsworth Gallery, London
Oceans, Sidney Cooper Gallery, Canterbury

Selected Group Exhibitions

1994
Appearances, Massimo Minini Gallery, Brescia

1995
Happy Squirrel, Club Bank, Eindhoven
ACE!, Hayward Gallery, London; Galerie Ursula Walbrol, Dusseldorf
Station Transformation, Tel Aviv
Sculptor's Drawings, Newlyn Art Gallery

1997
Belladonna, ICA, London
Pictura Britannica, MOCA, Los Angeles

1998
Il Passato nel Presente, The Tannery, London and Turin
New Art From Britain, Kunstraum Innsbruck

1999
Cognitive Landscapes, Galerie Dorothee De Pauw, Brussels
Thinking Aloud, Kettle's Yard, Cambridge

1999
Explorations of the Environment: Landscape Redefined, Barbara Gillman Gallery, Miami
Real places?, Westfalischer Kunstverein, Münster

2000
Lost, Ikon Gallery, Birmingham

2001
Close Encounters of the Art Kind, Victoria and Albert Museum, London
At Sea, Tate Liverpool
Unseen Landscapes, The Lowry, Salford

2002
Medicine Pump Rooms, Leamington Spa Art Gallery

2004
Off the Beaten Track, Longside Gallery, Yorkshire Sculpture Park, Wakefield

2004–05
Bad Behaviour, Longside Gallery; Aberystwyth Arts Centre; The Metropole Arts Centre, Folkstone; Glynn Vivian Art Gallery, Swansea; Newcastle upon Tyne University, Hatton Art Gallery; Millennium Court Arts Centre, Portadown; Djanogly Art Gallery, Nottingham; Tullie House, Carlisle

2005
Wild Landscapes, Compton Verney, Warwickshire
Taberei De Creatie Internationale, Miercurea Ciuc, Romania

2006
You'll Never Know: Drawing and Random Interference, Hayward Gallery, London
Repatriating the Ark, The Museum of Garden History, London
International Waters, Steven Wolf Fine Arts, San Francisco
Art at The Rockface, Norwich City Art Gallery

2009
A Duck for Mr. Darwin, BALTIC, Gateshead

2010
Edge of the World, Royal Botanic Garden, Edinburgh
So That May Come Back, Danielle Arnaud Gallery, London

2012
Galapagos, Bluecoat, Liverpool; The Fruitmarket Gallery, Edinburgh
Pertaining to Things Natural, Chelsea Physic Garden, London
Roots, Grizedale Arts, Northumberland

2015
VITA VITALE, Palazzo Garzoni, Venice Biennale
One and All, Somerset House, London
Periodic Tales: The Art of the Elements, Compton Verney, Warwickshire

2016
New Art Gallery Walsall

Cildo Meireles

Born in Rio de Janeiro, 1948. Lives in Rio de Janeiro

Selected Solo Exhibitions
1967
Desenhos, Museu de Arte Moderna, Salvador, Brazil

1975
Blindhotland/Ghetto: Virtual Spaces: Corners, Galeria Luiz Buarque de Hollanda e Paulo
Bittencourt, Rio de Janeiro
Eureka/Blindhotland, Museu de Arte Moderna, Rio de Janeiro

1981
Galeria Luisa Strina, São Paulo

1990
Missão/Missões How to Build Cathedrals & Cinza, ICA, London
Projects 21, MoMA, New York

1994
Volatile and Entrevendo, Capp Street Project, San Francisco

1999
Retrospective, New Museum, New York; Kiasma, Helsinki

2004
Descala and Strictu, Galerie Lelong, New York

2008–10
Tate Modern, London; MACBA, Barcelona; Museo Universitario Arte Contemporáneo, Mexico City

2014
Like a Needle in a Haystack, Kunsthal 44 Møen, Askeby, Denmark

2020
Museo de Arte Miguel Urrutia, Banco de la República, Bogotá

Selected Group Exhibitions
1965
Il Salao de Arte Moderna do Distrito Federal, Brasilia

1970
Information, MoMA, New York

1976
International Actuality, 37th Venice Biennale

1977
Biennale de Paris

1981
16th Bienal de São Paulo, Parque do Ibirapuera, São Paulo
The Sermon of the Mountain: Fiat Lux, Museum of Modern Art, Medellin, Colombia

1984
5th Sydney Biennale

1988
Brazil Projects, PS1, New York
Broken Music, Daadgalerie Gemeentemuseum, Berlin; The Hague; Le Magasin, Grenoble

1989
20th Bienal de São Paulo
Magiciens de la terre, Centre Pompidou, Paris

1990
Casino Fantasma, Casino Municipal, Venice; PS1, New York
The Rhetorical Image, New Museum, New York
Transcontinental, Ikon Gallery, Birmingham; Cornerhouse, Manchester

1992
documenta IX, Kassel

1993
Time and Tide. The 2nd Tyne International Exhibition of Contemporary Art, Newcastle upon Tyne

1996
Face à l'Histoire, Centre Pompidou, Paris

1997
You are Here, Royal College of Art, London

1998
Out of Actions: Between Performance and the Object 1949–1979, MOCA, Los Angeles

1999–2001
Global Conceptualism: Points of Origin 1950s–1980s, Queens Museum of Art, New York; Walker Art Center, Minneapolis; Miami Art Museum; MIT List Visual Arts Center, Cambridge, USA, Vancouver Art Gallery

2000
Gwangju Biennale

2001
Ars 01 – Unfolding Perspectives, Kiasma, Helsinki

2002
documenta 11, Kassel

2003
8th Istanbul Biennial
The Paper Sculpture Show, Sculpture Center, New York

2004
Liverpool Biennial

2005
Open Systems: Rethinking Art c.1970, Tate Modern, London

2007
New Economy, Artists Space, New York

2009
Italian Pavilion, 53rd Venice Biennale
Unbuilt Roads, e-flux project space, New York

2011
11th Biennale de Lyon

2012
Ends of the Earth: Land Art to 1974, MOCA, Los Angeles; Haus der Kunst, Munich

2013
Art Turning Left: How Values Changed Making 1789–2013, Tate Liverpool

2015
Resistance Performed – Aesthetic Strategies under Repressive Systems in Latin America, Migros Museum für Gegenwartskunst, Zurich

2016
Media Networks, Tate Modern, London

Lisa Milroy

Born in Vancouver, 1959. Lives in London

Selected Solo Exhibitions
1984
Fondation Cartier, Paris

1989
Third Eye Centre, Glasgow; Southampton City Art Gallery; Plymouth Art Gallery; Mary Boone
Gallery, New York

1995–96
Travel Paintings, Chisenhale Gallery, London; Ikon Gallery, Birmingham; Fruitmarket Gallery, Edinburgh

1999
Galerie der Stadt Schwaz, Innsbruck

2001
Tate Gallery, Liverpool

2007
Making Sense, Ikon Gallery, Birmingham

2010
Shouting from a Rock, Pharos Centre for Contemporary Art, Nicosia

2011
Act One, Seen Two, Barber Institute of Fine Arts, Birmingham

2012
Ivory Lamp Vine Bone Mars, Gallery North, Newcastle upon Tyne

2014
Grosse Geister, Artist Room: Lisa Milroy, Kunstmuseum Bonn

2018
Here & There: Paintings by Lisa Milroy, Parasol Unit, London

2020
Ensemble/Together, FRAC Occitanie Montpellier

Selected Group Exhibitions
1984
Problems of Picturing, Serpentine Gallery, London

1986
6th Sydney Biennale
42nd Venice Biennale

1987
Current Affairs: British Painting and Sculpture in the 1980s, Museum of Modern Art Oxford;
Mucsarnok, Budapest; Nemzeti Galeria, Prague; Zacheta National Gallery of Art, Warsaw

1988
The New British Painting, Contemporary Arts Center, Cincinnati; Chicago Public Library
and Cultural Center; Haggerty Museum, Marquette University, Milwaukee

1996
About Vision: New British Painting in the 1990s, Museum of Modern Art Oxford; Fruitmarket Gallery, Edinburgh

1998
11th Sydney Biennale
Urban, Tate Liverpool

2005
Raised Awareness, Tate Modern, London

2006
Fiction@Love, MoCA, Shanghai

2008
8 Visions, One Dream, Today Art Museum, Beijing

2009
Visual Deception, Nagoya City Art Museum
Mahlzeit (Essen in der Kunst), Galerie im Traklhaus, Salzburg

2015
Nature Morte: Contemporary Artists Reinvigorate the Still Life, Hå Gamle Prestegard, Stavanger, Norway; Konsthallen-Bohusläns Museum, Uddevalla, Sweden; National Museum, Warsaw; Guildhall Art Gallery, London

2018
Modern Art Revisited, Tottori Prefectural Museum, Museum of Modern Art, Saitama; Hiroshima City Museum of Contemporary Art; Yokosuka Museum of Art
Le rêve de la fileuse, Musée Fabre, Montpellier
Criminal Ornamentation, Attenborough Arts Centre, Leicester; Royal Albert Memorial Museum, Exeter; Longside Gallery, Arts Council Collection, Wakefield; Southampton City Art Gallery

2019
Architecture of London, Guildhall Art Gallery, London

Antoni Miralda
Born in Terrassa, Spain, 1942. Lives in Barcelona and Miami

Selected Solo Exhibitions
1966
Drawings 65, ICA, London

1970
Hanover Gallery, London

1971
(with Dorothée Selz) *Eat Art* Bankett, Restaurant Spoerri, Düsseldorf

1977
Breadline, Contemporary Arts Museum, Houston

1981
Wheat & Steak, Nelson-Atkins Museum of Art, Kansas City

1984
Santa Comida, El Museo del Barrio, New York

1988
Fundació Joan Miró, Barcelona

1990
Spanish Pavilion, 44th Venice Biennale
Philadelphia Museum of Art

1991
Honeymoon Project, Ikon Gallery, Birmingham

1995
Fundació La Caixa, Barcelona
Palau La Virreina, Barcelona

1996
IVAM, Valencia, Spain

1997
Galerie de France, Paris

2000
Food Pavilion, Expo 2000, Hanove

2004
Sabores y Lenguas, Museo de Bellas Artes de Caracas, Venezuela

2008
Power Food, Artium Centro-Museo Vasco de Arte Contemporáneo, Vitoria-Gasteiz, Spain

2010
Museo Nacional Centro de Arte Reina Sofía, Madrid

2016
MACBA, Barcelona

2017
Azkuna Zentroa, Bilbao

2019
Henrique Faria Fine Art, New York

Selected Events and Actions

1972
Edible Landscape, Museum of Contemporary Crafts, New York

1975
La Dernière Poutre, Centre Pompidou, Paris

1977
Fest fur Leda, documenta 6, Kassel

1984
(with Montse Guillén) *El Internacional Tapas Bar & Restaurant*, New York

2016
The Last Ingredients, Faena Art Center, Miami

2019
Five Feastables, Kaldor Public Art Projects, Art Gallery of New South Wales, Sydney

Selected Group Exhibitions

1968
The Obsessive Image 1960–1968, ICA, London

1969
XXV Salon de Mai, Musée d'Art Moderne, Paris

1978
Coca-Cola Polenta, Palazzo Grassi, Venice

1989
Magiciens de la terre, Centre Pompidou, Paris

1991
With This Ring ..., Ikon Gallery, Birmingham

2006
27th Bienal de São Paulo

2012
Barcelona Pavilion, 9th Shanghai Biennale

2015
Spanish Pavilion, Expo Milano 2015

Avis Newman

Born in London, 1946. Lives in London

Selected Solo Exhibitions

1982
Scenes (A Drawing Installation), Matt's Gallery, London

1984
Figure Who No One Is ... , Serpentine Gallery, London

1987
On the Margins of Forgetfulness, Lisson Gallery, London
Renaissance Society at the University of Chicago
This ... Dream's Navel, Galerie Akumabltory 2, Poznan, Poland

1990
Earth of Paradise, Arnolfini, Bristol

1993
Vicious Circle, De Appel, Amsterdam; Douglas Hyde Gallery, Dublin

1994
Works, Casa Masaccio, San Giovanni Valdarno, Arezzo

1995
Ikon Gallery, Birmingham

1998
Meridians, Lisson Gallery, London

2003
Avis Newman: Descriptions, MCA, Sydney

2013
Mobile Relations, East Gallery, Norwich University of the Arts

Selected Group Exhibitions

1982
Hayward Annual 1982: British Drawing, Hayward Gallery, London

1984–85
British Art Show: Old Allegiances and New Directions, 1979–1984, Birmingham Museum and Art Gallery; Royal Scottish Academy, Edinburgh, Mapping Art Gallery, Sheffield; Southampton City Art Gallery

1986
Falls the Shadow, Recent British and European Art, Hayward Gallery, London
Summer Group Show, Lisson Gallery, London
6th Biennale of Sydney
Aperto86, 42nd Venice Biennale

1987–88
The Analytical Theatre: New Art from Britain, New York; Akron Art Museum, Ohio; Alberta College of Art Gallery; University Art Museum, Santa Barbara; ICA, Philadelphia

1988
Vanities, Norwich University of the Arts
California 9; Signaturen, Museum of Contemporary Art, Ghent
The Impossible Self, Winnipeg Art Gallery

1989
Blasphemies, Ecstasies and Cries, Serpentine Gallery, London; Norwich School of Art; Herbert Read Gallery, Canterbury; Oriel Mostyn, Llandudno
A Propos de Dessin, Galerie Adrien Maeght, Paris

1990
Excavating the Present, Kettle's Yard, Cambridge

1994
Paula Rego, John Murphy, Avis Newman, Saatchi Gallery, London

1994–95
Inside the Visible, ICA, Boston; Washington Museum; Whitechapel Gallery, London; Perth Institute of Contemporary Art, Australia
Contemporary Art in the Bowes Museum, Barnard Castle, County Durham

1997
Something Old, Something New, Something Borrowed, Something Blue, Casa Masaccio, San Giovanni Valdarno, Arezzo
Material Culture, The Object in British Art of the 1980s and 90s, Hayward Gallery, London

1999–2000
La casa, il corpo, il cuore Konstruktion der Identitaten, National Gallery Prague; Museum Moderner Kunst Stiftung Ludwig Wien, Austria

2003
In Good Form, Longside Gallery, Yorkshire Sculpture Park, Wakefield

2004
Questionmark, Wait, Error, Understood, National Museum of Art, Kaunas, Lithuania

2009
Drawing of the World, College of Fine Art, Seoul National University

2010
On Line: Drawing Through the Twentieth Century, MoMA, New York

2013
5th Moscow Biennale of Contemporary Art

2014
Drawn Together: Artist as Selector,
Jerwood Gallery, Hastings

2017
*Meticulous Observations and Naming the
Money*, Arts Council Collection, Walker Art
Gallery, Liverpool

Lucia Nogueira
Born in Goiania, Brazil, 1950. Died 1998

Selected Solo Exhibitions
1990
Chisenhale Gallery, London
Mario Flecha Gallery, London

1992
Anthony Reynolds Gallery, London
*The Left Hand Does Not Know What the
Right Hand Does*, Espace Artère Sud,
Brussels

1993–94
Ikon Gallery, Birmingham; Camden Art
Centre, London

2005
Lucia Nogueira: Drawings, The Drawing
Room, London

2007
Serralves Museum of Contemporary Art,
Porto

2011
Drawings, Galeria Leme, São Paulo
Mischief, Kettle's Yard, Cambridge
Swing…Slip…Step and drawings, Anthony
Reynolds Gallery, London

Selected Group Exhibitions
1989
Promises, Promises, Serpentine Gallery,
London

1990
Galeria Ciento, Barcelona
*This Symphony Will Remain Always
Unfinished*, Terrain, San Francisco

1991
Gulliver's Travels, Galerie Sophia Ungers,
Cologne, Germany
Gymnopédies, Galeria Angels de la Motta,
Barcelona

1993
WaterCOLOUR, Curwen Gallery, London

1994
Hales Gallery, London
Le Shuttle, Kunstlerhaus Bethanien, Berlin

1995
Here and Now, Serpentine Gallery, London

1996
A Century of Sculptor's Drawings, Frith
Street Gallery and Karsten Schubert Gallery,
London
Contemporary Art at The Courtauld,
Courtauld Institute of Art, London

1997
Marks and Traces, Sandra Gering Gallery,
New York
Material Culture, Hayward Gallery, London
Pictura Britannica, MCA, Sydney; Art Gallery
of South Australia, Adelaide; Museum of
New Zealand Te Papa Tongarewa,
Wellington
The Little Object, The Freud Museum,
London

1999
Ein Hod 5th Sculpture Biennial, Israel
Sublime: The Darkness & the Light, John
Hansard Gallery, Southampton; Atkinson
Gallery, Street, Somerset; Storey Gallery,
Lancaster; Angel Row Gallery, Nottingham;
The Potteries Museum & Art Gallery,
Stoke-on-Trent; Laing Art Gallery, Newcastle
upon Tyne; Wolsey Art Gallery, Ipswich

2001
Home, Douglas Hyde Gallery, Dublin
Trauma, Dundee Contemporary Arts;
Firstsite, Colchester; Museum of Modern Art,
Oxford

2006
How to Improve the World, Hayward
Gallery, London
Lines of Enquiry, Kettle's Yard, Cambridge

2011
Modern British Sculpture, Royal Academy
of Arts, London
*The Life of the Mind: Love, Obsession and
Sorrow*, New Art Gallery Walsall
Watercolour, Tate Britain, London

2014
Revolver II, Matt's Gallery, London

2015
History is Now: 7 Artists Take on Britain,
Hayward Gallery, London

2017
The Frisson of The Togetherness,
Whitechapel Gallery, London

2018
33rd Bienal de São Paulo

Vong Phaophanit
Born in Savannakhet, Laos, 1961. Lives in
London

Selected Solo Exhibitions
1987
Just A Moment, Tea Ceremony, Spacex
Gallery, Exeter

1988
Just A Moment, Fragments, Chapter Arts
Centre, Cardiff

1990
In the Shadow of Words, Arnolfini, Bristol

1991–92
*Tok Tem Dean Kep Kin Bo Dai (What Falls
to the Ground But Can't be Eaten)*,
Chisenhale Gallery, London; Ikon Gallery,
Birmingham

1995
Phaophanit and Piper, Angel Row Gallery,
Nottingham; Site Gallery, Sheffield;
Cambridge Darkroom; The Minories,
Colchester

1996
Stephen Friedman Gallery, London

1997
Atopia, daadgalerie, Berlin; Royal Festival
Hall, London

1999
(with Claire Oboussier) *Scan*, Jerwood
Space, London; Hayward Gallery, London

2000
Field of Rods, 30 Kensington Church Street,
London

2001–03
Field of Labels, Loch Lomond and The
Trossachs National Park
Neon Wax Words, Asia Society, New York
Centre For Drawing, Wimbledon School of
Art, London

2004
(with Claire Oboussier) *Outhouse*, Woolton, Liverpool

2005
(with Claire Oboussier) *Life Lines*, Pier Hill, Southend-on-Sea

2009
(with Claire Oboussier) *Light Curtain*, Hull Truck Theatre

2011
(with Claire Oboussier) *Mute Meadow*, Derry~Londonderry

2012
(with Claire Oboussier) *Light Veils*, Weymouth Esplanade

2015
(with Claire Oboussier) *IT IS AS IF*, Block 366, London

Selected Group Exhibitions
1990
The British Art Show, McLellan Galleries, Glasgow; Leeds Art Gallery; Hayward Gallery, London

1991
Shocks to the System, Royal Festival Hall, London; Northern Centre for Contemporary Art, Sunderland; Ikon Gallery, Birmingham; Chapter Arts Centre, Cardiff; Royal Albert Memorial Museum, Exeter; Plymouth City Museum and Art Gallery; Maclaurin Art Gallery, Ayr

1993
Four Rooms, Serpentine Gallery, London
Sonsbeek, Arnhem, Netherlands
45th Venice Biennale
Turner Prize, Tate Gallery, London

1994
From Beyond the Pale, Irish Museum of Modern Art, Dublin

1996
Inclusion: Exclusion, Steirischer Herbst, Graz

1997
Pictura Britannica, MCA, Sydney; Art Gallery of South Australia, Adelaide
2nd Johannesburg Biennale

1998
Pictura Britannica, Museum of New Zealand Te Papa Tongarewa, Wellington

Crossings, National Gallery of Canada, Ottawa

1999
3rd Asia-Pacific Triennial of Contemporary Art, Queensland Art Gallery, Brisbane

2001
East of Eden, Spacex Gallery, Exeter

2002
Process of Renewal, Victoria and Albert Museum, London

2004
5th Shanghai Biennale

2006
(with Claire Oboussier) *The Quiet in the Land*, Luang Prabang, Laos
6th Gwangju Biennale

2007
Turner Prize A Retrospective 1984–2006, Tate Britain, London
(with Claire Oboussier) *Thermocline of Art. New Asian Waves*, ZKM | Center for Art and Media Karlsruhe

2008–10
The Tropics: View From the Middle of the Globe, Martin-Gropius-Bau, Berlin; Rio de Janeiro; Iziko South African National Gallery, Cape Town; Jim Thompson Art Center, Bangkok

2018
(with Claire Oboussier) 1st Thailand Biennale

2019
(with Claire Oboussier) 6th Singapore Biennale

Adrian Piper
Born in New York, 1948. Lives in Berlin

Selected Solo Exhibitions
1969
Three Untitled Projects, New York

1987–91
Adrian Piper: Reflections 1967–1987, The Alternative Museum, New York; Nexus Contemporary Art Center, Atlanta; Goldie Paley Gallery, Philadelphia; University of Colorado Art Gallery, Boulder; The Power Plant, Toronto; College of Wooster Art Museum, Ohio; Lowe Art Museum, Coral Gables; Santa Monica Museum of Contemporary Art; Washington Project for the Arts, Washington DC

1990
Out of the Corner, Whitney Museum of American Art, New York

1991–92
Ikon Gallery, Birmingham; Cornerhouse, Manchester; Cartwright Hall, Bradford; Kettle's Yard, Cambridge; Kunstverein München, Munich

1992
Political Drawings and Installations, 1975–1991, Cleveland Center for Contemporary Art; Carver Community Cultural Center, San Antonio; Herron Gallery, Indianapolis Center for Contemporary Art, Indianapolis; Women & Their Work, Austin

1999–2001
Adrian Piper: A Retrospective, Fine Arts Gallery, University of Maryland, Baltimore; New Museum, New York; The Andy Warhol Museum, Pittsburgh; Contemporary Arts Center, Cincinnati; Weatherspoon Art Gallery, Greensboro
MEDI(t)Ations: Adrian Piper's Videos, Installations, Performances and Soundworks, 1968–1992, MOCA, Los Angeles; New Museum, New York; The Andy Warhol Museum, Pittsburgh; Contemporary Arts Center, Cincinnati; Weatherspoon Art Gallery, Greensboro

2002–04
Adrian Piper: since 1965, Generali Foundation, Vienna; Institut d'art contemporain, Villeurbanne-Lyon; MACBA, Barcelona

2006
CPH Kunsthal, Copenhagen
Adrian Piper: The Mythic Being, Smart Museum of Art, University of Chicago

2008
Adrian Piper: Everything, Elizabeth Dee Gallery, New York

2017
Lévy Gorvy, New York

2018
Adrian Piper: A Synthesis of Intuitions, 1965–2016, MoMA, New York

Selected Group Exhibitions
1970
Information, MoMA, New York

1971
Biennale de Paris

1974
Persona, Artists Space, New York

1977
Biennale de Paris, Musee d'Art Moderne,
Paris

1980
*Issue: Twenty Social Strategies by Women
Artists*, ICA, London

1985
Tradition and Conflict, The Studio Museum
in Harlem, New York

1988
The Turning Point: Art and Politics in 1968,
Cleveland Center for Contemporary Art, USA

1989–1990
L'Art Conceptuel: Une Perspective, Musee
d'Art Moderne, Paris

1991
The Art of Advocacy, The Aldrich
Contemporary Art Museum, Ridgefield, USA

1992
documenta IX, Kassel (artwork withdrawn)

1992–93
9th Biennale of Sydney

1994–95
*Black Male: Representations of Masculinity
in Contemporary American Art*, Whitney
Museum of American Art, New York

1995
1ˢᵗ Johannesburg Biennale

1996
*Thinking Print: Books to Billboards
1980–95*, MoMA, New York

1998–99
*Out of Actions: Between Performance and
the Object, 1949–1979*, MOCA, Los
Angeles, Österreichisches Museum für
Angewandte Kunst, Vienna; Museu d'Art
Contemporani de Barcelona; Museum of
Contemporary Art, Tokyo; National Museum
of Art, Osaka

1999–2001
*Global Conceptualism: Points of Origin
1950s–1980s*, Queens Museum of Art, New
York; Walker Art Center, Minneapolis; Miami
Art Museum; MIT List Visual Arts Center,
Cambridge, Vancouver Art Gallery

2002
documenta 11, Kassel

2005
Systems, Tate Modern, London

2007–09
*Multitasking–Synchronität als kulturelle
Praxis*, Neue Gesellschaft für bildenden Kunst,
Berlin; Stedelijk Museum – Hertogenbosch,
Netherlands, Overbeck–Gesellschaft, Lübeck,
Germany; La Filature, Mulhouse, France;
Musée du Quai Branly, Paris

2010–11
Move: Choreographing You, Hayward
Gallery, London; Haus der Kunst, Munich;
K20, Düsseldorf

2012
La Triennale: Intense Proximité, Palais
de Tokyo, Paris

2014
Dallas Biennial, Texas

2015
56ᵗʰ Venice Biennale

2016
9ᵗʰ Berlin Biennale

Keith Piper

Born in Mtarfa, Malta, 1960. Lives in London

Selected Solo Exhibitions
1987
Another Empire State, Battersea Arts Centre,
London

1984
Past Imperfect, Future Tense, The Black Art
Gallery, London

1990
The Devil Finds Work, Transmission Gallery,
Glasgow

1991
A Ship Called Jesus, Ikon Gallery,
Birmingham; Camden Art Centre, London

1992
Tradewinds, Merseyside Maritime Museum,
Liverpool

1995
Reckless Eyeballing, Bonington Gallery,
Nottingham

1997
Western Passage, The Fabric Workshop
and Museum, Philadelphia

1998–99
Relocating the Remains, Ikon Gallery,
Birmingham; New Museum, New York

2000–01
Machine, Henie Onstad Kunstsenter, Oslo

2004
Crusade, Contemporary Art Museum,
St Louis

2007
The Abolitionist's Parlour, Ferens Art
Gallery, Hull

2017
Unearthing the Bankers Bones, New Art
Exchange, Nottingham; Bluecoat, Liverpool

2019
Body Politics. Work from 1982–2007,
Wolverhampton Art Gallery

Selected Group Exhibitions
1981
Black Art & Done, Wolverhampton Art
Gallery

1982–83
Pan-Afrikan Connection, Ikon Gallery,
Birmingham; Africa Centre, London; 38 King
Street Gallery, Bristol: Midland Group,
Nottingham; Herbert Art Gallery & Museum,
Coventry

1983
Beyond The Pan-Afrikan Connection,
Midlands Arts Centre, Birmingham

1984
Into the Open, Mappin Art Gallery, Sheffield
Black Art Now, The Black Art Gallery,
London

1986
From Two Worlds, Whitechapel Gallery,
London

1987
State Of The Nation, Herbert Art Gallery,
Coventry

1989
3ʳᵈ Havana Biennial
The Other Story, Hayward Gallery, London

1991
Interrogating Identity, Grey Art Gallery,
New York; Museum of Fine Arts, Boston;
Walker Art Center, Minneapolis

1992
Trophies of Empire, Arnolfini, Bristol

1994
4th Havana Biennial

1995
Boxer, Walsall Museum and Art Gallery

1997
2nd Johannesburg Biennale

1998
The Unmapped Body, Yale University Art
Gallery New Haven

2001–02
Race In Digital Space, MIT List Visual
Arts Center; The Studio Museum In Harlem
New York

2002
Terminal Frontiers, Castlefield Gallery,
Manchester

2004
The Black Atlantic, Haus der Kulturen der
Welt, Berlin

2006
*How to Improve the World: 60 Years
of British Art*, Hayward Gallery, London

2007
Uncomfortable Truths, Victoria and Albert
Museum, London

2010
*Afro Modern: Journeys Through the
Black Atlantic*, Tate Liverpool; Centro
Galego de Arte Contemporánea, Santiago
de Compostela, Spain

2011–12
Blk Art Group, Graves Gallery, Sheffield

2012
Migrations: Journeys into British Art, Tate
Britian, London

2015–16
No Colour Bar, Guildhall Gallery, London

2016
*Thinking Black. A Montage of Black Art
in Britain*, Van Abbemuseum, Eindhoven

2017
The Place Is Here, Nottingham Contempo-
rary; Middlesbrough Institute of Modern Art;
South London Gallery

2018–19
*Speech Acts: Reflection-Imagination-
Repetition*, Manchester Art Gallery

Donald Rodney
Born in Birmingham, 1961. Died 1998

Selected Solo Exhibitions
1986
*The Atrocity Exhibition & Other Empire
Stories*, The Black Art Gallery, London

1989
Crisis Exhibition, Chisenhale Gallery, London

1990
Critical, Rochdale Art Gallery

1991
Cataract, Camerawork, London

1997
9 Night in Eldorado, South London Gallery

2005
Donald Rodney Sketchbook Display, Tate
Britain, London

2008
In Retrospect, Iniva, London

2016
Re imaging Donald Rodney, Vivid Projects,
Birmingham

Selected Group Exhibitions
1982
The Pan Afrikan Connection, Trent
Polytechnic, Nottingham

1983
The Blk Art Group, Battersea Art Gallery,
London

1985
Heroes and Heroines, The Black Art Gallery,
London

1986
State of the Art, ICA, London

1987
The Devil's Feast, Chelsea School of Art,
London
Piper & Rodney, Prema Art Centre, Dursley,
Gloucestershire

1989
Searchlight, Ikon Gallery, Birmingham

1990
Trophies of the Empire, Arnolfini, Bristol
Let the Canvas Come to Life With Dark Faces,
Herbert Gallery, Coventry

1991
Shocks to the System, Royal Festival Hall,
London; Northern Centre for Contemporary
Art, Sunderland; Ikon Gallery, Birmingham;
Chapter Arts Centre, Cardiff; Royal Albert
Memorial Museum, Exeter; Plymouth City
Museum and Art Gallery; Maclaurin Art
Gallery, Ayr

1994
(with Rose Finn-Kelcey), *Truth, Dare,
Double-Dare ...* Ikon Gallery, Birmingham

1995
Care & Control, Hackney Hospital, London

1996
Body Visual, Barbican Centre, London
The Invisible & The Visible, Wellcome Trust,
London

1997
Transforming the Crown, Caribbean Cultural
Centre, New York

1998
Inside Out, East London Gallery, University
of London

2001
*Century City – Art and Culture in the
Modern Metropolis*, Tate Modern, London
*Homes for the Soul, Micro-architecture in
Medieval and Contemporary Art*, Henry
Moore Institute, Leeds

2000–01
The British Art Show 5, Inverleith House,
Royal Botanical Garden, Edinburgh;
Southampton City Art Gallery; National
Museum of Wales, Cardiff; Ikon Gallery,
Birmingham; Birmingham Museum and Art
Gallery

2003
*Self Evident: The Artist as Subject
1969–2002*, Tate Britain, London
*A Bigger Splash. British Art from Tate
1960–2003*, São Paulo

2005
State of the Art, Laing Art Gallery,
Newcastle upon Tyne

2006
How to Improve the World: 60 years of British Art, Hayward Gallery, London

2009
Niet Normaal – Difference on Display, Beurs van Berlage, Amsterdam
British Subjects: Identity and Self-Fashioning 1967–2009, Neuberger Museum of Art, New York

2010
The Surreal House, Barbican Centre, London

2011
The Blk Art Group, Graves Art Gallery, Sheffield
Donald Rodney Display, Science Museum, London

2012
Migrations, Journeys into British Art, Tate Britain, London
Focal Points: Art and Photography, Manchester Art Gallery

2013
Keywords, Iniva, London

2014
Static-Still Life Reconsidered, Birmingham Museum and Art Gallery

2015
At Home, Yorkshire Sculpture Park, Wakefield

2016
Black Art in Focus, Wolverhampton Art Gallery

2017
The Place is Here, Van Abbemuseum, Eindhoven; Nottingham Contemporary; South London Gallery
Blood: Life Uncut, Copeland Gallery, London
Corpus: The Body Unbound, Courtauld Institute of Art, London

2018
Within and Without: Body Image and the Self, Birmingham Museum and Art Gallery
The Atlantic Project, Plymouth Museums, The Box and Plymouth University

2018
Structures of Meaning | Architectures of Perception, Manarat al Saadiyat, Abu Dhabi

2019
Super Black, Firstsite, Colchester
Civic Duty, Cell Project Space. London
Generations. Connecting, Across Time and Place, Somerset House. London

Martha Rosler
Born in Brooklyn, New York. Lives in Brooklyn

Selected Solo Exhibitions
1977
Martha Rosler, New American Filmmakers, Whitney Museum of American Art, New York

1987
Focus: Martha Rosler, ICA, Boston

1989
If You Lived Here ... , Dia Art Foundation, New York
Housing is a Human Right, Times Square, New York

1990
Housing is a Human Right, Museum of Modern Art Oxford

1994
In the Place of the Public, Contemporary Arts Center, Cincinnati
Videotapes of Martha Rosler, Palais des Beaux Arts, Brussels

1995
Public Information: Desire, Disaster, Document, San Francisco Museum of Modern Art;
Center for Contemporary Arts, Glasgow

1998–2000
Positions in the Life World, Ikon Gallery, Birmingham; Institut d'art contemporain, Villeurbanne-Lyon; Generali Foundation, Vienna; MACBA, Barcelona; New Museum and International Center for Photography, New York

2005
London Garage Sale, ICA, London

2005–09
Martha Rosler Library, e-flux projects, New York; Frankfurter Kunstverein, Frankfurt; MuKHA, Antwerp; unitednationsplaza, Berlin; Institut national d'histoire d'art, Paris; Stills, Edinburgh; Herter Art Gallery, Amherst, USA

2010
As If, GAM, Turin

2012
Meta-Monumental Garage Sale, MoMA, New York

2014
Guide for the Perplexed: How to Succeed in the New Poland, Ujazdowski Castle Centre for Contemporary Art, Warsaw

2015
Below The Surface, Seattle Art Museum

2018
Martha Rosler: Irrespective, The Jewish Museum, New York

Selected Group Exhibitions
1979
Whitney Biennial, New York

1980
A Decade of Women's Performance Art, Contemporary Arts Center, New Orleans

1982
documenta 7, Kassel

1983
Whitney Biennial, New York

1986
2nd Havana Biennale

1995
25 Years of Video Art, MoMA, New York

1996
Inside the Visible, ICA, Boston; National Museum of Women in the Arts, Washington DC; Whitechapel Gallery, London; Art Gallery of Western Australia, Perth

2000
The Wounded Diva: Hysteria, Body, Technology in 20th Century Art, Kunstverein München, Städtische Galerie im Lenbachhaus und Kunstbau and Siemens Kulturprogramm, Munich; Galerie im Taxispalais, Innsbruck; Staatliche Kunsthalle Baden-Baden,

2003
50th Venice Biennale

2004
Liverpool Biennial
Taipei Biennial

2007
documenta 12, Kassel
Skulptur Projekte Münster

2011
3rd Singapore Biennale
12th Istanbul Biennial

2012
9th Shanghai Biennale

2017
Elements of Vogue: A Case Study in Radical Performance, Centro de Arte Dos de Mayo, Madrid

2017–18
6th Thessaloniki Biennale of Contemporary Art

2018
4th Kochi-Muziris Biennale

2019
BIENALSUR – International Contemporary Art Biennial of South America

2020
Supermarket, Jeu de Paume, Paris

Yinka Shonibare
Born in London, 1962. Lives in London

Selected Solo Exhibitions
1989
Byam Shaw Gallery; Bedford Hill Gallery, London

1994
Double Dutch, Centre 181 Gallery, London

1997
Present Tense, Art Gallery of Ontario, Toronto

1998
Alien Obsessives, Mum, Dad and the Kids, The Tabernacle, London; Norwich Art Gallery

1999
Dressing Down, Ikon Gallery, Birmingham; Henie Onstad Kunstsenter, Oslo; Northern Gallery for Contemporary Art, Sunderland; Mappin Art Gallery, Sheffield; Oriel Mostyn, Llandudno

2000
Camden Art Centre, London
Affectionate Men, Victoria and Albert Museum, London
Diary of a Victorian Dandy Project, Iniva, London; Castle Museum, Nottingham; Laing Art Gallery, Newcastle upon Tyne; Towner Art Gallery, Eastbourne

2002
Double Dress, Israel Museum, Jerusalem; Kiasma, Helsinki; Studio Museum in Harlem, New York; Padiglione d'Arte Contemporanea, Milan

2004
Turner Prize, Tate Britain, London
Yinka Shonibare, Double Dutch, Boijmans van Beuningen Museum, Rotterdam; Kunsthalle Vienna

2007
Jardin d'Amour, Musée du Quai Branly, Paris

2008
MCA, Sydney; Brooklyn Museum, New York; Smithsonian, Washington DC

2009
A Flying Machine for Every Man, Woman and Child & Other Astonishing Works, Santa Barbara Museum of Art

2010
Human Culture: Earth, Wind, Fire and Water, Israel Museum, Jerusalem

2012
Imagined as the Truth, San Diego Art Museum

2013
Royal Museums Greenwich, London
FABRIC-ATION, GL Strand, Copenhagen; Yorkshire Sculpture Park, Wakefield

2014
The British Library, Brighton Museum
Wroclaw Contemporary Museum, Poland

2015
William Morris Family Album, William Morris Gallery, London
Daegu Art Museum, South Korea

2016
End of Empire, Turner Contemporary, Margate
Yale Centre for British Art, New Haven

2017
Paradise Beyond, Gemeentmuseum Helmond, Netherlands

2018
End of Empire, Glynn Vivian Art Gallery, Swansea
Busan Museum of Art, South Korea

2019
Flower Power, Fukuoka Art Museum

Selected Group Exhibitions
1989
Black Art New Directions, Stoke-on-Trent City Museum & Art Gallery

1991
Interrogating Identity, Grey Art Gallery, New York; Museum of Fine Arts, Boston; Walker Arts Center, Minneapolis; Madison Art Centre, Wisconsin; Memorial Art Museum, Ohio

1992
Barclays Young Artists Award, Serpentine Gallery, London

1994
Where are they now …?, Byam Shaw Gallery, London
Seen/unseen, Bluecoat, Liverpool

1995
The Art of African Textiles: Technology, Tradition and Lurex, Barbican Centre, London

1996
10th Biennale of Sydney

1997
Sensation: Young British Art from the Saatchi Collection, Royal Academy of Arts, London; National Gallery, Berlin; Brooklyn Museum, New York
2nd Johannesburg Biennale

1998
Crossings, National Gallery of Canada, Ottawa

1999
Secret Victorians: Contemporary Artists and a 19th Century Vision, Ikon Gallery, Birmingham; Firstsite, Colchester; Arnolfini, Bristol; Middlesbrough Art Gallery; Museum and Art Gallery, Brighton; Armand Hammer Museum, Los Angeles

2000
5th Lyon Biennale
Intelligence: New British Art 2000, Tate Britain, London

2001
Authentic/Ex-centric: Conceptualism in Contemporary African Art, 49th Venice Biennale

2002
documenta 11, Kassel

2003
Looking Both Ways: Art of the Contemporary African Diaspora, The Museum for African Art, New York
Love Over Gold, Gallery of Modern Art, Glasgow

2004
African Art, African Voices: Long Steps Never Broke a Back, Philadelphia Museum of Art

2005
Take Two. Worlds and Views, MoMA, New York
Translation, Palais de Tokyo, Paris

2005–06
Africa Remix – Contemporary Art of a Continent, Museum Kunst Palast, Düsseldorf, Germany; Hayward Gallery, London; Centre Pompidou, Paris; Mori Art Museum, Tokyo; Moderna Museet, Stockholm

2006
Alien Nation, ICA, London
William Hogarth, Musée du Louvre, Paris; Tate Britain, London; Caixa Forum, Madrid
Contemporary Commonwealth, National Gallery of Victoria, Melbourne

2007
African Pavilion, 52nd Venice Biennale
Tomorrow Now: When Design Meets Science Fiction, Mudam Luxembourg – Musée d'Art Moderne Grand-Duc Jean
War and Discontent, Museum of Fine Arts, Boston

2008
The Essential Art of African Textiles: Design Without End, Metropolitan Museum of Art, New York

2009
3rd Moscow Biennale of Contemporary Art

2010
GSK Contemporary: Aware: Art Fashion Identity, Royal Academy of Arts, London
The House of Fairy Tales, Harris Museum and Art Gallery, Preston
Contemplating the Void, Guggenheim Museum, New York

2011
Kaunas Biennial
The African Continuum, United Nations, New York

2012
The Desire for Freedom: Art in Europe since 1945, Deutsches Historisches Museum, Berlin
Migrations: Journeys into British Art, Tate Britain, London

2013
Earth Matters: Land as Material and Metaphor in the Arts of Africa, Smithsonian National Museum of African Art, Washington DC

2014
Ship to Shore, John Hansard Gallery, Southampton
The Human Factor, Hayward Gallery, London

2015
Self: Image and Identity, Turner Contemporary, Margate
Staying Power: Photographs of Black British Experience 1950s–1990s, Victoria and Albert Museum, London

2016
BODY/PLAY/POLITICS, Yokohama Museum of Art

2017
Tous, des sang-mêlés, Musée d'Art Contemporain du Val-de-Marne, Paris

2018
Senses of Time, Smithsonian National Museum of African Art, Washington DC
Like Life: Sculpture, Color, and the Body, Met Breuer, New York

Nancy Spero
Born in Cleveland, USA, 1926. Died 2009

Selected Solo Exhibitions
1965
Galerie Breteau, Paris

1973
Codex Artaud, AIR Gallery, New York

1980–81
Women: Appraisals, Dance and Active Histories, University and college galleries in Massachusetts, New Jersey and New York

1985
Nancy Spero: The Black Paris Paintings 1959–1966, Hewlett Gallery, Carnegie-Mellon University, Pittsburgh

1987
ICA, London; Fruitmarket Gallery, Edinburgh; Orchard Gallery, Derry~Londonderry
MIT List Visual Arts Center, Cambridge, USA

1987–89
Works Since 1950, Everson Museum of Art, Syracuse; Museum of Contemporary Art Chicago; Mendel Gallery, Saskatoon; New Museum, New York, The Power Plant, Toronto

1991
A Commitment to The Human Spirit (with Leon Golub), UWM Art Museum/University of Wisconsin-Milwaukee

1993
Torture of Women, The First Language and The Hours of the Night, National Gallery of Canada, Ottawa

1994
The First Language and The Black and The Red, Malmö Konsthal

1998
Ikon Gallery, Birmingham

2002
Nancy Spero: A Continuous Present, Kunsthalle zu Kiel, Germany

2003
Other Worlds: The Art of Nancy Spero and Kiki Smith, BALTIC, Gateshead

2004
Weighing the Heart Against a Feather of Truth, Centro Galego de Arte Contemporanea, Santiago de Compostela, Spain

2008
Dissidances, Museo Nacional Centro de Arte Reina Sofia, Madrid; Museu d'Art Contemporani de Barcelona

2010–11
Centre Pompidou, Paris; Serpentine Gallery, London

2015
Slip of the Tongue, Punta della Dogana, Venice

2019–20
Nordiska Akvarellmuseet, Tjörn, Norway;
Museum Folkwang, Essen

Selected Group Exhibitions
1973
Women Choose Women, New York Cultural
Center

1977
Words at Liberty, Museum of Contemporary
Art Chicago

1980
Issue-Social Strategies by Women Artists,
ICA, London; University and college galleries
of Hartford, Ohio

1982
Sense and Sensibility, Midland Group,
Nottingham

1984
Art & Ideology, New Museum, New York

1985
Whitney Biennial, New York

1986
6th Biennale of Sydney
*Philadelphia Collects American Art-Since
1940*, Philadelphia Museum of Art

1987
Resistance (Anti-Baudrillard), White
Columns, New York
documenta 8, Kassel, Germany

1992
*Allegories of Modernism: Contemporary
Drawing*, MoMA, New York

1993
*43rd Biennial Exhibition of Contemporary
American Painting*, The Corcoran Gallery
of Art, Washington DC
Whitney Biennial, New York

1995
The Human Figure, A Modern Vision,
MoMA, New York
21st International Biennial of Graphic Art,
Modern Gallery, Ljubljana, Slovenia

1996
*Inside the Visible: Alternative Views of
20th Century Art Through Women's Eyes*,
ICA, Boston; National Museum for Women
in the Arts, Washington DC; Whitechapel
Gallery, London

1997
documenta X, Kassel, Germany

1998
Past / Present, International Biennale of Cairo

2000
Gwangju Biennale
*The American Century, Art and Culture,
Part II 1950–2000*, Whitney Museum of
American Art, New York

2001
49th Venice Biennale

2003
Other Worlds, BALTIC, Gateshead

2005
*Toward the Future: Through the Eyes of the
Artists Awarded the Hiroshima Art Prize*,
Hiroshima City Museum of Contemporary
Art, Japan
*Persistent Vestiges: Drawing from the
American-Vietnam War*, The Drawing
Center, New York

2006
Whitney Biennial, New York

2007
52nd Venice Biennale
27th Biennial of Graphic Arts, Centre of
Graphic Arts, Lubljana

2007–08
WACK! Art and the Feminist Revolution,
Geffen Center; MOCA, Los Angeles; National
Museum of Women in the Arts, Washington
DC; Vancouver Art Gallery; PS1, New York

2010
Shifting the Gaze: Painting and Feminism,
Jewish Museum, New York

2014
The Disasters of War, Louvre-Lens, France

2016
From Revolt to Postmodernity, 1962–1982,
Museo Nacional Centro de Arte Reina Sofia,
Madrid

2017
*Delirious. Art at the Limits of Reason
1950–1980*, Metropolitan Museum of Art,
New York

Born in Leeds, 1968. Lives in London

Selected Solo Exhibitions
1994
Anthony Reynolds Gallery, London

1996
Hypnodreamdruff, Tate Gallery, London

1998
Tuberama, Ikon Gallery, Birmingham

2003
Bunny Lake Drive-In, Fletcher Works,
Site Gallery, Sheffield

2005
Big V, Leeds Art Gallery

2007
Anthology Film Archives, New York

2010
Le Confort Moderne, Poitiers

2011
Theda with Sigune von Osten, The Pier
Theatre, Bournemouth

2012
The Lesson, Pinksummer Contemporary Art,
Genoa

2013
Before Le Cerveau Affamé, Cooper
Gallery, Dundee

2015
I, Cave, Middlesbrough Institute of
Modern Art

2017
Androgynous Egg, Frieze Projects, London
Hello. Come Here. I Want You, Frac
Franche Comté, Besançon, France

2019
The Eternal Ear, Matera Alberga,
Sextantio Le Grotte della Civita, Italy
Big V, Centre for Audio Visual
Experimentation, Leeds

Selected Group Exhibitions
1994
Andrea Rosen Gallery, New York
Serpentine Gallery, London

1995
Philadelphia Museum of Modern Art
Serpentine Gallery, London

1997
MOCA, Los Angeles

1998
Women's 20th Century Club, Los Angeles

2002
*Rapture, Art's Seduction by Fashion
Since 1970,* Barbican Centre, London

2008
Royal Academy of Arts, London

2014
Past the Future, Tate Britain, London
The Decade, Centre Pompidou-Metz
The Uplawmoor Show, Mure Hall, Glasgow
International

2015
The Nakeds, De La Warr Pavillion,
Bexhill-on-Sea
*Believe Not Every Spirit, but Try the
Spirits,* Monash University Museum of Art,
Melbourne

2016
*Of Other Spaces: Where Does Gesture
Become Event?* Cooper Gallery, Dundee
Lo Specchio Concavo, Base Arte
Contemporanea Odierna, Bergamo
Mycorial Theatre 2016, Pivô, São Paulo
Intimate Wine Reception, Chateau Shatto,
Los Angeles

2017
Fantasy Access Code, K11, Shangha

2019
Sixty Years, Tate Britain, London
Re-collections, Site Gallery, Sheffield
Static Steps, The Collection, Leeds Art
Gallery

Amikam Toren
Born in Jerusalem, 1945. Lives in London

Selected Solo Exhibitions
1967
Maserik Gallery, Tel Aviv

1976
Serpentine Gallery, London

1979
Replacing, ICA, London

1985
Subverting … a temporary edition,
Camerawork, London

1989
Rotterdam Kunststichtung

1990
Ikon Gallery, Birmingham

1991
Chisenhale Gallery, London
Arnolfini, Bristol

1998
Armchair Paintings 1989–1998,
Minerva-Bar Gallery, Tel Aviv

2000
Ramat-Gan Museum of Contemporary Art,
Tel Aviv

2003
Golem, Anthony Reynolds Gallery, London

2012
Moving in the Right Direction, Anthony
Reynolds Gallery, London

2013–14
Carrots, Ikon Gallery, Birmingham

2014
Neither a Teapot Nor a Painting, MOT
International, Brussels

2015
The End of the World as We Know It, Art
Seen – Contemporary Art Projects & Editions,
Nicosia

2017
Palpable, works from 1973–2002, Jessica
Silverman Gallery, San Francisco

2018
Safe City, Matt's Gallery, London
Noga Gallery of Contemporary Art, Tel Aviv

2020
This Way Up, Pataphysic.com

Selected Group Exhibitions
1967
5th Biennale de Paris

1976
Summer Show 5, Serpentine Gallery,
London

1984
Arte e Arti. Attualità e Storia, 41st Venice
Biennale
Problems of Picturing, Serpentine Gallery,
London

1993
The Portrait Now, National Portrait Gallery,
London

1997
L'empreinte, Centre Pompidou, Paris
Humanism 2020, 4th Ein Hod Sculpture
Biennale

2000–01
The British Art Show 5, Inverleith House,
Royal Botanical Garden, Edinburgh;
Southampton City Art Gallery, Southampton;
National Museum of Wales, Cardiff; Ikon
Gallery, Birmingham; Birmingham Museum
and Art Gallery

2005
Whatever Happened to Social Democracy,
Rooseum Center for Contemporary Art,
Malmö, Sweden

2008
Intimacy, ACCA, Melbourne

2009
*British Subjects: Identity and Self-Fashioning
1967–2009,* Neuberger Museum of Art,
New York

2010
No New Thing Under the Sun, Royal
Academy of Arts, London

2012
4th Guangzhou Triennial
The London Open, Whitechapel Gallery,
London
13th Venice Biennale of Architecture
Homenagem, Museu do Acude, Rio de
Janeiro

2013
Four Corners of the World, Hite Foundation,
Seoul

2014
Waywords of Seeing, Frac Ile-de-France,
Le Plateau, Paris
A View from a Window, Camden Art
Centre, London

2015
Unorthodox, Jewish Museum, New York
Imago Mundi: Map of the New Art,
Fondazione Giorgio Cini, Venice
Artists for Ikon, Ikon Gallery, Birmingham

2016
… and there was time, Helga de Alvear
Foundation Visual Arts Center, Cáceres, Spain

Suzanne Treister

Born in London, 1958. Lives in London

Selected Solo Exhibitions

1985
Edward Totah Gallery, London

1990
Ikon Gallery, Birmingham; Spacex, Exeter; Gallery Oldham; The Minories, Colchester; Darlington Arts Centre; Nottingham Castle Museum & Art Gallery

1994
Q. Would You Recognise a Virtual Paradise? and other paintings, Contemporary Art Centre of South Australia, Adelaide; ACCA, Melbourne

1996
Dying for Your Sins, Institute of Modern Art, Brisbane

1997
Dying for Your Sins, ACCA, Melbourne

1999
No Other Symptoms – Time Travelling with Rosalind Brodsky, Artspace, Sydney

2004
Operation Swanlake, Kunstlerhaus Bethanien, Berlin

2006
HEXEN 2039, CHELSEA space, Warburg Institute and Science Museum, London

2007
HEXEN 2039, New Art Gallery Walsall

2008
3 Projects, Annely Juda Fine Art, London

2012
The Real Truth. A World's Fair, Raven Row, London
HEXEN 2.0, Science Museum, London; Hartware MedienKunstVerein, Dortmund; D21 Kunstraum, Leipzig

2013
HEXEN 2.0, P.P.O.W, New York

2015
HEXEN 2.0, Fig-2, ICA, London
Rosalind Brodsky's Electronic Time Travelling Costumes and Cookery Shows, Schaufenster am Hofgarten, Kunstverein München, Munich

2016
HFT The Gardener, Exhibition Research Lab (ERL), Liverpool Biennial

2017
Works from Survivor (F), IMT Gallery, London

2018
Suzanne Treister's Journey to Bordeaux – Parallel Histories and Peripheral Narrratives, CAPC, Bordeaux

2019
The Escapist BHST (Black Hole Spacetime), Serpentine Galleries, London

2020
SURVIVORS, Vienna

2021
Technoshamanic Systems, Mattflix, Matt's Gallery, London

Selected Group Exhibitions

1988
Something Solid, Cornerhouse, Manchester
Interference, Riverside Studios, London

1993
The Return of the Cadavre Exquis, Drawing Center, New York

1995
Pretext:Heteronyms, Rear Window at Clink Street Studios, London

1996
On a Clear Day, ICA, London; Cambridge Darkroom; John Hansard Gallery, Southampton; Firstsite, Colchester; Focal Point Gallery, Southend-on-Sea; Gallery Oldham; Middlesbrough Art Gallery

1997
documenta X, Kassel

1998
Idea 98, The Tea Factory, Liverpool

1999
7th WRO Media Art Biennale, Warsaw

2000
CHEMISTRY: Art in South Australia 1990–2000, Art Gallery of South Australia, Adelaide

2003
Don't Call it Performance, Museo Nacional Centro de Arte Reina Sofía, Madrid; Centro Párraga, Murcia

2002
13th Biennale of Sydney

2004
transmediale.04, Berlin

2005
The Blur of the Otherworldly: Contemporary Art, Technology and the Paranormal, Center for Art, Design and Visual Culture, University of Maryland, Baltimore County

2006
Drawing from Turner, Tate Britain, London

2009
Reinventing Ritual: Contemporary Art and Design for Jewish Life, Jewish Museum, New York
Planet of Signs, FRAC Île-De-France | Le Plateau, Paris
Awake are only the Spirits, Hartware MedienKunstVerein (HMKV), Dortmund

2010
Cross-fades. Reconstructing the Future, Shedhalle, Zurich
Magic Show, Grundy Art Gallery, Blackpool; Tullie House Museum and Art Gallery, Carlisle; Chapter, Cardiff; Pump House Gallery, London

2011
Secret Societies. To Know, To Dare, To Will, To Keep Silence, Schirn Kunsthalle, Frankfurt; CAPC, Bordeaux
Outrageous Fortune: Artists Remake the Tarot, Focal Point Gallery, Southend-on-Sea; Queens Hall Arts Centre, Hexham; Jersey Arts Centre, St Helier; Midlands Arts Centre, Birmingham

2012
Intersections: Science in Contemporary Art, Weizmann Institute of Science, Rehovot, Israel
Plus ou moins sorcières 3/3: Hugger-Mugger, La Maison Populaire, Paris
Mutatis Mutandis, Secession, Vienna

2013
Systemics #2 – As We May Think (Or the Next World Library), Kunsthal Aarhus, Denmark
The Whole Earth. California and the Disappearance of the Outside, Haus der Kulturen der Welt, Berlin
A World of Wild Doubt, Hamburger Kunstverein, Hamburg

2014
10th Shanghai Biennale
8th Biennale de Montréal
Treasure of Lima: A Buried Exhibition, TBA21 – Academy, Thyssen-Bornemisza Art Contemporary, Vienna; Cocos Island, Costa Rica

2015
Infosphere, ZKM | Center for Art and Media Karlsruhe, Germany
Control Mode Feedback, HALLE 14, Leipzig
Air de Jeu, Extension du Domaine du Jeu, Centre Pompidou, Paris

2016
Perpetual Uncertainty, Bildmuseet, Umeå, Sweden
The Museum of Rhythm, Muzeum Sztuki ms1, Lodz
You Say You Want a Revolution: Records and Rebels 1966–70, Victoria and Albert Museum, London

2017
Parapolitik: Kulturelle Freiheit und Kalter Krieg, Haus der Kulturen der Welt, Berlin
Alien Matter, Transmediale 2017, Haus der Kulturen der Welt, Berlin
As Above, So Below: Portals, Visions, Spirits & Mystics, Irish Museum of Modern Art, Dublin

2018
Broken Symmetries, FACT, Liverpool
9th Busan Biennale
17th Tallinn Print Triennial

2019
BIO 26 – Common Knowledge, 26th Biennial of Design, Ljubljana
16th Istanbul Biennial
Age of You, Museum of Contemporary Art, Toronto

2020
We Never Sleep, Schirn Kunsthtalle, Frankfurt
Yerevan Biennial, Armenia
Broken Symmetries – Art x Physics, National Taiwan Museum of Fine Arts, Taichung

2021
7th Athens Biennale
ISKRA DELTA, 34th Ljubljana Biennale of Graphic Arts

Alison Turnbull
Born in Bogotá, 1956. Lives in London

Selected Solo Exhibitions
1989
Anne Berthoud Gallery, London

1990
Anne Berthoud Gallery, London

1997
Gallery A, London

2000–01
Houses into Flats, Milton Keynes Gallery; Museum of Modern Art Oxford

2003
Hospital, Matt's Gallery, London

2005
ArtSway, New Forest, Hampshire
World in a Chamber, University of Oxford
Black Borders, Galería Magda Bellotti, Madrid

2010
Observatory, Matt's Gallery, London

2012
Talbot Rice Gallery, Edinburgh

2013
De La Warr Pavilion, Bexhill On Sea

2014
Like a Secret Spring in a Well-ordered Machine, Shandy Hall, Coxwold, Yorkshire

2015
Another Green World – Linn Botanic Gardens: Encounters with a Scottish Arcadia, Royal Botanic Garden Edinburgh

2016
Cloud Diagram, Art Seen – Contemporary Art Projects & Editions, Nicosia

2018
If Mimicry Minded, Matt's Gallery, London

2020
Out of Line, Saicoro, Tokyo

Selected Group Exhibitions
1992–93
Bruise: Painting for the Nineties, Ikon Gallery, Birmingham; Cornerhouse, Manchester

1993
New Voices: New Works for the British Council Collection, Centre de Conferences Albert Borschette, Brussels
East, Norwich Art Gallery, Norfolk School of Art and Design

1997
Blueprint, Glasgow Print Studio

2002
British School at Rome

2004
Open Secret, Imperial War Museums, London

2005
Storey Gallery, Lancaster

2006
Responding to Rome, Estorick Collection of Modern Italian Art, London

2008
Darwin's Canopy, Natural History Museum, London

2009
Between the Lines – British Contemporary Drawing, Trinity Fine Art, London

2010
On the Edge of the World, Royal Botanic Garden Edinburgh

2010–11
Seeing in Colour, Style Art Gallery, Gyumri, Armenia; Qaboos University Cultural Centre, Oman; Azerbaijan State Academy of Fine Arts, Baku; Tbilisi State Academy of Arts, Georgia; Centre for Urban History, Ukraine; Bottega Gallery, Kyiv, Ukraine; National Gallery, Yerevan, Armenia

2012–13
Galápagos, Bluecoat, Liverpool; Fruitmarket Gallery, Edinburgh; Centro de Arte Moderna, Lisbon

2011
(with Rupert Ackroyd) *Green Oak Aqua Modern*, The Russian Club Gallery, London

2013
A Lasting Legacy: The House and Collection of Victor Skipp, Kettle's Yard, Cambridge

2016
Seeing Round Corners: the Art of the Circle, Turner Contemporary, Margate

2018
In the Labyrinth, Large Glass, London

2019
From Narrow Provinces, Cample Line, Thornhill, Scotland

2020
Into the Labyrinth, Large Glass, London; Dalby Forest, North Yorkshire

Shelagh Wakely
Born in Madingley, 1932. Died 2011

Selected Solo Exhibitions
1977
Some Encounters With Reality, Serpentine Gallery, London

1979
Towards the inside of a container, ICA, London; LYC Museum & Art Gallery, Cumbria

1982
If a Fan Becomes a Fountain, John Hansard Gallery, Southampton

1980
The Palace Was Closed On Mondays, The Fountains Were Not Playing, Piwna 20/26, Warsaw

1991
British School at Rome

1992
Gold Dust, Ikon Gallery, Birmingham

1993
Aguadorado, Museu do Açude, Rio de Janeiro

1994
Rainsquare, South London Gallery, London

1997
Paisagem Inutil & The Practice of Enchantment, Instituto Brasil-Estado Unidos, Rio de Janeiro

1999
Minerva Gallery, Tel Aviv

2002
A Space For Dreaming, Angel Row Gallery, Nottingham

2012
Homenagem, Museu do Acude, Rio de Janeiro

2014
A View from a Window, Camden Art Centre, London

2016
Spaces Between Things, Richard Saltoun Gallery, London

2018
A Different Kind of Reality, Galleria Tiziana Di Caro, Naples

Selected Group Exhibitions
1976
Alison Wilding and Shelagh Wakely, AIR Gallery, London

1979
6th International Print Biennale, Bradford
4th Cleveland International Drawing Biennale

1980
British Art 1940–80 from the Arts Council Collection, Hayward Gallery, London

1981
2nd Biennale of European Graphic Art, Baden-Baden
16th Bienal de São Paulo

1984
41st Venice Biennale
Concepts of Space in Contemporary Art, National Museum, Warsaw

1991
An English Summer, British Art in Northern Italy, Palazzo Ruini, Reggio Emilia

1986
La Jouisseuse Drawing, Kettle's Yard, Cambridge

1996
Beyond Consumption, LIFE/LIVE la scène artistique au Royaume-Uni, Musée d'Art Moderne de la Ville de Paris; Centro Cultural de Belem, Lisbon

2000
Structurally Sound, 4 British Artists, EX-Teresa, Mexico City

2003
Work About The Transitory and Immaterial, Roaming Room, Bristol

2010
Drawings and Installation, Roaming Room, Bristol

2018
Speech Acts: Reflection-Imagination-Repetition, Manchester Art Gallery

Maxine Walker
Born in Birmingham, 1962. Lives in Birmingham

Selected Exhibitions
1986
South of the River: Monocrone Womens Photography Collective, South London Gallery

1986
Unknown Show, Pyramid Art Gallery, London

1987
SAFF, South London Gallery

1987
Not Just Sitting Pretty, Pavilion, Leeds
Three Women Photographers (with Ingrid Pollard and Jenny Mckenzie), Commonwealth Institute, London

1988
The British At Home, Impressions Gallery, York
My Family, My History, Myself, Untitled Gallery, Sheffield

1989
UK – UK, Jamaica Arts Centre, New York
Through the Looking Glass: Photographic Art in Britain 1945–1986, Barbican Centre, London
Intimate Distance: Five Female Artists, The Photographers' Gallery, London
Decent Exposure, Central Library, Birmingham
Seeing Things, Gas Hall, Birmingham

1990
Still Lives, Sharp Voices, Birmingham Photography in the 1980s, Birmingham Museum and Art Gallery
Homes, Ikon Gallery (touring), Birmingham
At Home, Victoria and Albert Museum, London

1991
Body Adornment, Nottingham Castle Museum & Art Gallery

1992
Shifting Borders, Laing Art Gallery, Newcastle upon Tyne
Some European Outlooks, Saaremaa Museum, Estonia

1993
Exposure, CCA, Glasgow

1995
Self Evident, Ikon Gallery, Birmingham; Netherlands Photo Museum, Rotterdam

1996
Light House Media Centre, Wolverhampton
Being There, Birmingham Museum and Art Gallery

1996
Prospect 96, Frankfurter Kunstverein

1997
Shifting Terrains, Zone Gallery, Newcastle upon Tyne

2015
Staying Power: Photographs of Black British Experience, 1950s–1990s, Victoria and Albert Museum; Black Cultural Archives, London

2019
UNTITLED and *Shining Lights: Black Women in Photography in the 1980s–90s*, Autograph, London

Mark Wallinger
Born in Chigwell, 1959. Lives in London

Selected Solo Exhibitions
1987
Serpentine Gallery, London

1990
School, Sophia Ungers, Cologne

1991
Capital, Grey Art Gallery, New York; ICA, London; Manchester Art Gallery

1995
Ikon Gallery, Birmingham; Serpentine Gallery, London

1998
The Four Corners of the Earth, Delfina Foundation, London

1999
Ecce Homo, The Fourth Plinth, Trafalgar Square, London
Lost Horizon, Museum für Gegenwartskunst, Basel
Mark Wallinger is Innocent, Palais des Beaux Arts, Brussels

2000
Threshold to the Kingdom, The British School at Rome
Credo, Tate Liverpool

2001
British Pavilion, 49th Venice Biennale
Cave, Milton Keynes Gallery; Southampton City Art Gallery
Time and Relative Dimensions in Space, Oxford University Museum of Natural History
No Man's Land, Whitechapel Gallery, London

2003
Via Dolorosa, Städtische Galerie im Lenbachhaus, Munich, Germany
The Sleep of Reason, The Wolfsonian, Florida
Threshold to the Kingdom St Michael's Castle, State Russian Museum, Saint Petersburg

2004
The Underworld, Laing Art Gallery, Newcastle upon Tyne
Sleeper, Neue Nationalgalerie, Berlin
Presence 4. Mark Wallinger, Speed Art Museum, Kentucky

2005
Easter, Hangar Bicocca, Milan
Museo de Arte Carillo Gil, Mexico City

2006
Threshold to the Kingdom Convent of St. Agnes of Bohemia, National Gallery Prague
Out of Place, New Art Gallery Walsall

2007
Kunstverein Braunschweig, Germany
State Britain, Tate Britain, London; Musée d'Art Contemporain du Val-de-Marne, Paris

2008
Kunstmuseum Aarau, Switzerland

2009
The Russian Linesman, Frontiers, Borders and Thresholds, Hayward Gallery, London; Leeds Art Gallery; Glynn Vivian Art Gallery, Swansea

2011
Museum De Pont, Tilburg

2012
BALTIC, Gateshead
Sinema Amnesia: Mark Wallinger, Turner Contemporary, Margate

2016
Self Reflection, Freud Museum, London
MARK WALLINGER MARK, Serlachius Museum / Art Museum Gösta, Mänttä, Finland; Fruitmarket Gallery, Edinburgh; Dundee Contemporary Arts; Centro per l'Arte Contemporanea Luigi Pecci, Prato

2018
The Human Figure in Space, Jerwood Gallery, Hastings

Selected Group Exhibitions
1981
New Contemporaries, ICA, London

1985
Prelude, Kettle's Yard, Cambridge

1986
Canvas: New British Painting, John Hansard Gallery, Southampton

1987
Stuart Brisley, Ken Currie, Glenys Johnson, Mark Wallinger, Serpentine Gallery, London

1988
Something Solid, Cornerhouse, Manchester
The New British Painting, Contemporary Arts Center, Cincinnati; Chicago Cultural Center; Haggerty Museum, Marquette University, Milwaukee; South Eastern Center for Contemporary Art, Winston-Salem; Grand Rapids Art Museum

1989
Territories, Chisenhale Gallery, London

1990
Australian Sculpture Triennial, National
Gallery of Victoria, Melbourne

1991
Kunstlandschaft Europa, Kunstverein
Karlsruhe
Confrontaciones, Palacio de Velasquez,
Madrid

1993
Young British Artists II, Saatchi Collection,
London

1994
Here and Now, Serpentine Gallery, London

1995
The Art Casino, Barbican Centre, London
The British Art Show, Manchester
The Turner Prize, Tate Britain, London

1996
10th Biennale of Sydney

1997
Sensation, Royal Academy of Arts, London;
Hamburger Bahnhof, Berlin
5th Istanbul Biennale
2nd Johannesburg Biennale

1998
Wounds, Moderna Museet, Stockholm
1st Biennale de Montreal

1999
Fourth Wall, National Theatre, London

2000
Seeing Salvation, National Gallery, London

2001
*Century City: Art and Culture in the
Modern Metropolis*, Tate Modern, London
Purloined, The Studio Museum in Harlem,
New York

2002
Glynn Vivian Gallery, Swansea
Real Life, Tate St. Ives

2003
Independence, South London Gallery
Warum! Ebenbild – Abbild – Selbstbild,
Martin-Gropius Bau, Berlin
Sanctuary, Gallery of Modern Art, Glasgow
Body Song 2003 (The Lark Ascending),
ICA, London

2005
Monuments for the USA, White Columns,
New York
Variety, De La Warr Pavillion, Bexhill-on-Sea
Italian Pavillion, 51st Venice Biennale
The World is a Stage, Mori Art Museum,
Tokyo

2006
Glasgow International

2007
Turner Prize 2007, Tate Liverpool
Skulptur Projekte Münster
*Dateline Israel: New Photography and
Video Art*, Jewish Museum, New York

2008
Folkestone Triennial

2009
The British Pavilion at the Venice Biennale,
Whitechapel Gallery, London
2nd Athens Biennale

2010
17th Biennale of Sydney

2011
A Threepenny Opera, S1 Artspace, Sheffield
The Wonders of the Visible World,
Northern Gallery for Contemporary Art,
Sunderland

2012
Metamorphosis: Titian 2012, National
Gallery, London

2014
*The Human Factor: The Figure in
Contemporary Sculpture*, Hayward Gallery,
London

2015
How to Construct a Time Machine, MK
Gallery, Milton Keynes

2016
Seeing Round Corners, Turner
Contemporary, Margate
*Collected by Thea Westreich Wagner and
Ethan Wagner*, Centre Pompidou, Paris
I am Van Dyck, Dulwich Picture Gallery,
London

2017
The Art of Dissonance, SeMA, Seoul
Museum of Art

2018
BRONZE AGE c. 3500 BC – AD 2017,
Firstsite, Colchester

2019
The Classical Now, King's College London,
London

2020
World Without End, Dublin City Gallery
The Hugh Lane

John Yeadon
Born in Burnley, 1948. Lives in Coventry

Selected Solo Exhibitions
1977
Against Racialism, Lanchester Polytechnic,
Coventry

1978
*The Crisis of Empire and National
Liberation*, Transport House, Coventry

1981
Two Communist Banners, Lea House,
Coventry

1984
Dirty Tricks, Herbert Art Gallery & Museum,
Coventry; Pentonville Gallery, London

1986
The Shining City on the Hill, Transmission
Gallery, Glasgow

1988
*Unbelievable Stories, inc. The Travails of
Blind Bifford Jelly*, Lanchester Gallery,
Coventry Polytechnic

1991–92
*Chronicles & Continuing Tales, The
Travails of Blind Bifford Jelly*, Ikon Gallery,
Birmingham;
CCA, Glasgow; Royal Festival Hall, London

1993
Yeadon's Back Sides, Concourse Galley,
Coventry Polytechnic

1997
A Tragical Comedy or Comical Tragedy,
New End Gallery, London

1999
Vilma Gold Gallery, London

2002
John Yeadon, Por Amor à Arte Galeria, Porto

2003
Variations on a Theme, Ellen Terry Building, Coventry University

2006
Vanitas, Acacia Café, Herbert Art Gallery & Museum, Coventry

2010
FAT: The Mortality of the Eater and Eaten, Gallery 150, Leamington Spa

2012
Ghosts I Have Known, Browns, Coventry

2013
Englandia, Coventry/Dresden Arts Exchange, Johannstadthalle, Germany

2017
Control Rooms, Class Room, Coventry

2018
What's The Meaning Of This? – John Yeadon At 70: A Retrospective View, Newsroom Gallery, CET Building, Coventry
Three Witches – John Yeadon At 70, The National Museum of Computing, Bletchley Park

2019
Fearful Symmetry, Incorporating Unbelievable Stories and Ventriloquist Dummies, Lanchester Research Gallery, Coventry University

Selected Group Exhibitions
1977
Lest We Forget – People's Jubilee, Alexandra Palace, London

1981
Artery 10th Anniversary, Edinburgh Festival

1982
Artists for Peace, Scottish Trades Union Congress, Glasgow

1983
Midland View Two, Leicester Polytechnic; Milton Keynes Central Library; MAG Worcester – Worcester City Art Gallery & Museum; Ikon Gallery; Midland Group, Nottingham
The Nude, Herbert Art Gallery & Museum, Coventry

1984
21 for 21, Ikon Gallery, Birmingham; Hong Kong Arts Centre

1984–85
The British Art Show: Old Allegiances and New Directions 1979–1984, Birmingham Museum and Art Gallery; Ikon Gallery, Birmingham; Royal Scottish Academy, Edinburgh; Mappin Art Gallery, Sheffield; Southampton City Art Gallery

1987
The State of the Nation, Herbert Art Gallery & Museum, Coventry

1987
Critical Realism, Nottingham Castle Museum & Art Gallery; Edinburgh Arts Centre; Stirling Smith Art Gallery & Museum; Camden Art Centre; Worcester City Art Gallery & Museum; Winchester Art Gallery

1988
The Invisible Man: Representations of Male Sexuality, Goldsmiths, London

1990
Post Morality, Kettle's Yard, Cambridge

1998
Animals in Art, Herbert Art Gallery & Museum, Coventry

2002
A Woman's Place, Invisible Histories, Herbert Art Gallery & Museum, Coventry

2008
Drawing Breath/ Respirar Arte, Fundação Júlio Resende – Lugar do Desenho, Porto

2010/12
400 Women, Shoreditch Town Hall, London; Sugar City, Amsterdam

2012
Artery 1971–1984, Rob Tufnell, London

2014
Coventry/Dresden Arts Exchange, Galerie 2. Stock, Rathaus, Dresden

2017
Bienal Internacional De Arte Gaia, Portugal
The Future: Coventry Biennial of Contemporary Art, CET Building, Coventry

2019
The Lie of the Land, MK Gallery, Milton Keynes
Condition Humaine, Coventry/Dresden Arts Exchange, Kreuzkirche, Dresden and Coventry Cathedral

We are very grateful to the following individuals for their help towards the realisation of this exhibition:

Thalia Allington-Wood
Adrian Bland
Stefania Bonelli
Nuala Bradley
Russ Bradley
Julie Brown
Axel Burrough
Vanley Burke
Jill Constantine
Andrée Cooke
Photi Giovanis
Marian Hall
Nicola Heald
Isabelle Hogenkamp
David Juda
Deborah Kermode
Soweto Kinch
Angela Kingston
Herman Lelie
John Leslie
Nadine Lockyer
Niki Longhurst
Elizabeth Macgregor
Lynn Maliszewski
Desirée Martínez
Mike McKernan
Stewart Meese
Hannah Murray
David Owen
Anne Parouty
Mungo Parks
Wayne Partridge
Laura Peterle
Roma Piotrowska
Megan Piper
Anthony Reynolds
Deborah Robinson
Fabio Rossi
Dan Rowlinson
Mary Sabbatino
Deborah Smith
Nick Smith
Stephen Snoddy
Polly Staple
Rohan Stephens
Diane Symons
Nicholas Thomas
Toby Watley
Stuart Whipps

Lenders

Annely Juda Fine Art, London
Anthony Reynolds Gallery, London
Arts Council Collection, Southbank Centre, London
Birmingham City Council
Birmingham Museums Trust
Callicoon Fine Arts, New York
Cathy Wills Collection, London
Collection Adrian Piper Research Archive Foundation Berlin
Matt's Gallery, London
Mitchell-Innes & Nash, New York
Museum of Contemporary Art Australia
P.P.O.W. Gallery, New York
Richard Saltoun Gallery
Tanya Bonakdar, New York
Tate
The British Council Collection
The Estate of Edward Allington
The Estate of Rose Finn-Kelcey
The Estate of Donald Rodney
The New Art Gallery Walsall
The Tiqui Atencio Collection
And those who wish to remain anonymous

A Very Special Place
IKON IN THE 1990s

Ikon Gallery, Birmingham, 18 June – 30 August 2021
Curated by Jonathan Watkins
Assisted by Melanie Pocock, Thomas Ellmer and Kirstie North

ISBN: 978-1-911155-29-4

Ikon Gallery
1 Oozells Square, Brindleyplace, Birmingham, B1 2HS, UK
T: +44 (0) 121 248 0708
www.ikon-gallery.org

Ikon Gallery Limited trading as Ikon
Registered charity no. 528892

Edited by Jonathan Watkins
Texts by Jonathan Watkins and Elizabeth Macgregor
Designed and produced by Herman Lelie
Layouts by Stefania Bonelli
Repro by Dexter Premedia, London
Printed by EBS, Italy

Front and back cover: Nancy Spero, installation, Ikon Gallery, 1998
Inside front cover and front paper: Shelagh Wakely, *Gold Dust*, installation, Ikon Gallery, 1992
Title page: Ikon Gallery, John Bright Street
Inside back cover: Rigo, *Ocean*, 1997

Images courtesy the artists, their estates, galleries and representatives except all rights reserved, DACS/Artimage 2021 pp. 56, 58–59, 94–95, 105, 107; Autograph pp. 114–115; Arts Council Collection, Southbank Centre, London pp. 52, 86–87, 101; British Council Collection pp. 29, 80–81, 116–118; Kalli Rolfe Contemporary Art p. 62; Tate pp. 60, 64–65, 68, 70–71, 77, 85, 90–91, 93; The Tiqui Atencio Collection p. 83; Richard Saltoun Gallery p. 55

Photography by Daniella Baptista pp. 58–59; Birmingham Museums Trust p. 69; The British Council pp. 29, 80–81, 116–118; Damian Griffiths p. 83; Gary Kirkham pp. 78–79; Andra Nelki p. 101; Phaophanit and Oboussier Studio pp. 94–95; Tate pp. 60, 64–65, 68, 70–71, 77, 85, 90–91, 93; Stuart Whipps pp. 51, 109, 112, 113; and Edward Woodman p. 53

Images © courtesy the artists, their estates, galleries and representatives except Adrian Piper Research Archive Foundation, Berlin p. 97; and The British Council pp. 29, 80–81, 116–118

Zarina Bhimji pp. 58–59: Commissioned by Ikon Gallery, 1992. Re-fabricated by Sharjah Art Foundation as part of the *Black Pocket* exhibition, Sharjah, UAE, 2020

Distributed by Cornerhouse Publications
2 Tony Wilson Place, Manchester, M15 4FN, UK
publications@cornerhouse.org
T: +44 (0)161 200 1503   F: +44 (0)161 200 1504

This project has been supported by Elonex, The Grimmitt Trust, Paul Mellon Centre and The Owen Family Trust

Ikon is supported using public funding by Arts Council England and Birmingham City Council

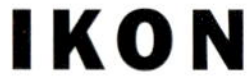
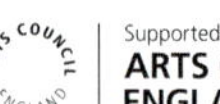
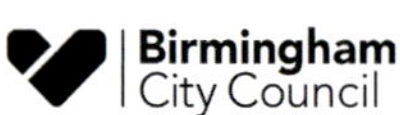
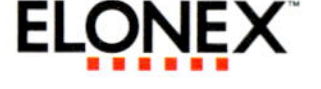
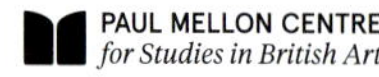